I0427220

Canon EOS R6 Mark II
User Guide

A Comprehensive Guide to Discovering the Secrets to Stunning Shots, Creative Techniques, and Beyond with Your Canon Powerhouse

McBunny Albert

Copyright © 2024 **McBunny Albert**

All Rights Reserved

This book or parts thereof may not be reproduced in any form, stored in any retrieval system, or transmitted in any form by any means—electronic, mechanical, photocopy, recording, or otherwise—without prior written permission of the publisher, except as provided by United States of America copyright law and fair use.

Disclaimer and Terms of Use

The author and publisher of this book and the accompanying materials have used their best efforts in preparing this book. The author and publisher make no representation or warranties with respect to the accuracy, applicability, fitness, or completeness of the contents of this book. The information contained in this book is strictly for informational purposes. Therefore, if you wish to apply the ideas contained in this book, you are taking full responsibility for your actions.

Printed in the United States of America

TABLE OF CONTENTS

TABLE OF CONTENTS III

INTRODUCTION 1

Canon EOS R6 Mark II: Features 2
Key features of the Canon EOS R6 Mark II 5
Canon EOS R6 Mark II: Build and Handling 6
Canon EOS R6 Mark II: Viewfinder and Screen 9
Canon EOS R6 Mark II: Mastering Autofocus 10
Canon EOS R6 Mark II: Impressive Performance 11
Canon EOS R6 Mark II: ISO and noise 13

CHAPTER ONE 14

MEET YOUR CANON EOS R6 II 14

Overview 14
Charging the Battery 14
    LC-E6 .... *14*
    LC-E6E *15*
Inserting and removing batteries 16
    Inserting the battery *17*
    Battery Removal Procedure *18*
Inserting and Removing Cards 18
    Inserting Cards *18*
    Card 1 .... *19*
    Card 2 .... *19*
    Formatting the Card *20*
    Caution *21*
Using the Screen 22
    Turning on the Power *23*
Setting the Date, Time, and Time Zone 23
Change the Interface Language 27
Automatic Sensor Cleaning 28
    First things first *28*
Initial Setup 31
    Power Options *31*
    Mounting a Lens *33*
    Adjusting Diopter Correction with expertise *33*
Mastering Basic Navigation 34
    Choosing a Metering Mode *35*
    Choosing a Focus Mode (AF Operation) *36*
    Selecting AF Area *36*
Transferring Photos to Your Computer 38
Frequently Asked Questions 39

CHAPTER TWO **40**

YOUR VISUAL ROADMAP **40**

OVERVIEW 40
FRONT VIEW 40
THE BUSINESS END 42
    Right-Side Controls 44
MASTERING THE TOUCH SCREEN 46
    Flexible View 46
    Touch Operation 47
    Going Topside 48
    Underneath Your Camera 50
FREQUENTLY ASKED QUESTIONS 51

CHAPTER THREE **52**

RECOMMENDED SETTINGS **52**

OVERVIEW 52
CHANGING DEFAULT SETTINGS 52
    Resetting to Factory Defaults 52
    Still Photo Shooting Menu Defaults 53
    AF Menu Defaults 53
CONFIGURE MENU SETTINGS 54
    Set-up Menu Defaults 54
    Recommended Default Changes 54
    Default, All Purpose, Sports: Outdoors, Sports; Indoors 55
    Stage Performances, Long Exposure, HDR, Portrait 55
FREQUENTLY ASKED QUESTIONS 55

CHAPTER FOUR **56**

NAILING THE RIGHT EXPOSURE **56**

OVERVIEW 56
GETTING A HANDLE ON EXPOSURE 56
CHOOSING A METERING MODE 59
CHOOSING A SHOOTING MODE 61
    Aperture-Priority Mode 62
    Shutter-Priority Mode 62
    Program AE Mode 63
    Flexible-Priority Mode 65
    Manual Exposure Mode 65
ADJUSTING EXPOSURE WITH ISO SETTINGS 66
    Dealing with Visual Noise 67
    Making EV Changes 68
BRACKETING PARAMETERS 69
    Number of Exposures 70

Bracketing Sequence..70

Bracketing Auto Cancel..71

Increment between Exposures..71

Creating a Bracketed Set..71

WORKING WITH HDR 73

Using HDR Mode 74

Moving Subjects Mode 76

Dynamic Range Mode 76

FIXING EXPOSURES WITH HISTOGRAMS 77

Tonal Range..77

Histogram Basics..79

Understanding Histograms 79

Exposing to the Right 80

DISCOVERING BASIC ZONE MODES 80

Scene Intelligent Auto Mode..80

Special Scene Mode 83

FREQUENTLY ASKED QUESTIONS 84

CHAPTER FIVE 85

MASTERING THE MYSTERIES OF FOCUS 85

OVERVIEW 85

AUTO OR MANUAL FOCUS? 85

HOW FOCUS WORKS 86

Contrast Detection 87

Phase Detection..88

AF Pixel Layout..88

Dual Pixel CMOS AF 89

Dual Pixel RAW Focus Adjustments....................................90

Circles of Confusion and Focus 90

WORKING WITH THE AF SYSTEM 92

AF Operation 92

One-Shot AF 93

AI Focus..94

Servo AF..94

AF Area 95

Spot AF..95

1-Point AF 95

Expand AF Area 95

Expand AF Area: Around 95

Flexible Zone AF 1..96

Whole Area AF 96

SUBJECT TRACKING 96

MANUAL FOCUS 98

Magnified View 99

Focus Peaking 99

Focus Guide *100*

FINE-TUNING YOUR AUTOFOCUS 100

Back-Button Focus *101*

Activating Back-Button Focus *102*

FREQUENTLY ASKED QUESTIONS 104

CHAPTER SIX **105**

ADVANCED TECHNIQUES **105**

OVERVIEW 105

CONTINUOUS SHOOTING 105

MORE EXPOSURE OPTIONS 106

A Tiny Slice of Time *106*

Working with Short Exposures *107*

LONG EXPOSURES 108

Three Ways to Take Long Exposures *108*

Working with Long Exposures *109*

DELAYED EXPOSURES 110

Self-Timer *111*

TIME LAPSE AND INTERVAL PHOTOGRAPHY 111

Using Interval Photography *111*

Star Trails *112*

SHOOTING PANORAMAS 113

FREQUENTLY ASKED QUESTIONS 115

CHAPTER SEVEN **116**

CHOOSING YOUR LENS ARSENAL **116**

OVERVIEW 116

YOUR FIRST LENSES 116

CANON RF-MOUNT LENSES 118

Zoom lenses *119*

Prime Lenses *121*

USING ADAPTED LENSES 123

CANON RF-MOUNT ADAPTERS 124

IMAGE STABILIZATION AND YOU 125

WHAT LENSES CAN DO FOR YOU 126

USING WIDE-ANGLE LENSES 127

AVOIDING POTENTIAL WIDE-ANGLE PROBLEMS 128

Issue: Converging lines *128*

Issue: lines that appear to be bowing outward *128*

Issue: The presence of light and dark areas is observed when using a polarizing filter *128*

USING TELEPHOTO AND TELE-ZOOM LENSES 129

AVOIDING TELEPHOTO LENS PROBLEMS 129

Issue: Flat faces in portraits *130*

Issue: Blurriness caused by camera shake *130*

Issue: Color fringes observed..*130*

Issue: Lines that exhibit a concave curvature *130*

Issue: Decreased contrast due to flare *131*

FREQUENTLY ASKED QUESTIONS 131

CHAPTER EIGHT **132**

MASTERING LIGHT **132**

OVERVIEW 132

LIGHT THAT'S AVAILABLE 132

Continuous Lighting Basics *133*

Living with Color Temperature...*134*

WHITE BALANCE BRACKETING 134

Daylight...*135*

Incandescent/Tungsten/Halogen Light *136*

Fluorescent Light/LEDs *136*

FREQUENTLY ASKED QUESTIONS 136

CHAPTER NINE **137**

ELECTRONIC FLASH BASICS..**137**

OVERVIEW 137

HOW ELECTRONIC FLASH WORKS 137

Ghost Images *137*

Avoiding Sync-Speed Problems *138*

DETERMINING EXPOSURE 138

Guide Numbers *139*

GETTING STARTED WITH ELECTRONIC FLASH... 139

Flash Exposure Compensation and FE Lock..*141*

Flash Range *141*

EXTERNAL SPEEDLITE CONTROL... 142

Flash Firing *142*

E-TTL II Metering *142*

Continuous Flash Control *142*

Slow Synchro *143*

Flash Function Settings..*144*

Flash C.Fn Settings *145*

Clear Settings *146*

FREQUENTLY ASKED QUESTIONS 146

CHAPTER TEN **147**

WORKING WITH WIRELESS FLASH **147**

OVERVIEW 147

WIRELESS EVOLUTION 147

ELEMENTS OF WIRELESS FLASH 147

Flash Combinations *147*

Controlling Flash Units...148
WHY USE WIRELESS FLASH?...149
   Key Wireless Concepts...*150*
   Which Flashes Can Be Operated Wirelessly?.....................................*150*
SETTING UP A SENDER/CONTROLLER FLASH..152
   Using a Speedlite as an Optical Sender..*152*
   EL-1..*152*
   580EX...*153*
   Using the Speedlite 430EX III-RT as Radio Sender............................*153*
   Setting up a Receiver Flash...*153*
FREQUENTLY ASKED QUESTIONS...154

CHAPTER ELEVEN...**155**

CUSTOMIZING WITH THE SHOOTING MENU..**155**

OVERVIEW..155
ANATOMY OF THE MENUS...155
SHOOTING MENU OPTIONS...157
   Image Quality...*157*
   Dual Pixel RAW..*159*
   HDR Shooting [HDR PQ]...*160*
   ISO Speed Settings...*161*
   Highlight Tone Priority..*162*
   Anti-Flicker Shooting...*163*
   High-Frequency Anti-Flicker Shooting..*164*
   Custom White Balance...*167*
   Dust Delete Data..*169*
   OVF Sim View Assist..*171*
   High-Speed Display..*173*
   High ISO Speed Noise Reduction...*174*
FREQUENTLY ASKED QUESTIONS...175

CHAPTER TWELVE...**176**

THE PLAYBACK AND WIRELESS MENUS..**176**

OVERVIEW..176
PLAYBACK MENU OPTIONS...176
   Protect Images..*176*
   Erase Images...*177*
   Rating..*179*
   Change Movie Rotate Info...*180*
   RAW Processing (RAW/DPRAW)...*181*
   Photobook Set-up...*182*
   Quick Control RAW Processing...*184*
   Cloud RAW Image Processing...*185*
   HEIF→JPEG Conversion...*187*

Magnification..*188*

Switch Main Dial/Quick Control Dial 2..*188*

Highlight Alert...*189*

HDMI HDR Output...*189*

AF Point Disp...*189*

FREQUENTLY ASKED QUESTIONS...190

CHAPTER THIRTEEN...**191**

SET-UP MENU...**191**

OVERVIEW...191

FILE NUMBERING...191

FILE NAME..193

FORMAT CARD...194

ADD MOVIE ROTATE INFORMATION...195

DATE/TIME/ZONE..196

AUTO ROTATE...196

LANGUAGE...197

VIDEO SYSTEM...198

MODE GUIDE...198

FEATURE GUIDE...198

Beep..*199*

Choose the USB Connection App..*199*

Custom Shooting Mode (C1–C3)...*200*

FREQUENTLY ASKED QUESTIONS...202

CONCLUSION..203

INDEX..**204**

INTRODUCTION

The Canon EOS R6 Mark II establishes a new standard for the performance of hybrid cameras. This camera is expertly crafted for action-packed moments, allowing you to capture motion in exhilarating ways. It excels at capturing stunning 24.2MP full-frame stills at an impressive 40fps, as well as shooting breathtaking 6K RAW video at 60p.

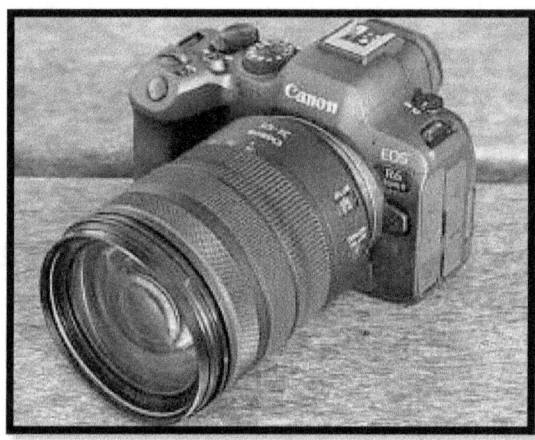

Canon carefully considered the feedback from users of the EOS R6 and elevated the camera's already impressive feature set to new heights. With a host of over 70 enhancements, the EOS R6 Mark II takes its predecessor's strengths to new heights. Notable upgrades include the addition of an In-Body Image Stabilizer (IBIS) and advanced intelligent subject detection.

Here's a quick overview of the Canon EOS R6 Mark II:

- The price for the body only is $3,561 / £2,779.
- **Price**: $3,981 / £3,129 with RF 24-105mm STM lens
- With a 24.2MP full-frame sensor, this camera delivers exceptional image quality.
- ISO range of 100-102,400 (standard)
- Shoot at an impressive 40 frames per second.
- Record videos in stunning 4K resolution at a smooth 60 frames per second.
- The camera features a high-resolution 3.69m-dot OLED EVF with a magnification of 0.76x.
- The camera features a 3-inch, 1.62m-dot vari-angle screen.

The more affordable model quickly gained recognition as the practical option for most photographers, even though its high-resolution counterpart received more attention. The firm has recently released a significant update for it, with the EOS R6 Mark II now equipped with a new 24MP sensor, replacing the previous 20MP chip. Additionally, there are a variety of feature updates, along with some noteworthy design and interface adjustments.

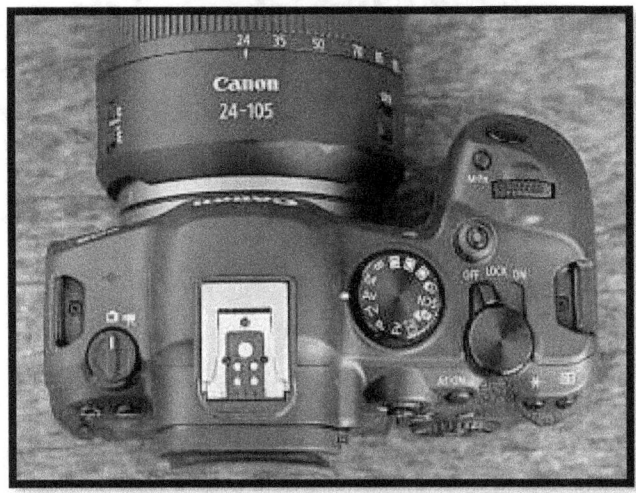

Priced at $2500 / £2,779 for the body-only option, the EOS R6 Mark II enters the market with a reasonable increase compared to its discontinued predecessor. The previous model was initially sold for £2500 and can now be found on the secondhand market for around £1,429 / $1700 in excellent condition. It faces tough competition from some lower-priced alternatives, particularly the impressive 33MP Sony Alpha A7 IV ($3051 / £2,399) and the Panasonic Lumix S5 II ($2288 / £1799). Canon is surely counting on its remarkable headline specifications, such as 40fps shooting and an advanced subject recognition autofocus system, to maintain the loyalty of its current DSLR users and entice them to invest in the R system.

Canon EOS R6 Mark II: Features

First, let's discuss the 24.2MP Dual Pixel CMOS AF II sensor. Although it shares the same resolution as the high-end EOS R3, it does not utilize the same stacked architecture for ultra-fast readout, as professional. Canon asserts that it provides low-light performance comparable to the EOS R6's 20MP chip. It offers a standard sensitivity range from ISO 100 to ISO 102,400, which can be extended up to ISO 204,800.

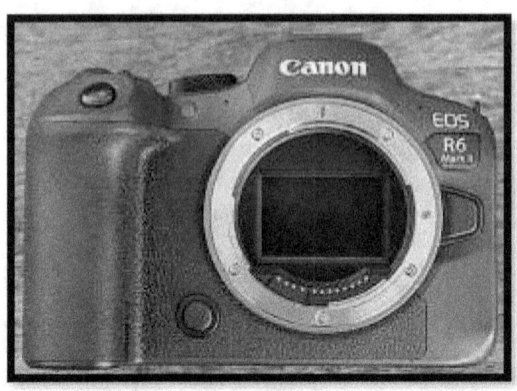

Regarding autofocus, the EOS R6 Mark II enhances the subject detection AF system that was previously featured in the EOS R3. The camera has expanded its recognition capabilities to include aircraft, trains, horses (including zebras), as well as humans, cars, animals, and birds. AF tracking is available in all focus modes, and Canon assures that autofocus remains operational even in extremely low light conditions of up to -6.5EV. This camera stands out as the fastest in its class, with the ability to capture 12 frames per second in full-resolution raw using its mechanical shutter. It goes above and beyond with an impressive 40 fps when using the electronic shutter. If speed is not a top priority, there are also options for 20 fps and 5 fps settings. Choose the raw burst mode option, and the camera will capture shots at an impressive 30 frames per second, allowing you to have a buffer of up to 15 frames before fully pressing the shutter button. With this feature, you can effortlessly capture those precious moments that might otherwise slip away.

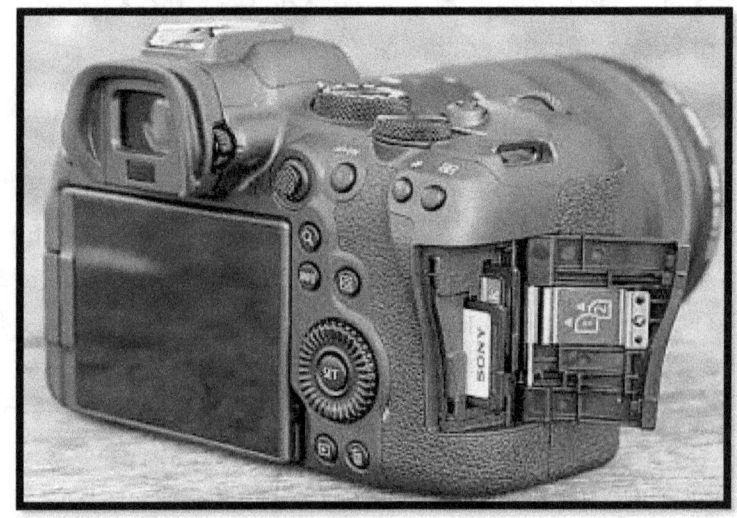

The buffer has an impressive depth, allowing for the capture of 190 JPEG or 140 CRAW files in a single burst. Canon's CRAW format allows for the creation of smaller raw files without compromising quality, enabling you to store more files on a memory card. This seemingly minor feature offers practical benefits that are truly valuable. The camera's in-body image stabilization is a great feature for low-light shooting, as it offers up to 8 stops of shake correction. Canon's RF lenses are equipped with optical stabilization, ensuring optimal performance by seamlessly integrating the in-lens and in-body systems. The system can also be used with adapted manual-focus lenses, including Canon's old FD-mount optics. However, similar to the original EOS R6, the process of inputting the lens's focal length to ensure the system functions correctly can be quite lengthy and cumbersome.

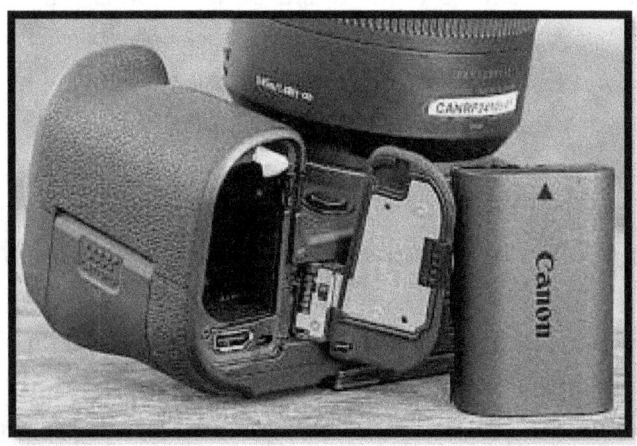

The video capabilities of this product are truly impressive. With the EOS R6 Mark II, you can enjoy the benefits of 4K recording at 60 fps, capturing stunning footage with enhanced detail thanks to 6K oversampling. Additionally, it can output 6K 60p ProRes raw to an external recorder via HDMI and offers Full HD slow motion recording at 180fps. Canon has included its new multi-function shoe, which accepts various digital audio accessories, along with the firm's EL-5 flash. Exciting new video features incorporate focus breathing compensation to rectify any alteration in the angle of view while adjusting the focus at various distances. Additionally, there is a **'face only AF'** function that prevents the camera from attempting to refocus when a human subject exits the frame. There is also a movie pre-recording option available, allowing you to continuously buffer 3 or 5 seconds of footage before you begin filming. This ensures that you capture every important moment of action without any interruptions.

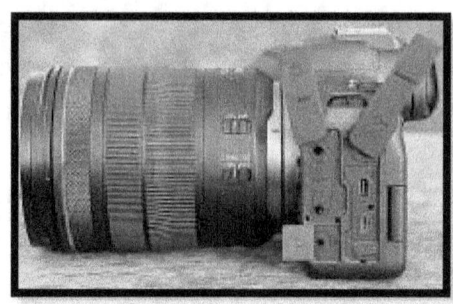

Connectivity has been enhanced with the inclusion of Bluetooth 5 and 5 GHz Wi-Fi, allowing seamless wireless connection between the camera and various devices such as smartphones, tablets, and computers. The Camera Remote app from Canon is available for both Android and iOS devices. It provides a wide range of features, allowing users to control their cameras remotely over Wi-Fi. With this app, you can enjoy a live view feed and have extensive control over various camera settings. Additionally, you can transfer photos to your phone for easy sharing, even if the camera is turned off and stored in your bag. This camera offers some unique features that are not commonly found in other models. For instance, it comes with a convenient Bluetooth remote control for effortless operation. Moreover, you can conveniently update the camera's firmware using your smartphone. Connecting the camera to a mobile device through its USB-C port provides a reliable connection. This enables the use of Camera Remote, allowing a phone or tablet to function as an external monitor. It's quite puzzling why other cameras don't offer this feature. Similar to other modern models, the EOS R6 Mark II can function as a 4K webcam for video calls, eliminating the need for extra software installation on your computer.

Key features of the Canon EOS R6 Mark II

Canon has enhanced the already impressive EOS R6 with a range of notable improvements.

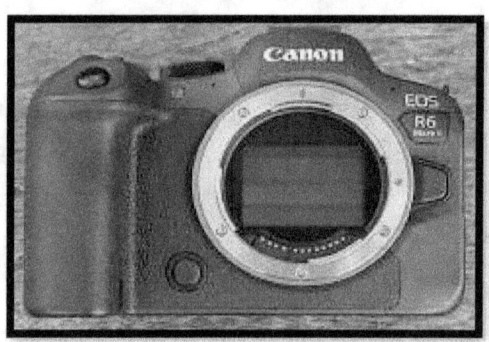

- **Lenses**: Canon's RF lens range offers a wide selection of 29 full-frame optics, catering to various needs and budgets. From affordable zoom lenses to high-quality ultra-telephoto primes, professionals have plenty of options to choose from. EF lenses can be used with an adapter.
- **Connectors**: Canon has included a 3.5mm stereo microphone and headphone sockets and a 2.5mm E3-type remote release connector, strategically placed to avoid obstructing the articulating screen. In addition, there are Micro HDMI and USB-C ports. Unfortunately, an infrared remote release is no longer supported.
- **Battery Power:** Canon's standard LP-E6N battery has a power rating of 450 shots when using the viewfinder, or 760 shots with the LCD. It has the convenience of in-camera charging, and a mains charger is included in the package.
- **Storage**: Files are recorded to two SD UHS-II card slots, ensuring reliable and efficient data storage. You have the option to use them either simultaneously or sequentially or to record different file types for each.
- **Multi-function shoe**: Canon has introduced a versatile multi-function shoe that can be used with various digital audio accessories and their latest flash units, such as the Speedlite EL-5.
- **Vertical grip**: The Mark II is compatible with the same BG-R10 battery grip as the EOS R5 and the original R6, which is priced at $299 / £379.

Canon EOS R6 Mark II: Build and Handling

The EOS R6 Mark III closely resembles its predecessor in terms of its external design. The handling of the R6 was exceptional, which is quite impressive. We have the same magnesium alloy chassis and glass fiber-reinforced polycarbonate shell when it comes to building quality. Although it may not exude the same level of durability as the Canon EOS 5D-series DSLRs of the past, it does significantly reduce the weight of the camera. The camera offers a secure hold and feels well balanced in the hand, even with larger lenses like the Canon RF 100-500mm f/4.5-7.1L IS USM. Additionally, the body is weather-sealed, providing the expected level of protection. The control layout has been updated with significant improvements, drawing inspiration from Canon's EOS DSLRs. With the inclusion of the customary front and rear control dials for adjusting exposure settings, a supplementary thumb dial has been added to the top plate specifically for ISO adjustments. Canon offers a unique and highly practical feature that allows for temporary ISO adjustments in Auto ISO mode. More so, there is a conventional exposure mode dial with three custom positions, as well as an AF multi-controller joystick that is finally enabled by default. Canon's higher-end RF lenses feature individual lens control dials that offer the flexibility to customize exposure settings. On the more affordable RF lenses, the manual focus ring is responsible for this function, but it may not perform as effectively.

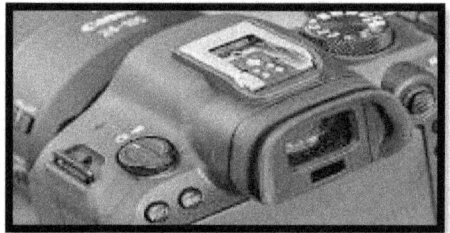

When compared to the original EOS R6, there have been a few updates. One noticeable change is the relocation of the on/off switch to the top left, which now serves as a stills/video mode selector. This feature provides convenient access to all the exposure modes for video recording, including the C positions. It presents a video-optimized interface featuring a 16:9 preview and the ability to save settings individually. The power switch has been relocated to the right side of the top plate for improved accessibility, although it is not as convenient as having it near the shutter button like on most other brands. It now features a central lock position, which is reminiscent of older Canon DSLRs, and replaces the separate lock button found on the R6. You can deactivate various controls on the camera, such as the control dials, joystick, touchscreen, and lens control ring.

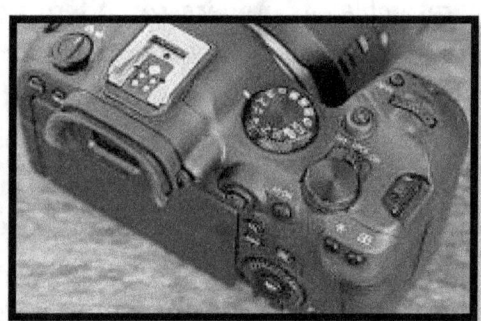

Canon has introduced an enhanced Dial Function option, enabling users to conveniently adjust pairs of settings simultaneously by pressing the M-Fn button located beside the shutter release and utilizing the front and rear dials. Meanwhile, the top dial allows you to select from the different pairs of functions. This provides convenient access to various settings such as white balance, metering, drive, and focus modes, flash exposure compensation, ISO, picture style, and AF area. You have the flexibility to customize this according to your preferences, with the addition of exposure compensation being the only other available option. Unfortunately, scrolling through the subject detection modes is not possible, which is quite disappointing.

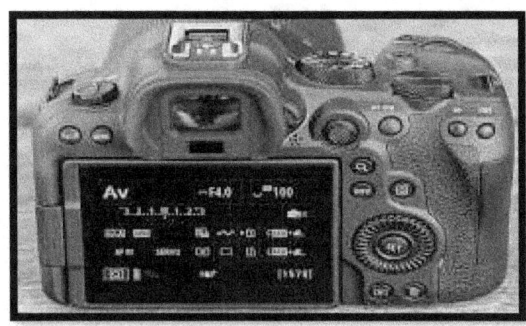

You can change other important settings by accessing the onscreen quick menu. Simply press the Q button on the back to activate it. This button is located in the center of a tightly packed group of ten controls, all of which can be easily operated using the right thumb. In reality, this is not as daunting as it may seem, since you probably won't be using a large number of them simultaneously. The controls can be easily customized, although there is little or no reason to do this since all the buttons have practical functions and the default layout is highly effective. Another option, however, is to repurpose the video record button for capturing still images. Alternatively, if you prefer a more personalized shooting experience, you might consider adjusting the depth of field preview button located on the front of the camera.

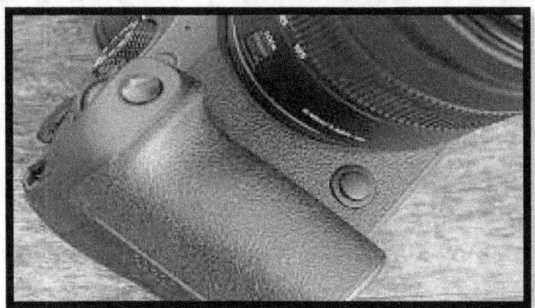

Canon consistently offers a touchscreen interface that seamlessly integrates with the camera's functionality, enhancing the user experience without overshadowing the physical controls. The menus of Canon cameras are well-organized and easy to navigate. Additionally, there is a customizable My Menu feature that allows you to group your frequently used settings for quick access. This feature is quite convenient, as it allows you to access certain useful options, like the mechanical/electronic shutter selection and raw burst mode, without having to navigate through the main menu. The shooting experience provided by the EOS R6 Mark II is truly exceptional, rivaling that of top-tier cameras.

Canon EOS R6 Mark II: Viewfinder and Screen

Canon has maintained the same 3.69m-dot EVF and 3in, 1.62m-dot fully articulated touchscreen on the R6, ensuring a professional experience for composing and viewing your images. The viewfinder boasts impressive features, including a 0.76x magnification and a high refresh rate of 120fps. However, in extremely bright conditions, visibility may be slightly challenging.

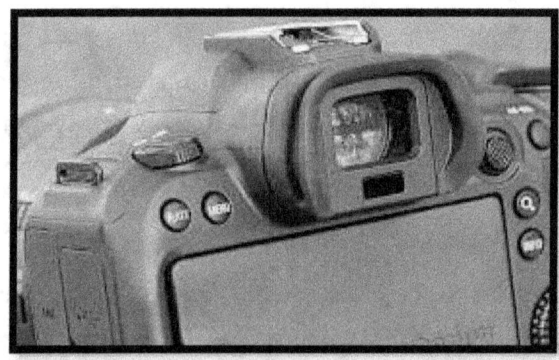

Canon provides a convenient feature that allows you to preview color, white balance, and exposure compensation by default. This makes it effortless to visualize the outcome of your images. In addition, you have the option to overlay grid lines, electronic levels, and an RGB live histogram to help you assess exposure with precision. By pressing the info button, you can effortlessly switch to a sleek and organized view that enhances your composition experience. When you shift your gaze from the viewfinder, the camera will seamlessly transition to the LCD screen below. This provides a precise preview, thanks to its side-hinged, fully articulated design that allows for shooting from a tripod or at unique angles in both portrait and landscape formats. Additionally, it can be positioned in a forward-facing direction to capture selfies or for vlogging purposes. In comparison to the original R6, there have been a few minor yet practical updates. Additionally, the EOS R6 Mark II now features the OVF View Assist mode, inspired by the EOS R3. This mode enhances shadow details and ensures accurate color reproduction, providing users with a viewing experience reminiscent of traditional SLR cameras. Mastering this technique is especially valuable in situations with extreme lighting differences, or when it is necessary to decrease exposure to preserve important highlights. The depth-of-field preview can be easily accessed through a button located on the front of the camera, similar to what you would find on a traditional DSLR. Canon has introduced a new menu setting that allows for full-time depth of field preview. This feature keeps the lens stopped down to the chosen aperture at all times. I might consider using this mode during the day, but in low light conditions, it can cause the viewfinder's refresh rate to decrease too much, resulting in a noticeably choppy view.

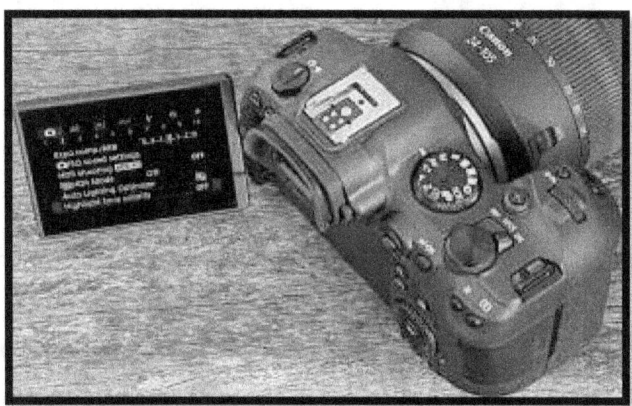

There is a valuable update available for video mode. During recording, a red outline flashes around the display, visible in both the viewfinder and on the LCD. One drawback is the absence of a tally light on the camera's front to indicate its recording status.

Canon EOS R6 Mark II: Mastering Autofocus

Similar to Canon's other cameras; autofocus is achieved through the use of the company's Dual Pixel CMOS AF technology. This innovative technology enables each sensor pixel to be used for phase detection autofocus. You have the option to select from 4897 points that are spread out across the entire frame. Additionally, you can choose from various sizes of focus areas. With three custom options at your disposal, you can precisely define the height and width of the focus zone. This feature proves to be incredibly useful when you have prior knowledge that your subjects will be situated in a specific area of the image, such as cars on a racecourse. Mastering the art of cycling through area modes is a breeze. Simply press the AF Area button and then M-Fn.

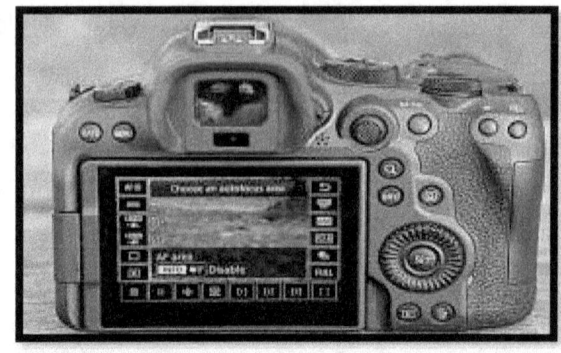

True to its professional nature, the EOS R6 Mark II excels in single-shot AF, effortlessly and silently focusing on static subjects with remarkable speed and reliability. The conventional tracking mode is highly effective and can be effortlessly activated by simply pressing the SET button on the back. Sony could benefit from observing Canon's approach in this matter. Nevertheless, the most recent AF systems focus on AI-based subject recognition and tracking, especially with continuous AF. Canon has implemented an incredibly advanced system on the EOS R6 Mark II, surpassing even their flagship EOS R3 model. The R6 could detect and track humans and animals, but the Mark II takes it a step further by recognizing a broader range of animals as well as vehicles like cars, trains, and planes. There is also a spot recognition setting available, allowing the camera to focus on the key element of the subject, such as the front windscreen of a vehicle. What you may not be aware of is the impressive eye control focus of the EOS R3, as well as the high readout speed of its stacked sensor, which typically results in improved AF tracking accuracy.

Canon EOS R6 Mark II: Impressive Performance

The EOS R6 Mark II showcases exceptional speed and responsiveness, catering to the needs of professional photographers. It's important to note that enabling Bluetooth can slightly delay the otherwise instant start-up. It is crucial to keep your firmware up to date and, if you are still experiencing issues, you may want to consider disabling Bluetooth. The camera operates with a high level of professionalism, emitting only a subtle and discreet sound when the shutter is fired. By using the electronic shutter mode, you can achieve complete silence. However, it's important to note that there is a potential risk of encountering rolling shutter distortion. Metering, auto white balance, and color are all characteristics of Canon's signature reliability. When using the standard evaluative metering mode, it's important to consider the focus point. If you choose to focus on a darker area of the scene, there is a possibility of losing important highlight details that cannot be recovered. However, it is quite simple to observe this through the viewfinder, allowing you to make the necessary adjustments to the exposure when needed (note that it is not visible in OVF View Assist mode).

The auto white balance is typically accurate, resulting in well-balanced out-of-camera JPEGs that are ready to be shared without much adjustment. For optimal results, shooting in raw format is recommended, particularly if you plan on making substantial tonal adjustments post-shooting. The EOS R6 Mark II's 24MP sensor provides an impressive dynamic range, enabling effortless retrieval of shadow detail by at least three stops. Pushing beyond a certain point will reveal noticeable artifacts, where Canon seems to be applying noise reduction to the darkest tones in the raw file. This implies that the level of flexibility offered by the top-notch full-frame sensors may not be fully achieved; however, it is still more than sufficient for the majority of practical scenarios. The continuous shooting performance is quite impressive, however, as always; the devil lies in the details. When using the mechanical shutter at its impressive 12 fps frame rate, live view between frames is not available. Instead, you are provided with a swift review of your captured images. This can pose a challenge when attempting to track moving subjects. For live view between frames, shooting at 7fps is your best option, with an impressive 230-shot buffer. To achieve a top speed of 40fps, you'll need to switch to the electronic shutter. However, accessing this setting requires navigating through the menus, which can be a bit inconvenient. It would have been more user-friendly if it were accessible directly as a drive-mode setting. Due to the lack of sensor stacking, a noticeable rolling shutter effect is present. Although not severe enough to cause obvious distortion, it may result in the background's vertical lines appearing slanted when panning, which could pose challenges when capturing subjects like motorsport. Additionally, the camera offers electronic shutter modes at 20fps and 5fps. However, it's worth noting that the faster options feature a flickering outline around the image to signal when the camera is shooting, whereas at 5fps, the entire display flashes on and off.

Accessing raw burst mode can be done through the menu. The camera captures footage at a smooth 30 frames per second, allowing you to buffer up to 15 frames before fully pressing the shutter button. When capturing bursts, they are saved as a single file. Later, during playback, you have the option to extract individual frames as either raw or JPEG files. It functions adequately, although it lacks the smoothness found in OM System's Pro Capture mode.

Canon EOS R6 Mark II: ISO and noise

The EOS R6 Mark II boasts a 24MP sensor, resulting in a notable 10% increase in linear resolution compared to its predecessor. Although this is not entirely unwelcome, it can be considered a modest improvement. The sensor produces high-quality images at low ISOs and remains reliable even at moderately high settings. As one gains experience, the influence of noise becomes increasingly apparent in the level of detail and color accuracy. Every photographer establishes their threshold for what they consider to be unacceptable. **Here are the specifications**:

- **Price**: The body only of this camera is priced at $2,499 / £2,779.
- **Sensor**: It features a 24.2MP Dual Pixel CMOS II sensor, measuring 35.9 x 25.9mm.
- **Output size**: The camera captures images at a resolution of 6000 x 4000 pixels.
- **Focal length magnification**: 1x
- **Lens mount**: Canon RF
- **Shutter speeds** range from 30-1/8000 sec (mechanical) to 30-1/16,000 sec (electronic).
- **Sensitivity range**: ISO 100-102,400 (standard), ISO 50-204,800 (expanded)
- **Exposure modes** available include PASM, Fv, B, Scene, and 3x Custom.
- **Metering options** include evaluative, partial, spot, and center-weighted.
- **Exposure compensation** can be adjusted from -3 EV to +3 EV in 0.3 EV increments.
- **Continuous shooting** at a rapid 12fps with the mechanical shutter, or an impressive 40fps with the electronic shutter.
- Enjoy a 3-inch fully articulated **screen** with a high resolution of 1.62m-dots.
- Immerse yourself in the **viewfinder** with a stunning 3.69m-dot OLED display, boasting a fast refresh rate of 120fps and a magnification of 0.76x.
- Benefit from a generous 4897 **autofocus points** for precise and accurate focusing.
- **Video capabilities** include shooting in 4K up to 60fps and Full HD up to 180fps.
- **External microphones** can be connected either through a 3.5mm stereo jack or via the multi-function shoe.
- The camera supports 2x UHS-II SD memory cards.
- Powered by an LP-E6N Li-ion battery.
- Battery life lasts for approximately 450 shots when using the electronic viewfinder (EVF) and 760 shots when using the LCD screen.
- The camera has dimensions of 138.4 × 98.4 × 88.4 mm.
- With the battery and memory card included, the camera weighs 670g.

CHAPTER ONE
MEET YOUR CANON EOS R6 II

Overview

Chapter one discusses how you can set up your Canon EOS R6 Mark II including inserting a memory card, setting the time and date, selecting a shooting mode, and so on.

Charging the Battery

1. Remove the protective cover that comes with the battery.

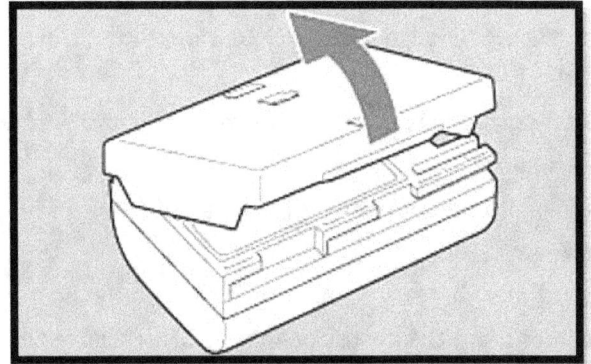

2. Ensure that the battery is completely inserted into the charger.
3. Charge the battery.

LC-E6

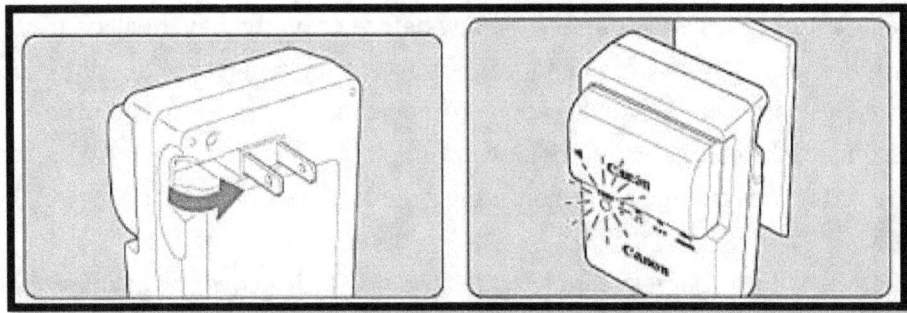

- Extend the charger prongs and securely insert them into a power outlet.

LC-E6E

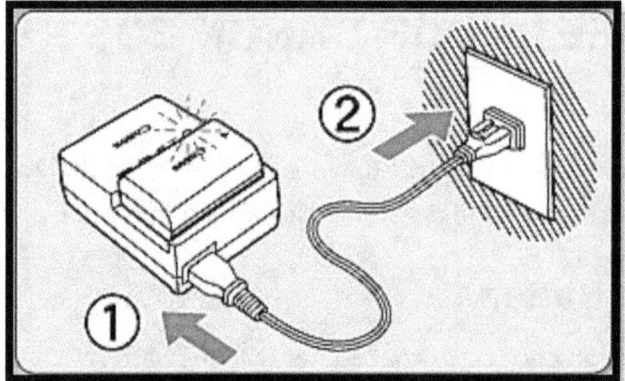

- Ensure that the power cord is securely connected to the charger and then plug it into a power outlet.
- The recharging process will begin automatically and you will notice the charge lamp blinking in orange.
- Charging a fully drained battery typically takes around 3 hours at a room temperature of 23°C/73°F.

The charging time of the battery can vary significantly based on factors such as the surrounding temperature and the current capacity of the battery.

- Charging in low temperatures (5–10°C/41–50°F) may take longer for safety reasons, usually up to approximately 4 hours.

After purchasing, the battery does not come fully charged.

- Ensure the battery is fully charged before use.
- Make sure to charge the battery the day before or on the day it will be used.
- Batteries gradually lose their charge over time, even when they are not in use.
- Once the battery is fully charged, it is important to remove it from the device and disconnect the charger from the power outlet.
- Attach the protective cover in a different orientation to indicate the battery's charging status.

Once the battery is fully charged, simply attach the protective cover by aligning the battery-shaped hole $<\square>$ with the blue sticker on the battery. When the battery is drained, simply attach the protective cover in the opposite direction.

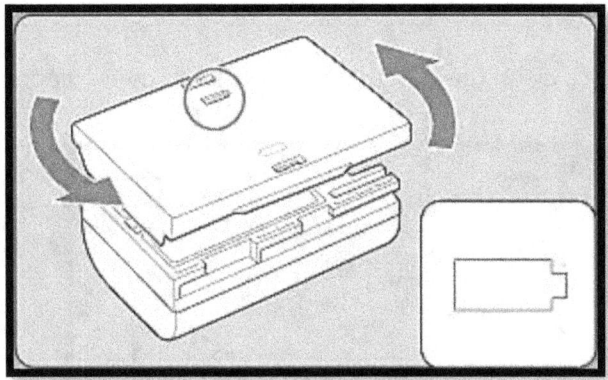

- **Remember to remove the battery when the camera is not in use**.

Leaving the battery in the camera for an extended period can lead to a gradual release of power current, causing excessive discharge and ultimately reducing the battery's lifespan. It is recommended to keep the battery stored with the protective cover attached. It is important to note that storing the battery when it is fully charged may have an impact on its performance.

- **The battery charger is designed to be compatible with power outlets in foreign countries**.

This battery charger is designed to work with a power source that ranges from 100 V AC to 240 V AC and operates at a frequency of 50/60 Hz. When needed, make sure to connect a plug adapter that is compatible with the country or region you are in. For optimal safety, refrain from connecting to portable voltage transformers.

- **If the battery is running out of power quickly even after being fully charged, it may be a sign that the battery needs to be replaced**.

Ensure the battery's recharge performance is up to par and consider investing in a new battery.

Inserting and removing batteries

Ensure that you have a fully charged Battery Pack LP-E6NH (or LP-E6N/LP-E6) ready to be inserted into the camera.

Inserting the battery

1. Gently slide the lock on the battery compartment cover to open it.

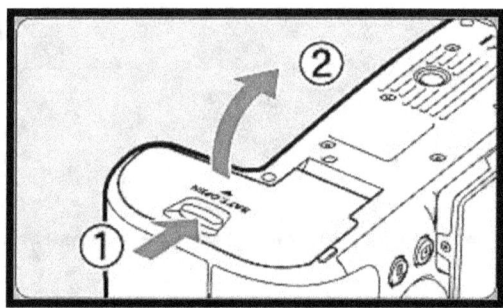

2. Proceed to insert the battery.

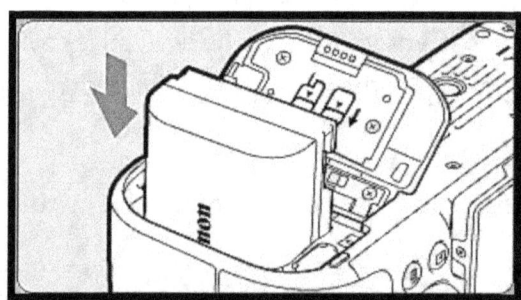

- Insert the end with the electrical contacts in a precise manner.
- Ensure that the battery is securely inserted by locking it in place.

3. Close the cover.

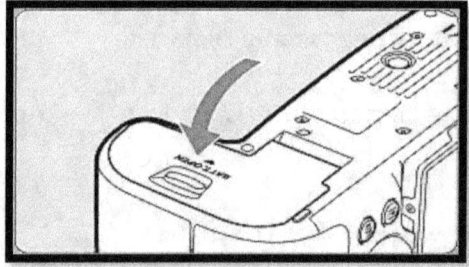

- Ensure that the cover is securely closed by applying pressure until it audibly snaps into place.

Battery Removal Procedure

1. Carefully open the cover and proceed to remove the battery.

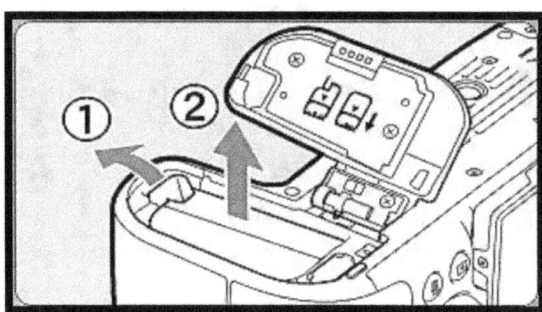

- Press the battery lock lever indicated by the arrow and carefully remove the battery.
- Always remember to attach the protective cover to the battery to avoid any potential short-circuits.

Inserting and Removing Cards

This camera is compatible with two different types of memory cards. Recording is feasible as long as there is at least one card in the camera. When two cards are inserted, you have the option to choose a single card for recording or simultaneously record the same image on both cards.

Inserting Cards

1. Open the cover by sliding it.

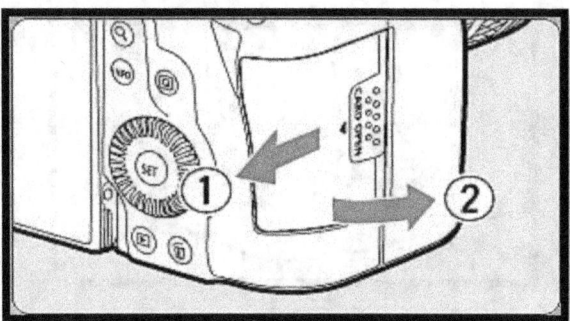

2. Proceed to insert the card.

Card 1

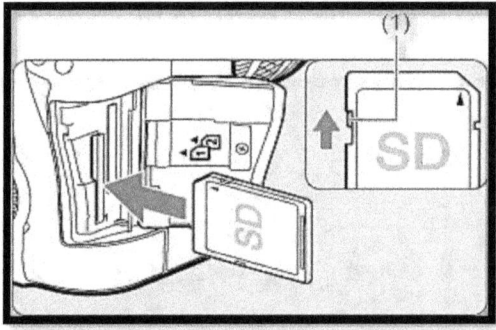

Card 2

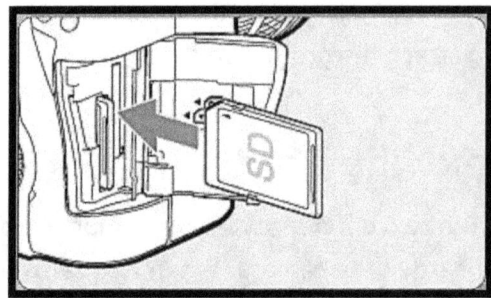

- The card in the back card slot is [1], and the one in front of it is [2].
- Ensure that the card's label side is facing toward you and insert it until you hear a click, indicating it is securely in place.
3. Close the cover.

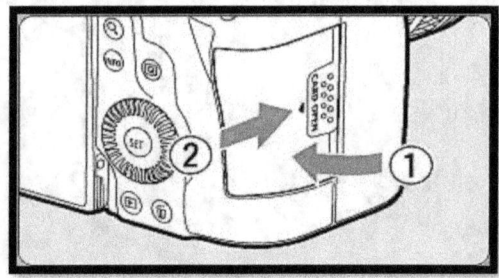

- Ensure the cover is securely closed by sliding it in the indicated direction until it snaps into place.

4. Make sure to set the power switch to the <ON> position.

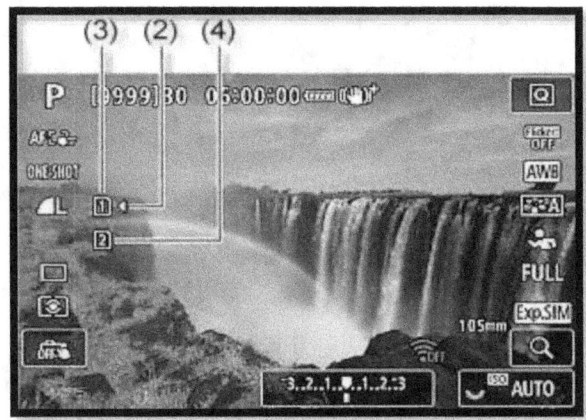

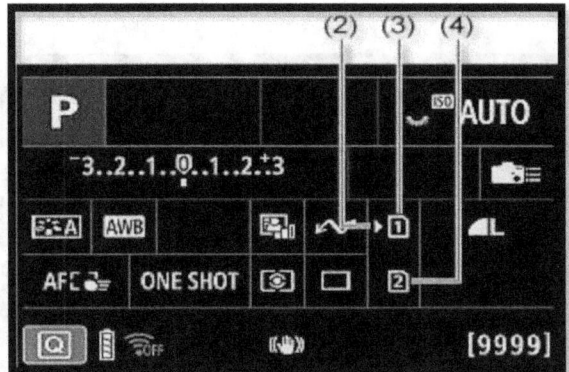

(2) Icon for selecting a card (3) Card 1 (4) Card 2

- Icons representing loaded cards are displayed on the shooting screen when you press the <INFO> button and on the Quick Control screen (). Selected cards are marked with

  [ⵣ] for recording.

Formatting the Card

For optimal performance, it is recommended to format the card with this camera if it is new or has been previously formatted by another device.

1. Begin by opening the cover.

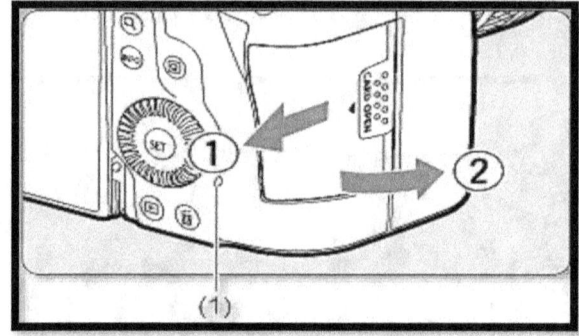

- Make sure to set the power switch to the correct position.
- Make sure the access lamp (1) is not illuminated before opening the cover.
- If the screen displays "Saving...", close the cover.

2. Remove the card.

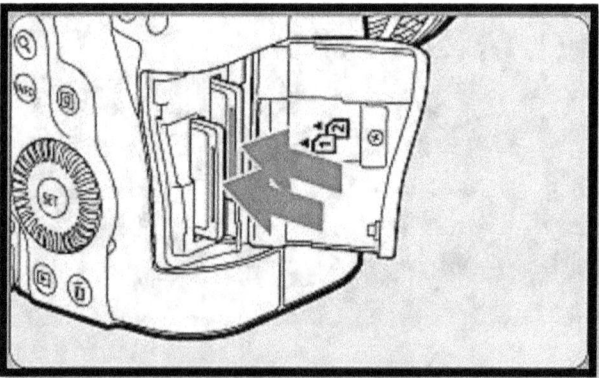

- Push the card in gently and it will be ejected.
- Ensure that you pull the card out in a straight manner and proceed to close the cover.

Caution

Refrain from removing cards right away when you see a red [⏻⬛▯▯▯▯▯▯] icons appear while shooting. The cards may be experiencing high internal camera temperature, which could cause them to become hot. Before removing the cards, first set the power switch to the <OFF> position and take a break from shooting. It is important to handle hot cards with care after shooting to prevent any potential damage from dropping them. Exercise caution when handling cards.

- Note that the number of shots you can take may vary based on factors such as the capacity of your memory card and your chosen settings for image quality and ISO speed.
- Make sure to set "**Release shutter without card**" to "**Disable**" to avoid any mishaps of forgetting to insert a card.

Using the Screen

You can adjust the orientation and tilt of the screen.

1. Adjust the screen to a different position.

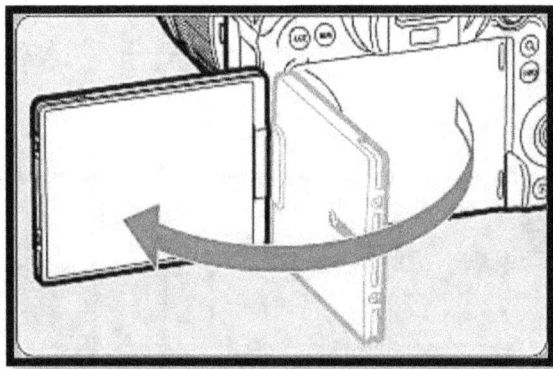

2. Rotate the screen.

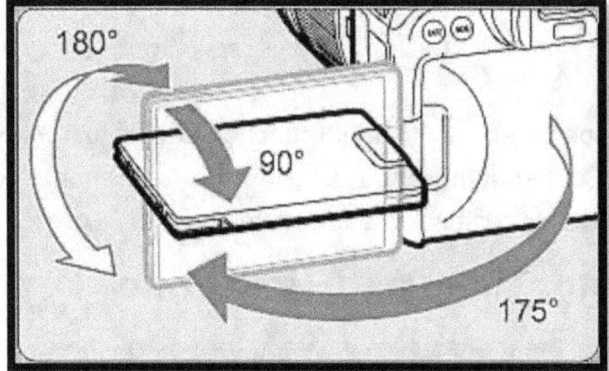

- When the screen is extended, you have the flexibility to adjust its angle or orientation to capture the desired subject.
- The indicated angles are only approximate.

3. Position it in your direction.

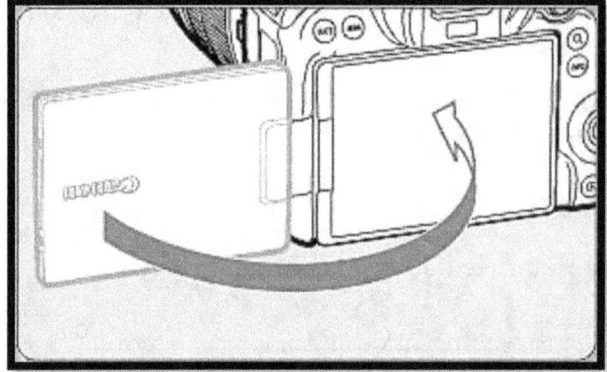

- Typically, it is recommended to use the camera with the screen facing you.

Turning on the Power

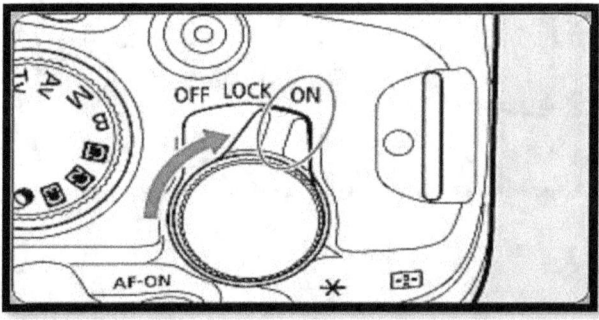

- The camera is turned on. This mode is specifically designed for capturing still photographs.
- The camera is powered on. The multi-function locking feature is currently activated.
- The camera is currently powered off and is not operational. Remember to set the power switch to this position when the camera is not in use.

Setting the Date, Time, and Time Zone

To set the time zone, follow these steps when you turn on the power for the first time or if the date/time/zone has been reset. By establishing the time zone initially, you can effortlessly modify this setting in the future to ensure the date and time is accurately synchronized. Make sure to properly set your date and time so that the captured images will include accurate shooting information.

1. Choose the **Date/Time/Zone option**.

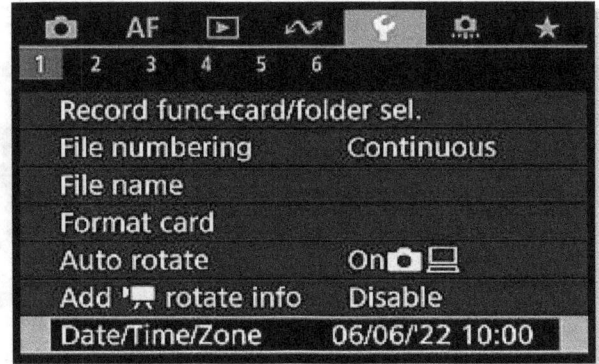

2. Set the time zone with precision.

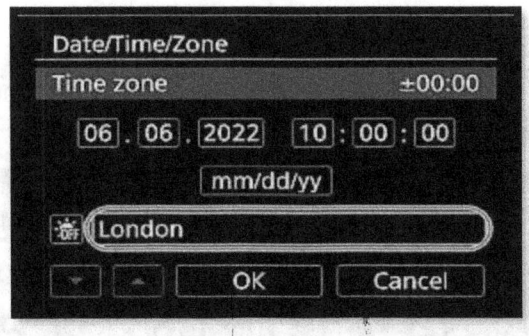

- Adjust the < ⊙ > dial to choose the desired time zone.

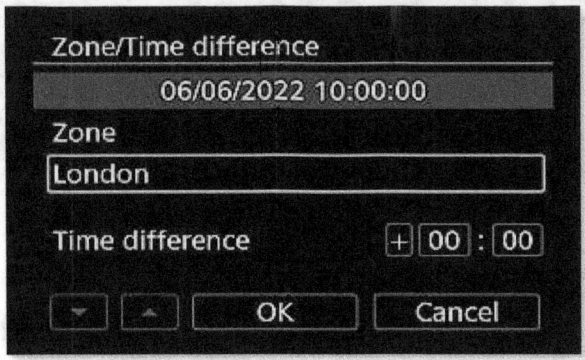

- Press the < (SET) > button.

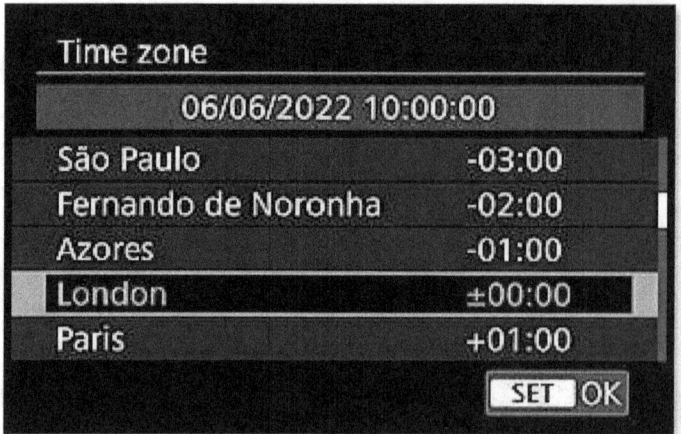

- Choose the time zone.
- If your time zone is not listed, you can easily set the difference from UTC by pressing the <**MENU**> button.

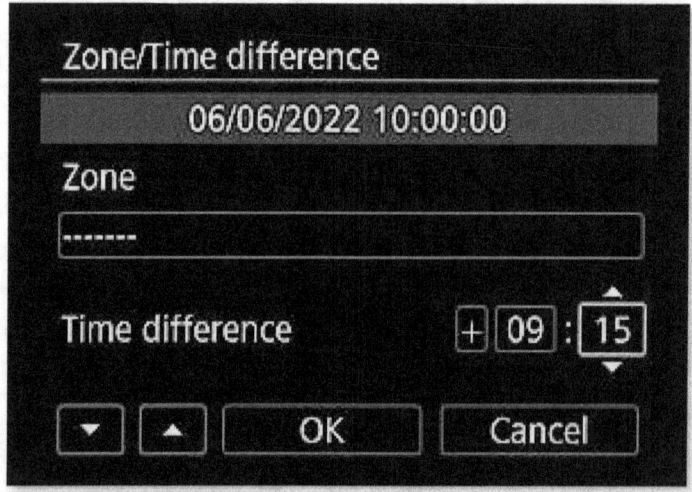

- Choose a time difference option (+–/hour/minute), and then press the < (SET) > button.
- Once you have positioned the item, simply press the < (SET) > button.
- Once you've entered the time zone or time difference, simply select [OK].
3. Set the correct date and time.

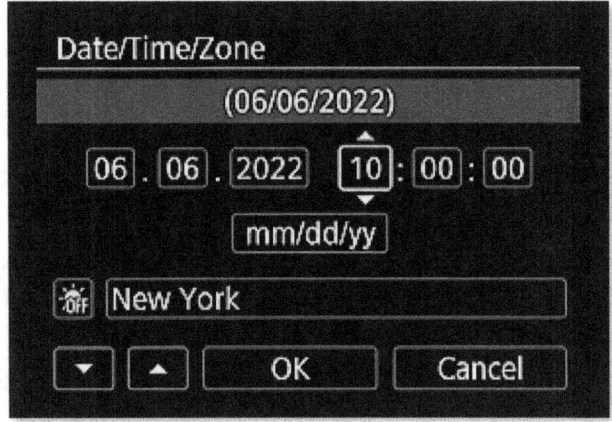

- Choose an item and then press the < (SET) > button.

- Once you have positioned the item, simply press the < (SET) > button.

4. Set daylight saving time.

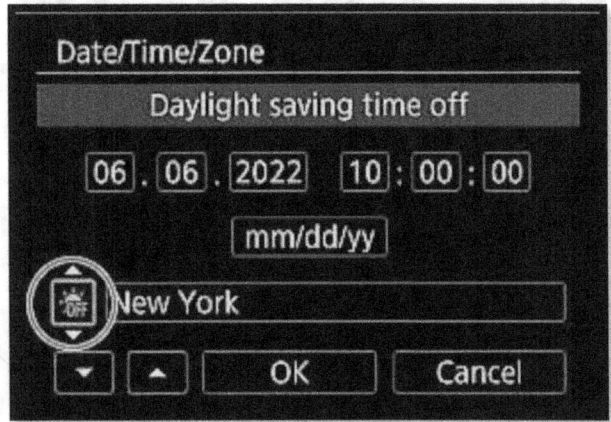

- Adjust it as needed.

- Choose [☀OFF] or [☀], and then press the < (SET) > button.

- When daylight saving time is [☀] enabled, the time set in step 3 will advance by 1 hour. If [☀OFF] is set, the daylight saving time will be deactivated and the time will be adjusted by moving back 1 hour.

5. Leave the setting.

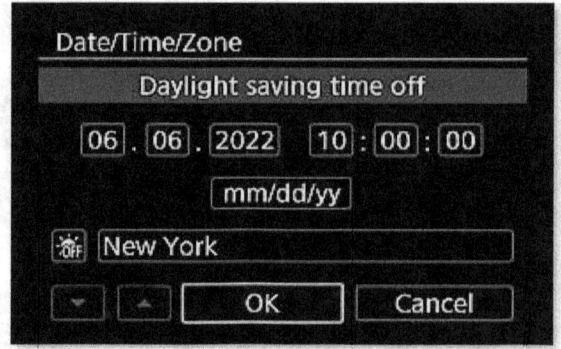

- Click on [**OK**].

Change the Interface Language

1. Choose **Language**.

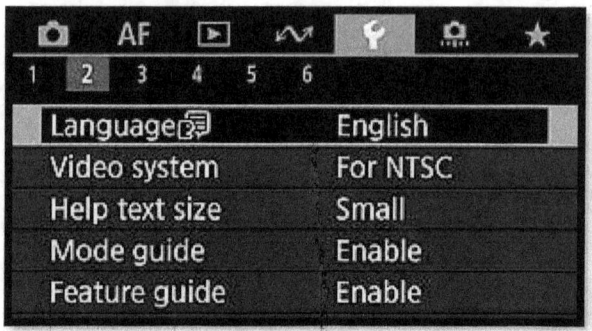

2. Choose the preferred language.

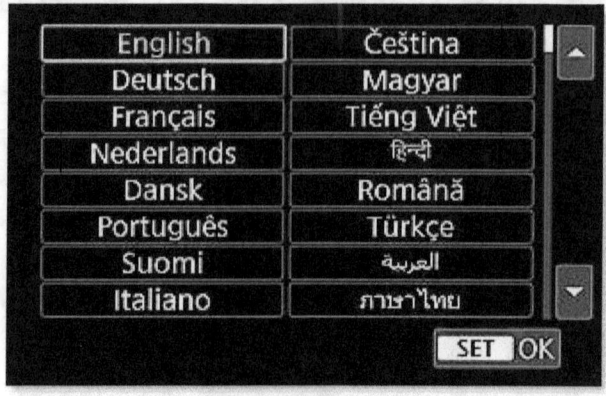

Automatic Sensor Cleaning

- When the power switch is set to the off position, the sensor will be cleaned automatically, which may produce a slight sound. While performing the sensor cleaning, the screen will show [·⊡⁺]. To activate automatic sensor cleaning when the power switch is turned on, you can configure this in the sensor cleaning settings.

- If you toggle the power switch on and off quickly, the [·⊡⁺] icon may not appear. However, this does not mean that there is a problem with the camera.

First things first

You can start by meticulously unpacking the camera and thoroughly verifying its contents. Ensure that the box contains the following items:

- **The camera itself (Canon EOS R6 II digital camera):** You need to thoroughly inspect the camera upon receiving it. Ensure that the color LCD screen on the back is free from any scratches or cracks. Check that the memory card and battery doors open smoothly. Once a fully charged battery is inserted and the lens is mounted, the camera should power up without any issues. Occasionally, defects like these can occur, although they are uncommon. Your dealer likely tampered with the camera or it could have been a customer return. It is advisable to purchase your camera from a reputable retailer that can provide you with a brand-new camera straight from the factory.

- **Lens (Not compulsory):** Upon its release, this camera was offered as a standalone body or in different kit options, including the body with either the 24-105mm f/4L lens or the more budget-friendly 24-105mm f/4.7-7.1 zoom lens. Dealers were also open to bundling the camera body with additional lenses, including the RF 35mm f/1.8 IS Macro STM, RF 28-70mm f/2.8L IS USM, and RF 50mm f/1.2L USM. However, if you were looking for a more affordable option or wanted to explore Canon's new mirrorless system, you most likely choose one of the versatile 24-105mm lenses. Many professional photographers who have heavily invested in Canon DSLR gear may have chosen to forgo the RF-mount option and instead opted for one of the three available mount adapters to use with their current lenses.

Lens Recommendation: The 24-105mm f/4L version is an excellent choice for an enthusiast camera. It is comparable to the Canon EF-mount 24-105mm lens and performs exceptionally well at this level.

- **Battery Pack LP-E6NH**: Ensure that the Battery Pack LP-E6NH is fully charged with its 7.2V, 1865mAh capacity before using it. Ensure that a protective cover is always used on the battery when it is not inside the camera to prevent any contact shorting.
- **Neck Strap**: Canon offers a neck strap adorned with your camera model, ensuring a professional look. Although it lacks adjustability, this product may not be the optimal choice for you. Additionally, it may attract the attention of unsavory individuals who are observant enough to recognize its high-end nature.
- If you bought a kit, you may also want to consider lens accessories. When you buy a camera with a lens, you'll be delighted to find that it comes with some fantastic accessories, such as the LF-N1 rear lens cap. The lens will come with a front lens cap that fits perfectly and might even include a case. The RF 24-105 f/4 L IS USM lens is accompanied by a Canon E-77 II and LP1319 lens case, for instance.
- **Camera cover RF-5**: Using a body cap is essential for preventing dust from entering your camera when a lens is not attached. It is essential to always have a body cap and rear lens cap with you. The body cap and rear lens cap can be conveniently stored together when not in use, ensuring compactness.
- **Instructional guides:** Canon continues to offer a printed manual for users. This book may appear small at first glance, but it is surprisingly dense. While approximately one-third of its pages are in English, the remaining content repeats the same information in Spanish and French.
- **Complete the warranty and registration card**: Make sure to keep these safe. Registering your camera by mail is optional and not necessary to maintain your warranty. However, it is advisable to keep the paperwork and purchase receipts/invoices from your retailer in case you need Canon service support in the future.

Canon categorizes certain items as optional accessories, although some of them may be deemed essential by both you and me. Consider the following items that are not included in the box, but may be worth considering before making a purchase.

Here is a rough list of them in order of importance:

- **Memory card:** It is necessary to have a memory card, as the camera does not come with one.

RECOMMENDED: Getting a memory card with a minimum size of 32GB. However, if you can, opting for a 64GB or larger card would be even more beneficial.

- **LP-E6NH/LP-E6**: When using your camera extensively, the battery life may not be as long as you're accustomed to. This is because the camera's sensor and either the electronic viewfinder or rear-panel LCD screen remain active for extended periods. According to Canon's estimates, you can expect around 320 to 450 shots from a single battery when using the electronic viewfinder, and up to 580 to 760 shots when working with the back-panel LCD monitor. It's quite simple to surpass that number in just a few hours of capturing sports action at 12 fps (or 40 fps with the electronic shutter). Even batteries can unexpectedly fail or lose their charge if left unused for a week or two.

RECOMMENDED: Invest in an additional battery, ensure it remains fully charged, and bid farewell to any concerns. The latest version of the LP-E6NH is highly recommended as it offers the convenience of being charged inside the camera using the USB Power Adapter PD-E1. However, if you are upgrading from a previous model that uses the original LP-E6 batteries and happens to have some spares, you can still make use of them.

- **Add-on Speedlite:** Similar to high-end enthusiast cameras, these cameras do not come with a built-in electronic flash. Therefore, you will require an external Speedlite like the Canon Speedlite 600EX II-RT or the top-of-the-line EL-1 (which comes with a hefty price tag of $1,100!). If you're interested in reducing the weight you need to carry, the Canon Speedlite EL-100 could be a great option. It offers a more modest output that is ideal for fill purposes.

RECOMMENDATIONS: Your add-on flash can serve as the primary light source for your photo, or it can be adjusted to provide a softer light to fill in any shadows. If you engage in frequent flash photography, it is highly recommended to consider a Speedlite as an essential accessory. To achieve optimal flexibility in lighting your subject, it is recommended to utilize two flash units. One flash unit should be mounted on the camera and used as a trigger, while the other flash unit should be positioned off-camera and wirelessly triggered as a receiver. The three flash units mentioned above are versatile and can be used in different roles. Additionally, Canon provides the ST-E2 and ST-E3-RT transmitter/triggers that can be mounted on the accessory shoe and act as masters.

- **Mount Adapters**: If you happen to possess a collection of Canon EF and EF-S lenses, Canon provides three adapters that enable you to use those lenses on any R-series camera. There are three options available for your EF/EF-S lenses. The first is a mount adapter, the second adds a customizable control ring similar to RF optics, and the third includes a drop-in filter carrier for using a single-size filter behind the rear element of the lens. It encompasses polarizers and variable neutral-density filters, and the feature is compatible with lenses that typically cannot accommodate screw-in filters, such as the Canon EF 11-24mm f/4L USM or Canon Tilt/Shift TS-E 17mm f/4L lenses.

- **AC Adapter Kit AC-E6N**: This device is used with a DC coupler, the DR-E6, that replaces the LPE6NH battery and powers the camera from the AC current. It is designed to provide a professional-level power solution for your camera.

RECOMMENDATIONS: There are various scenarios where this feature can be useful. For example, when you're cleaning the sensor manually and want to ensure that the shutter doesn't accidentally activate. It's also handy when you're shooting indoors for long periods, such as tabletop photos, portraits, or class pictures. Additionally, it's great for remote shooting and time-lapse photography, as well as reviewing images on your television or transferring files to your computer. This AC adapter can supply the substantial power required by all of these devices.

- **Remote controls:** Using a wired or wireless remote control to trip the shutter is a more convenient option than relying on the self-timer to trigger your tripod-mounted camera without any vibration.

Remote Recommendations: The Canon BR-E1 wireless remote control is a great option for remote camera control. It uses Bluetooth technology, allowing you to operate your camera from a distance of up to 16 feet without the need for a direct line of sight. Additionally, it is compatible with the PZ-E1 Power Zoom Adapter, enabling you to remotely adjust the zoom position and movement of the EF-S 18-135mm f/3.5-5.6 IS USM lens. The lens is specifically designed for APS-C cameras and does not provide full-frame coverage for the R6 II. Additionally, it features an AF button that allows for autofocus while shooting videos. Alternatively, you may consider using wired remotes such as the Canon RS-60E remote switch.

Initial Setup

Power Options

To ensure optimal performance of your Canon EOS R6 II, it is important to have a fully charged battery. Therefore, the initial task at hand is to recharge the LP-E6NH lithium-ion battery pack that comes with your camera. With a fully charged power source, you can expect to capture around 400 shots, give or take, depending on your preference for using the LCD or viewfinder to compose your shots. This estimate is derived from the standardized tests outlined in the Camera & Imaging Products Association (CIPA) document DC-002.

Rechargeable batteries naturally experience self-discharge even when they are not in use, whether they are inside the camera or still in their original packaging. Typically, lithium-ion power packs of this type experience a gradual loss of charge daily, even when the camera is not in use. Li-ion cells gradually lose power due to an ongoing chemical reaction, even when the camera is turned off. It is highly probable that the battery you bought with your camera is no longer functioning optimally. Consequently, it would be wise to recharge it before embarking on a photography session. There is a wide selection of battery chargers for your camera. Most owners find the compact LC-E6 charger to be their go-to choice. Investing in one of the optional charging devices provides more than just extra features. It gives you a backup power source to keep your camera running until you can replace your primary charger.

Presented below is a comprehensive list of power options for your reference:

- **LC-E6:** This charger is perfect for the camera and can also be used with earlier models that use the LC-E6 or LC-E6N batteries. It's incredibly convenient due to its compact size and built-in wall plug prongs, allowing you to connect it directly to your power strip or wall socket without the need for a cord.
- **LC-E6E**: This product is comparable to the LC-E6 as it charges a single battery, but it does require a cord for operation. That can be beneficial in specific circumstances. For instance, if your power outlet is located in a hard-to-reach spot, you can plug in the cord and route it in a way that allows the charger to sit on a more accessible surface, such as your desk.
- **CBC-E6 Car Battery Cable**: It comes with the Car Battery Cable CB-570, which can be easily plugged into your vehicle's lighter or accessory socket. With the vehicle battery option, you can continue capturing stunning shots even in remote areas without access to AC power.
- **Battery Grip BG-R10:** This accessory is designed to hold one or two LC-E6NH batteries, allowing you to power your device like a professional. Enhance your shooting capabilities by doubling your capacity and gaining extra controls for vertical shooting. These include an additional shutter release, Main dial, Quick Control dial, M-Fn button, AF-ON, AE lock/FE lock, and AF point selection controls. With the included power adapter, you can conveniently charge LP-E6NH batteries directly in the camera.

Mounting a Lens

The recommended lens-mounting procedure prioritizes safeguarding your equipment against any accidental damage and reducing the presence of dust. When using your camera without a lens, simply choose the lens you wish to use and gently loosen the rear lens cap, without removing it completely. Most people position the lens they intend to attach in a vertical slot within the camera bag. This ensures its safety and allows for easy access when needed. To ensure optimal protection, it is recommended to gently remove the rear lens cap just before lifting it off the back of the lens. Next, you can remove the body cap by gently rotating it towards the shutter release button. It is important to always mount the body cap when there is no lens on the camera. This will effectively prevent dust from entering the camera's interior and potentially causing damage to the sensor. (Ensuring optimal performance of the sensor-cleaning mechanism and minimizing dust accumulation is highly recommended.) Additionally, the body cap serves as a protective barrier against potential damage from external objects, such as fingers, if proper caution is not exercised.

After removing the body cap, take off the rear lens cap and set it aside. Then, carefully attach the lens to the camera by aligning the raised red indicator on the lens barrel with the red line on the camera's lens mount. Ensure that the lens is securely seated by rotating it away from the shutter release. Ensure that the focus mode switch on the lens is set to AF (autofocus) and the stabilizer switch is turned on. To ensure optimal portability, make sure to remove the lens hood if it is bayoneted on the lens in the reversed position. Simply twist it off and remount it facing outward. Using a lens hood is essential for safeguarding the front of your lens against any unexpected knocks, and unwanted smudges, and minimizing the impact of unwanted light that can cause flare on your images.

Adjusting Diopter Correction with expertise

For individuals with less-than-optimal eyesight, a slight optical adjustment in the viewfinder can often be advantageous. If you're someone who wears glasses but wants to work without them, you can make use of the camera's built-in diopter adjustment. This feature allows you to adjust the correction from -4 to +2, giving you the freedom to work without your glasses while still maintaining clear vision. Ensure the camera is powered on, and then carefully adjust the diopter control situated to the right of the viewfinder. Look through the viewfinder and continue adjusting until the indicators appear perfectly sharp.

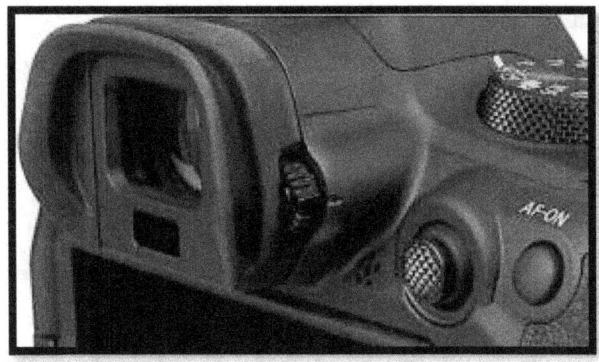

Mastering Basic Navigation

The following contains the basic navigation you should know when using the Canon EOS R6 Mark II:

- **Main Dial:** The wheel (main dial) on top of the camera, positioned behind the shutter release button, serves multiple purposes. It allows you to navigate through menus, make adjustments in the Quick Control screen, shift the focus point horizontally, and modify settings like shutter speed.
- **Quick Control dial 1:** The circular disc found on the rear panel of Canon cameras has been referred to as the Quick Control dial since the days of film photography. Referred to as Quick Control dial 1, this function allows for vertical movement within a menu tab, cycling through 10 available settings on the Quick Control screen, adjusting the focus point, or modifying settings like aperture.

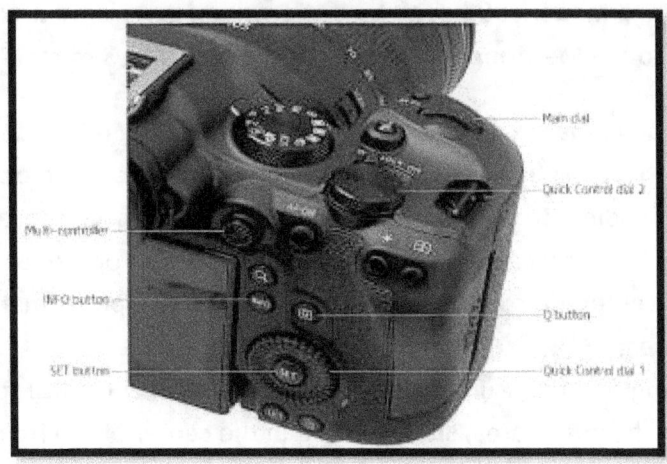

- **Quick Control dial 2**: Canon could have chosen to label the second dial at the top-rear edge of the same panel differently to distinguish it from the Main dial. This dial allows for seamless navigation between main menu tabs, allowing you to effortlessly switch from the Shooting menu to the AF menu without having to go through each tab within the main menus. It replicates the vertical focus point movement of Quick Control dial 1 and duplicates the setting adjustment function of the Main dial within the Quick Control screen.
- **Multi-controller**. You can effortlessly shift this button in eight different directions using just the tip of your finger. In addition, it can be pressed inward to serve as a Set/Return/Enter button for selecting certain options. Use it for tasks such as fine-tuning white balance, adjusting the autofocus point, zooming in on specific areas of the image, or making quick adjustments using the Control screen.
- **INFO button**: Switches the data displayed on the screen, allowing you to cycle through different screens by pressing it multiple times.
- **Q button**: Access the Quick Control menu with ease. When a menu is displayed on the screen, the Q button seamlessly navigates between main menu tabs, similar to the Quick Control dial 2.
- **SET button:** Functions as a confirmation tool for menu selections and adjustments.

Choosing a Metering Mode

Now, let's move on to the metering mode setting. Ensure that the camera is set to one of the semi-automatic or manual modes, rather than Scene Intelligent Auto (A+), for the following settings.

To select the Metering mode, you have two options. You can either use the Quick Control screen or navigate to the Metering mode entry in the Shooting 3 menu.

- **Using evaluative metering**: Using the standard metering mode, the camera employs its intelligent capabilities to analyze your image and select the optimal exposure by considering readings from numerous zones within the image sensor.
- **Partial metering**: Using a professional approach, you can opt for partial metering. The exposure is centered around a specific spot, covering approximately 5.9 percent of the image area.
- **Spot metering:** The exposure is calculated from a smaller central spot, approximately 3 percent of the image area, situated right in the center of the frame.

- **Center-weighted averaging metering:** The camera effectively meters the entire scene, with a particular focus on the central area of the frame.

Choosing a Focus Mode (AF Operation)

Switching between automatic and manual focus is quite a straightforward approach. Simply adjust the AF/MF selector on the lens attached to your camera (if available). When using a semi-automatic shooting mode, it is important to select the right focus mode, which Canon refers to as AF operation. It instructs the camera on when to focus while AF is active. To configure the autofocus mode, simply access the viewfinder or the Quick Control display on the LCD screen. From there, you can easily navigate to the AF operation icon to adjust the focus mode. It is positioned to the left of the Metering mode icon in the Quick Control screen and is the second option in the left column of the other two views. Select one of the available options: One-Shot or Servo. If the lens is set to manual focus, both options will be unavailable, and an MF indicator will be displayed as the icon.

Here are the options available to you:

- **One-Shot:** In this mode, also known as single autofocus, the focus point is locked when the shutter button is pressed down halfway. When the image is in focus at the active focus points, green boxes will appear. However, if the camera is unable to achieve sharp focus, orange boxes will be displayed. The focus will stay locked until you let go of the button or capture the image. This mode is most effective when your subject remains still.
- With **Servo AF**, you can achieve precise focus by partially depressing the shutter button. This mode constantly keeps an eye on the frame and adjusts focus if there is any movement from the camera or subject. Capturing sports and moving subjects is made easier with this mode.

Selecting AF Area

This camera provides a wide range of selectable focus positions integrated into the sensor, allowing for precise focus calculation. In Scene Intelligent Auto mode, the camera automatically selects the focus point using the face detection and tracking mode. In the other semi-automatic and manual exposure modes, you have the option to let the camera automatically select the focus point or manually choose the desired focus point. There are a total of eight focus point selection options available on your camera, allowing for both automatic and manual selection.

Here is the list:

- **Spot AF** enables the manual selection of a single, smaller AF point.
- **1-point autofocus:** You have the option to manually choose a larger AF point that is approximately three times the size of the Spot AF area.
- **Expand the AF area:** You have the option to manually choose a single AF point, along with the four points positioned above, below, and to the left/right of it.
- **Expand the AF: Around**: It is possible to manually choose a single AF point and also have the option to select up to eight points surrounding it, including above, below, left, right, and diagonally from the selected point.
- **Flexible Zone AF 1:** The AF points are organized into square-shaped zones that cover approximately one-sixth of the frame, allowing you to choose the desired zone for focusing. In this Zone mode and the two subsequent ones, the EOS camera will automatically detect faces, if they are present, and make an effort to focus on them.
- **Flexible Zone AF 2 (Vertical):** The AF points are organized into larger, vertically oriented zones, allowing you to choose the specific zone you want to use.
- **Flexible Zone AF 3 (Horizontal):** The AF points are positioned within a wider horizontal zone that you can customize.
- **Whole Area AF:** The camera calculates the focusing area dynamically, taking into account factors such as subject distance, identified people, animals, or vehicles, and subject motion.

Aside from the Quick Control menu, the R6 II provides various alternative methods for selecting the AF method.

Here's how to select the autofocus areas on your camera:

1. **Hit the AF point selection button:** The location of the camera is towards the right side at the back. Pressing this button is necessary whenever you need to switch the AF area selection mode or choose a specific AF point once the mode is selected.
2. **Switch between different modes:** Press the AF point selection button and quickly follow it up by pressing the M-Fn button. Keep pressing the M-Fn button to cycle through the eight available modes.
3. **Choose the AF area mode:** When you press the M-Fn button, the display will promptly show all the available AF area options. The highlighting will be modified to indicate the selected mode. When choosing the AF area, you can press the INFO button and

switch between the Whole area or AF points only subject tracking in Servo AF mode. Press **SET** to confirm.

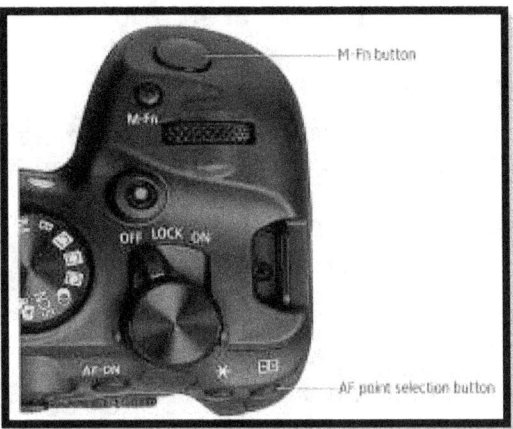

Transferring Photos to Your Computer

To complete your photo-taking session, you'll need to transfer the photos you've captured to your computer. This will allow you to print them, review them in more detail, or make any necessary image edits. With your camera, you can effortlessly generate print orders directly within the device. To transfer your images, you have two options. You can either use a cable to transfer them directly from the camera to the computer, or you can remove the memory card from the camera and use a card reader to transfer the images. Typically, the latter option is considered the superior choice due to its faster speed and minimal impact on your camera's battery life. If you find yourself in a situation where you have a cable and a computer but no card reader, such as when using a friend's computer or at an Internet café, you can still make a cable transfer.

To transfer images from a memory card to the computer using a card reader, follow these steps:

1. First and foremost, turn off the camera.
2. Open the memory card door and gently press the card to release it for removal.
3. Place the memory card into the memory card reader. The software installed on your device will automatically detect the files stored on the card and provide you with the option to transfer them. You can also access the card as a mass storage device on your

desktop, allowing you to easily transfer files by simply dragging and dropping them onto your computer.

To transfer images from the camera to a Mac or PC, follow these steps:

1. First of all, turn off the camera.
2. Carefully remove the cover that is shielding the camera's USB terminal, and then connect the provided USB Type-C cable to the terminal.
3. Connect the other end of the USB cable to a USB Type-C port on your computer. If your device does not have a USB Type-C terminal, you may need to use an optional Type-C-to-USB-A adapter.
4. Go on to turn on the camera. Typically, your installed software will automatically detect the camera and prompt you to transfer the pictures. Alternatively, the camera may appear on your desktop as a mass storage device, allowing you to easily drag and drop the files to your computer.

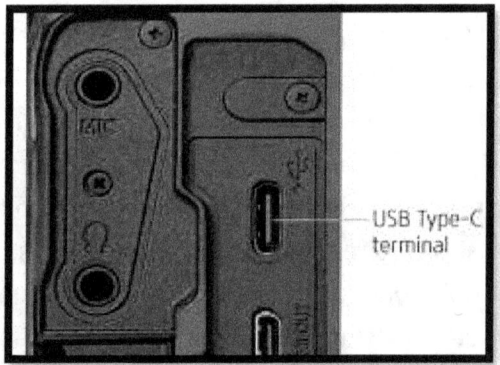

Frequently Asked Questions

1. How do you charge the Canon EOS R6 Mark II?
2. How do you insert and remove the batteries?
3. How do you turn on the power?
4. How do you insert and remove memory cards in the camera?
5. How do you set the date and time zone?
6. How do you change the interface language?
7. How do you transfer photos to your computer?
8. How do you choose a metering and focus mode?
9. How do you mount a lend on the camera?

CHAPTER TWO
YOUR VISUAL ROADMAP

Overview

Chapter two further takes you down the lane to learn about the different controls in the Canon EOS R6 Mark II including mastering the front view of the screen, the touch screen, under the camera, the right-side controls, and a whole lot more.

Front View

As you continue snapping, your subjects will see the front of the camera. The front, however, is the surface your fingers curl around when you hold the camera, and there are just three buttons to push, all within easy reach of your left hand's fingers, plus the shutter button and Main dial, which are on the top/front of the hand grip. The lens itself has extra settings. **The following are the other major components you should know:**

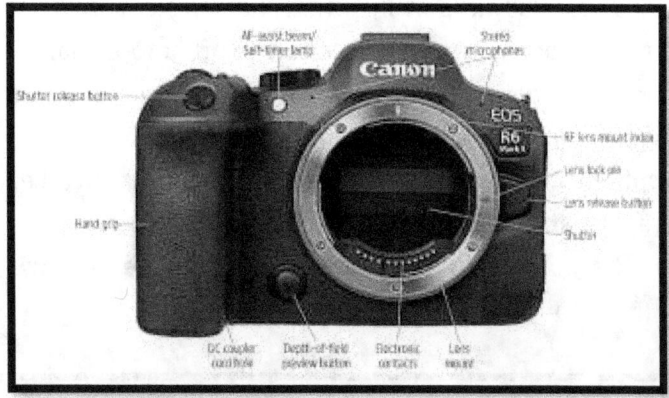

- **Shutter release button**: The shutter release button is angled on top of the hand grip. To lock exposure and focus (in One-Shot mode and Servo AF modes with non-moving subjects), press this button halfway down.
- **Self-timer light with AF-assist beam:** This LED flashes when more light is required to aid focusing. When using the self-timer, this bulb flashes to indicate the countdown until the shot is captured.

- **DC coupler cable access:** This cover, which is located on the inner edge of the hand grip, opens to enable the DC power cord to connect to the camera via the battery compartment.
- **Hand grip**: This gives a secure grip and also houses the camera's battery.
- **Depth-of-field preview button**: When pushed, the lens is stopped down to the aperture that will be used to capture the photograph, giving a preview of the depth-of-field.
- **Lens mount:** This strong flange takes a corresponding bayonet on the back of any lens or accessory you put on the camera.
- **Lens release button**: Press and hold this button to unlock the lens, allowing you to rotate it out of the camera.
- **Lens lock pin**: When the release button is pressed to unlock the lens, this pin on the lens flange retracts.
- **RF lens mount index:** To align it as you install it on the camera, line this mark with the corresponding red detent on the barrel of your RF or mount adapter lens.
- **Shutter**: When you turn off the camera, the shutter closes, protecting the delicate sensor, which is especially important when changing lenses. When you switch on the camera, the shutter opens, so be sure to turn it off before changing lenses.
- **Electronic contacts:** These connections are linked to corresponding locations on the lens, allowing the camera and lens to interact electrically.
- **Stereo microphones:** A stereo set of microphones is situated on each side of the front of the camera, just above the lens mount on the R6 II.

Added controls can be found on the camera's side. The following are the major components:

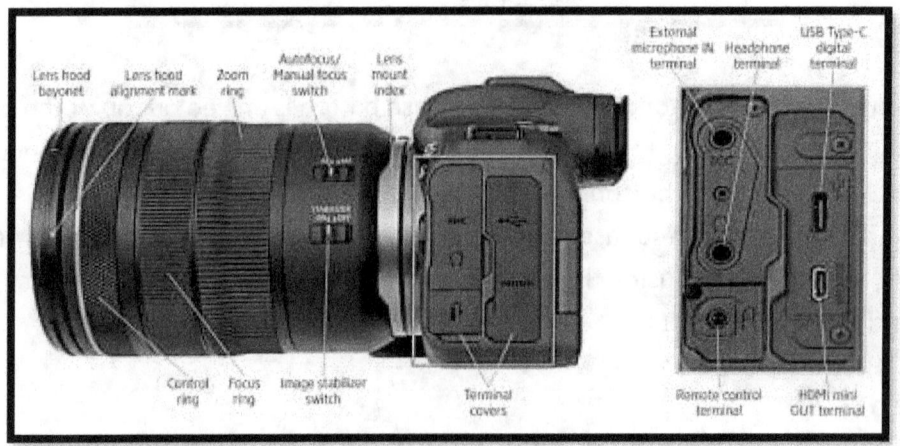

- **Lens hood bayonet**: Canon sells lens hoods that are custom-made for each lens; they connect to the grooved attachment that rings the front of the lens in both forward and backward orientations. The hood prevents unwanted light from entering the lens, which diminishes contrast and creates flare. When shooting, always wear a hood to protect yourself from harm caused by crashes and other incidents. Filters are made to shatter easily (which is how filter producers urge you to purchase extra filters to "**save**" your lens) and are best used when you need to filter anything or are working in damp or dusty conditions.
- **Lens hood alignment mark**: Align a matching indication on your lens hood and spin it to attach it to the front of your lens.
- **Control ring:** This function allows you to configure the aperture, shutter speed, ISO, and exposure compensation.
- **Focus ring**: Rotate this ring to manually focus or fine-tune autofocus.
- **Zoom ring:** Zoom in or out by turning this ring.
- **Image stabilizer switch:** This toggle toggles image stabilization on and off. When the camera is placed on a tripod, you should turn off IS.
- **Autofocus/Manual focus switch:** Canon autofocus lenses contain a switch that allows you to switch between automatic and manual focus.
- **Terminal covers**: The interface ports and terminals of the camera are protected from dust and moisture by these three rubber covers.

The Business End

The R6 II's rear panel is jam-packed with more than a dozen distinct controls, buttons, and knobs. That may seem to be a lot to understand, but you'll discover that the camera has a respectable number of specialized controls that allow you to make regular modifications more rapidly than visiting a standard menu every time you want to alter a setting.

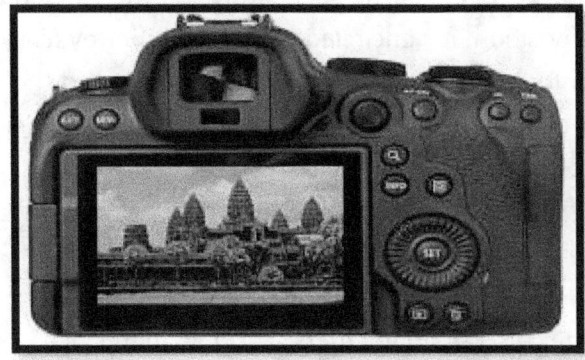

The following are the important buttons and components, as well as their functions:

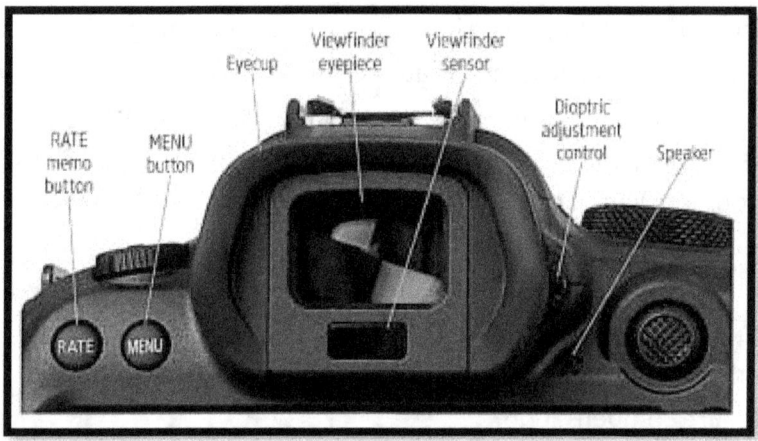

1. **MENU button:** The menu shown on the camera's LCD screen or electronic viewfinder is summoned/exited. This button is also used to quit a submenu and return to the main menu when dealing with submenus.

2. **RATE button:** This button's default behavior is to enable you to "**rate**" photos as they are playing. During picture playback, pressing numerous times assigns one through five-star ratings to the image, or clears all ratings. You can additionally program the RATE button to do two operations, one when pressed alone and the other when pressed while holding the RATE button down and moving the Quick Control dial 1. Rate/picture Jump and Protect/Image Jump (which, during picture review, jumps to the next image by an increment you define in the Playback 6 menu) are two of these choices.

3. **Dioptric adjustment control:** Adjust your eyesight by rotating this dial while gazing through the viewfinder.

4. **Viewfinder eyepiece/eyecup:** By looking through the viewfinder eyepiece, you may frame your composition. It's encircled by a soft rubber eyecup/frame that blocks out unnecessary light when squeezing your eye closely up to the viewfinder, as well as protecting your eyeglass lenses from scratches (if used). The electronic viewfinder of the R6 II features 3.69 million pixels.

5. **Viewfinder sensor:** When your eye (or any other object) approaches the viewfinder eyepiece, this sensor detects it. The camera alternates between the two automatically by default, but you may arrange it to switch exclusively manually by using the Screen/Viewfinder Display option in the Set-up 4 menu.

Right-Side Controls

The following are the primary controls found on the right-hand-side and their functions:

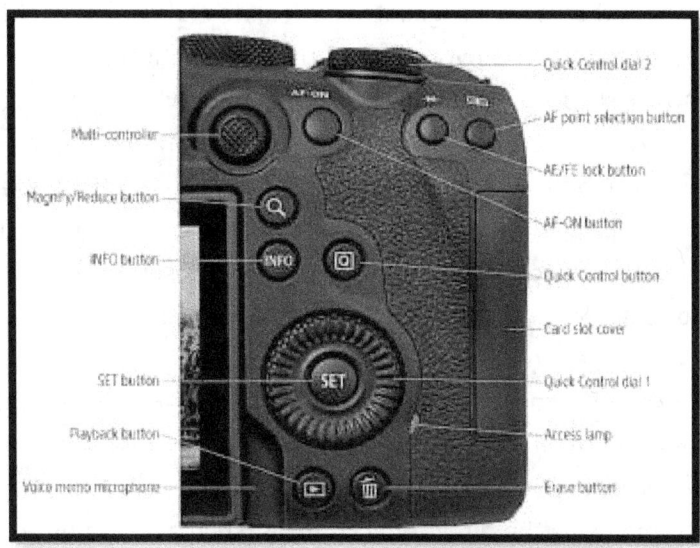

1. **(QCD-1) Quick Control Dial 1:** It is basically used to go through menus and pick photography parameters such as f/stop or exposure compensation value. It also acts as a backup controller for various functions that are established with other controls, such as AF point selection.

2. **(QCD-2) Quick Control Dial 2:** When browsing menus, the second QCD dial leaps immediately from one main heading to the next, allowing you to skip from the Shooting menus to the AF menu, and then to the Playback, Network, Set-up, and Custom Function menus without having to visit each of the tabs in the separate groups. To go from, for example, Shooting 1 to Shooting 2 to Shooting 3, and so forth, rotate the Main dials situated just rearward of the shutter release button. The QCD-2 is also utilized for additional directional operations. The QCD-2 (Quick Control Dial 2) is also known as the Rear dial.

3. **AF-ON button:** To engage the focusing mechanism without having to partly depress the shutter release, use this button. When used with other buttons, this function enables you to lock exposure and focus individually. Lock exposure by halfway pushing the shutter release or the AE lock button; autofocus by halfway pressing the shutter release or the AF-ON button.

4. **AE/FE (auto exposure/flash exposure) lock button:** It locks the exposure or external flash exposure that the camera sets when you partly depress the shutter button in shooting mode. The exposure lock indicator (*) is displayed in the display's bottom left corner. Press the * button again to recalculate exposure while the shutter button is still half depressed. When you release the shutter button or snap the image, the exposure is unlocked. Maintain the * button held when shooting to maintain the exposure lock for consecutive images. When using an external flash, pushing the * button fires an additional pre-flash when you partly depress the shutter button, allowing the machine to calculate and lock the exposure before capturing the photo.

5. **AF point selection button:** This button has two purposes:

- **AF area mode selection:** Press this button once, then continually press the M-Fn button to cycle between the possible AF area modes, which include Spot AF, 1-Point AF, Expand Area AF, Expand Area AF (Around), Zone AF 1, Zone AF 2, Zone AF 3, and Whole Area AF.

- **AF point movement:** When you press this button, you may move the AF point or zone across the frame using the directional controls, such as the multi-controller, in all AF area modes except Whole Area AF.

6. **Multi-controller:** When shifting focus points, moving a zoomed area, browsing menus, and performing other operations, this joystick-like button can be adjusted in eight distinct ways.

7. **Magnify/Reduce button.** This button has two functions: shooting and playback.

- **Shooting mode:** Once pressed, this button will magnify the screen by 5X, 10X, and ultimately 1X (full frame). While the picture is enlarged, you may use the multi-controller to manipulate the zoomed region.

- **Playback mode.** Press and release this button. Then, rotating the QCD-2 to the right, gradually zoom in on a still picture. There are 15 magnification increments ranging from 1X to 10X; the starting magnification may be specified using the Magnification option in the Playback 5 menu. Zoom out to full-frame mode and then to 4-, 9-, 36-, and 100-image index views by rotating the QCD-2 to the left. Press SET in any index or enlarged view to display a full-frame view of the currently highlighted picture.

8. **SET button:** When making a decision, this button acts as a SET/ENTER control to activate or confirm your choice.

9. **Card slot cover:** To unlock and obtain access to the camera's dual card slots, slide towards the rear of the camera.

10. **The Q (Quick Control) button:** When in shooting mode, press this button to bring up the Quick Control panel, which offers you access to a variety of options. When you're examining photographs in Playback, a new Quick Control panel appears, allowing you to protect or rate images, modify the jump method, resize, crop, rotate, and many other things.

11. **Access lamp:** This bulb shows that the memory card is being accessed when it is illuminated or blinks.

12. **Erase button:** This button deletes the presently displayed picture in Playback mode.

13. **Playback button:** The most recent picture is shown.

14. **INFO button:** Changes the information shown in shooting and playback modes. It's also used in certain menu panels to go to more information or alternatives.

Mastering the Touch Screen

The LCD 3.0-inch display screen on your camera is articulated and can be positioned in a variety of positions. It is also touch-sensitive for quick menu and focus selection. The articulation function allows you to capture images in a range of positions. When you touch the screen, you can conduct various common tasks, including menu navigation/selection functions.

Flexible View

The adjustable screen allows you to examine and evaluate your photographs in ways that the electronic viewfinder cannot. **Here are a few to think about:**

- **Selfie mode:** Swing the LCD out of the body and rotate it such that the screen faces the same direction as the lens. Place the camera on a tripod or any other temporary support, then position yourself (alone or in a group) for a selfie. With the self-timer or remote control, you may see the picture that the camera will take before snapping the photo. If you choose, the camera may quickly show the snapshot so you can analyze it and adjust postures before taking another photo.

- **Share the fun:** When the LCD is in the "**selfie**" position, you may share the photograph you're going to capture with your subject even if you're not in the shot. It works best when the camera is mounted on a tripod. Before you photograph, your subject may assess the position, change his or her hair, or turn to their "**good**" side. When you transfer your gaze to the viewfinder, the LCD preview disappears and you can see the image as you snap the shot.

- **Waist-level view**: You can tilt the screen back with the LCD swinging out, giving you a waist-level preview of the photo you're going to snap. That viewpoint is particularly beneficial for capturing low-lying things without crouching or getting down on your hands and knees. It's also excellent for semi-stealth photography since it eliminates the need to raise the camera to your eye to create a picture.
- **Periscope view:** The screen can rotate to face entirely downward, allowing you to hold the camera over your head and shoot in periscopic mode. Excellent for shooting above crowds, especially during parades.
- **Screen protection**: Swivel the screen so that the back of the LCD faces outward, and you have solid protection—at least from scratches and moderate impacts.

Touch Operation

For many expert shooters, certain touch-friendly tasks, such as browsing menus, may be no faster than the button/dial methods we are used to and may be much more problematic for those with big fingers or those who need/want to wear gloves. However, as you grow more acclimated to interacting with the camera's screen, there are various applications for the touch screens that border on spectacular. It can even be used while looking through an electronic viewfinder. **Here are some examples of what you can do:**

- **While using the EVF, move the focus point:** As you preview your picture via the viewfinder, you may move the AF point or Zone AF frame around by touching the screen with one finger and dragging. Simply enable Touch & Drag AF in the AF 4 menu and choose one of many techniques for designating the active region of the screen and how the point or zone travels.
- **Touch the shutter/focus point**: By touching the screen while watching the touch screen, you may define the precise focus point (or zone) you desire. If you've engaged the Touch Shutter function (via an icon in the bottom left corner of the screen), the camera can concentrate on the spot you just picked or even capture a photo. If you want to shift the focus point by dragging it around the screen, hit the point selection button and then swipe your finger around the touch screen.
- **Text entry**: If you've ever had to type in copyright information, rename the My Menu tab, or perform any other text-entry operation using the camera's buttons and dials, you'll appreciate the ability to simply tap on the virtual keyboard to enter data, such as photographer and copyright information.

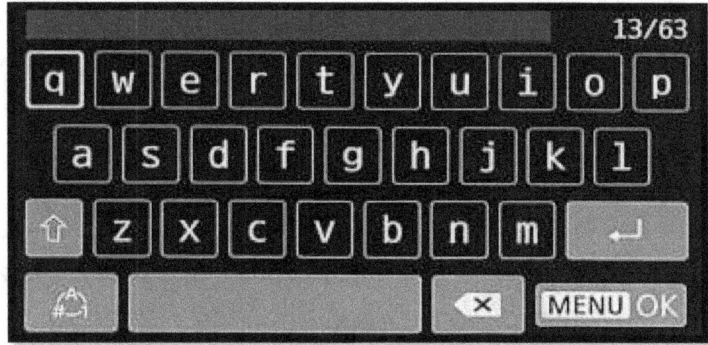

Going Topside

The camera's top surface has its own set of commonly used controls.

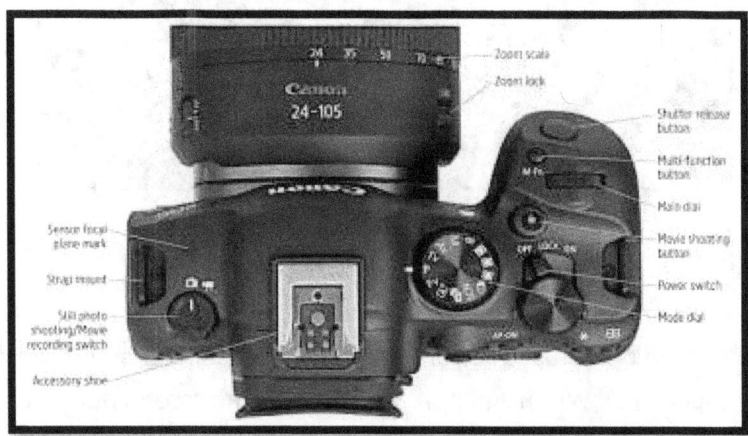

The main controls, as well as two extra lens control functions, are shown below.

- **Zoom scale**: The current zoom focal length is shown. This is only available with zoom lenses.
- **Zoom lock:** When the zoom is set to its widest setting, you may toggle this switch to keep it there. This prevents "**zoom creep**" when the lens is directed downward.
- **Shutter release button:** To lock in exposure and focus, push this button just partially. To snap the photo, press the button down. When the camera has switched off the auto-exposure and focusing functions, tapping the shutter release button reactivates both. When a review picture is shown on the back-panel color LCD, pressing this button clears the image and reactivates the auto exposure and focusing functions.
- **M-Fn button**: This multi-function button serves two purposes:

Dial-up functions: If you hit this button alone, a pop-up horizontal list of functions will appear by default. The display shows the available functions in pairs. When a function is highlighted, you can change the parameters for the top function by rotating the Main dial, and the bottom function by rotating the QCD-1. If you want other functions to show here, you can add or remove them.

Autofocus area selection mode: In the upper-right corner of the camera's back, press the AF point selection button. Using the Custom Controls functionality, you may assign hundreds of different functions to this control.

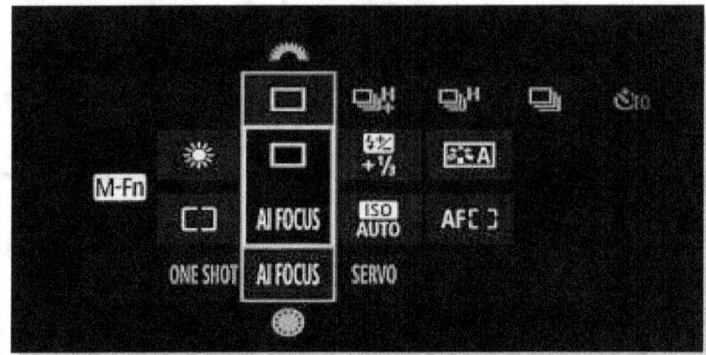

- **Main dial:** This dial is used to adjust a variety of shooting parameters. When two settings are available (for example, shutter speed/aperture in Manual shooting mode), the Main dial is used for one (for example, shutter speed) and the QCD-1 for the other (aperture). When a picture is shown on the screen during playback, this dial also defines the leaps that skip a certain number of photos during playback of previously taken shots. Jumps maybe 1 picture, 10 images, 100 images, by date, by screen (that is, by thumbnail screens when using Index mode), by date, or by folder. This dial is also used to navigate between tabs when the **MENU button** is held, and it is used to modify pairs of settings inside certain menus (in combination with the QCD-1).

- **Movie shooting button**: To begin recording video, press; to stop, press again. If you choose, you can remap this button for any of 40 different purposes.

- **Power switch**: To turn on the camera, rotate to the far right, and the far left to turn it off. The camera is turned on in the center Lock position; however, specific controls may be frozen to prevent them from being modified accidentally. To unlock those controls, move from the Lock position. You have the option of locking the main dial,

QCD-1, QCD-2, multi-controller, control ring, or touchscreen panel. Use the Multi-Function Lock item in the Set-up 5 menu to choose which of these to lock.

- **Accessory shoe**: When you require an external Speedlite, slide an electronic flash into this multi-purpose accessory shoe. A dedicated flash unit, such as one from Canon, can exchange exposure, zoom setting, white balance information, and other data between the flash and the camera via the various contact points displayed.
- **Sensor focal plane mark:** Precision macro and scientific photography necessitates knowing the exact location of the sensor's focus plane. The plane is represented by the symbol on the side of the pentaprism.
- **Strap mount**: A neck strap attaches to this attachment, and a corresponding mount is located on the other side of the camera.
- **Mode dial:** Rotate the cursor to pick one of the various exposure modes and one of the camera's user settings.

Underneath Your Camera

There's not much going on with your camera's bottom panel.

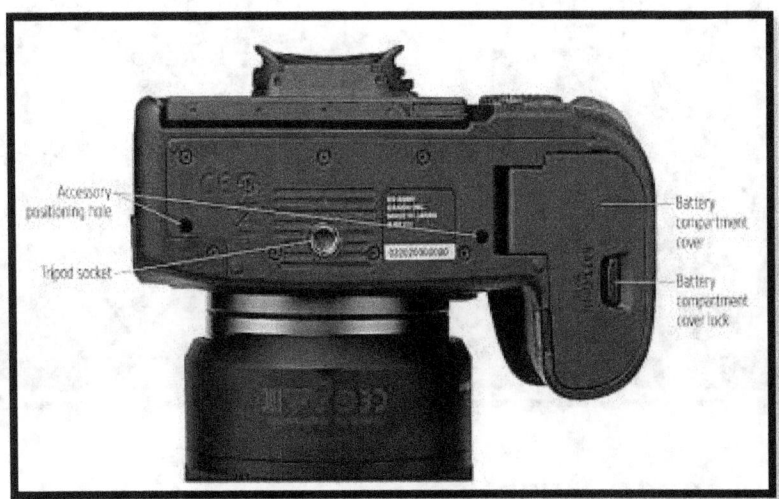

The following can be found below the camera:

- **Tripod socket:** It is used to secure the camera to a tripod and to lock on the optional BG-R10 battery grip.
- **Accessory positioning holes:** Install corresponding studs on the BG-R10 grip to offer extra electricity to your camera, allowing you to shoot more exposures on a single

charge. For simpler vertical shooting, it also has a vertically oriented shutter button, a Main dial, AE lock/FE lock, and AF point selection settings.

- **Battery compartment cover/lock/door/door release:** To open the battery compartment cover and access the LP-E6NH battery, or to insert the BG-R10 battery grip, slide the cover lock clasp towards the center of the camera. To remove the battery, retract the battery release tab and press the white button.

When the battery door latch is open, press down on the little black battery compartment door release level that extends from the hinge to attach the grip. This will allow you to remove the battery door, as seen in the image on the right. Then, take out the camera's battery and insert the grip into the battery cavity, matching the pin on the grip with the little hole on the other side of the tripod socket. Tighten the tripod socket screw on the grip to secure it to the bottom of your camera.

- **Electronic contacts:** The grip contacts will join with the electrical contacts.

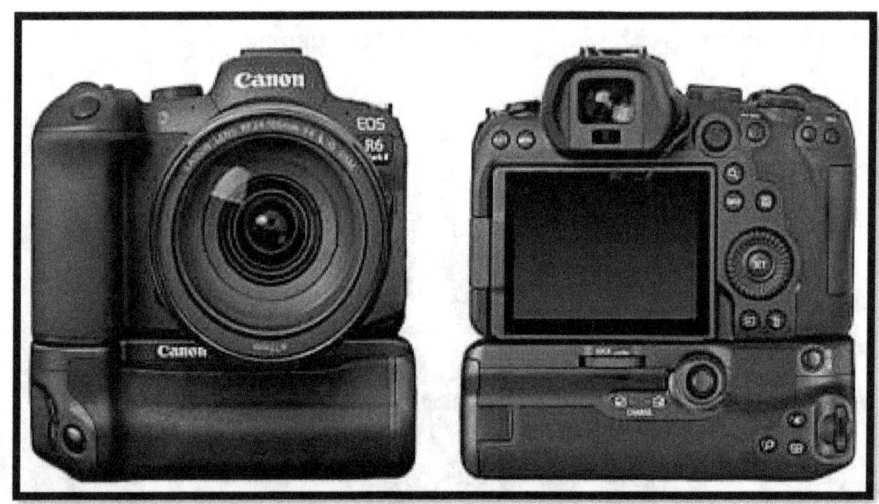

Frequently Asked Questions

1. How do you master the touch screen on the camera?
2. What are the front controls and their functions?
3. What are the back controls and their functions in the Canon EOS R6 II?
4. What are the top controls and their functions?

CHAPTER THREE
RECOMMENDED SETTINGS

Overview

In this chapter, you will learn about the different recommended settings in Canon EOS R6 Mark II and how you can change the default settings as well.

Changing Default Settings

Even if you're new to using a Canon digital camera, making adjustments to the default settings is simply straightforward.

Resetting to Factory Defaults

To ensure that the camera is set to the factory defaults before making any changes, it is advisable to double-check the current settings. Indeed, it is possible that the settings of a recently purchased camera could have been altered either at the retailer or during a demonstration. Typically, the Reset Camera option in the Set-up 6 menu is the preferred choice. It offers two options: Basic Settings and Other Settings. Restoring the default adjustments for camera shooting functions and menu settings is a feature available in Basic Settings. No matter how you've configured your camera, it will be set to the following: One-Shot AF mode, Evaluative metering, single-shot drive mode, JPEG Fine Large image quality, Automatic ISO, sRGB color mode, Automatic White Balance, Auto Lighting Optimizer Off, and Standard Picture Style. All adjustments made to exposure compensation, flash exposure compensation, and white balance will be reset, and any bracketing for exposure or white balance will be undone. Erasing custom white balances and Dust Delete Data.

Restoring the factory defaults for various settings can be done through the Other Settings option. This includes Customized Quick Controls, Shooting Information Display, Root Certificate, Communication Settings, Custom Shooting Modes (1–3), Copyright Information, Customized Controls, Custom Functions (C.Fn), and My Menu. In the Custom Functions 3 menu, there is an option called Clear Customized Settings. This allows you to reset the Customize Buttons and Customize Dials settings. Additionally, in the Custom Functions 5 menu, you will find an option called Clear All Custom Functions. The following tables display the default settings after using the resetting option in the Basic Settings menu. They provide

a wide range of menu settings, including some functions that are not strictly settings. Additionally, camera settings like Drive mode are also included.

Still Photo Shooting Menu Defaults

Image Quality	Large, Fine	Clarity	0
Dual Pixel RAW	Disable	Shooting Creative Filters	Off
Cropping/Aspect Ratio	Full	Lens Aberration Correction	
Digital Tele-Converter	Off	Peripheral Illumination Correction	Enable
Exposure Compensation/Auto	0	Distortion Correction	Disable
Exposure Bracketing		Digital Lens Optimizer	Standard
ISO Speed Settings		Long Exposure Noise Reduction	Disable
ISO Speed	Auto	High ISO Speed Noise Reduction	Standard
ISO Speed Range	Minimum: 100	Dust Delete Data	Erased
	Maximum: 102,400	Multiple Exposure	Disable
Auto Range	Minimum: 100	RAW Burst Mode	Disable
	Maximum: 25,600	Focus Bracketing	Disable
Minimum Shutter Speed for Auto	Auto	Drive Mode	Single Shooting
HDR PQ Settings	Off	Interval Timer	Disable
HDR Mode	Off	Bulb Timer	Disable
Auto Lighting Optimizer	Off	Silent Shutter Function	Off
Highlight Tone Priority	Off	Shutter Mode	Electronic
Anti-Flicker Shooting	Disable		1st-curtain
High Frequency Anti-Flicker Shooting	Off	Release Shutter Without Card	On
External Speedlite Control		IS (Image Stabilizer) Mode	On
Flash Firing	Enable	Digital IS	Off
E-TTL Balance	Standard	Touch Shutter	Off
E-TTL Metering	Evaluative (Face Priority)	Image Review	2 seconds
		Review Duration	2 seconds
Continuous Flash Control	E-TTL Each Shot	Viewfinder Review	Disable
Slow Synchro	1/250-1/200 to 1/60 Second Auto	High-Speed Display	Off
		Metering Timer	8 seconds
Flash Function Settings	—	Display Simulation	Exposure
Flash Custom Function Settings	—	Optical Viewfinder Simulated View Assist	Off
White Balance	AWB (Ambience-priority)	Shooting Information Display	—
Custom White Balance	Canceled	Viewfinder Display Format	Display 1
WB Shift/Bracket	0,0/+−0	Display Performance	Power Saving
Color Space	sRGB		
Picture Style	Auto		

AF Menu Defaults

AF Operation	One-Shot AF	AF Method Selection Control	M-Fn
AF Area	Whole Area AF	Multi-controller Sensitivity—AF Point Select	0
Whole Area Tracking Servo AF	On		
Subject to Detect	People	Orientation-Linked AF Point	Same for both Vertical/Horizontal
Eye Detection	Auto		
Switching Tracked Subjects	1	Limit Subject to Detect	All Selected
Servo AF	Case A (Auto)	Left/Right Eye Detection	All Enabled
One-Shot AF Release Priority	Focus Priority	MF Peaking Settings	Off
Preview AF	Disable	Level	High
Lens Drive when AF Impossible	On: Continue Focus Search	Color	Red
		Focus Guide	Off
AF-assist Beam Firing	On	Movie Servo AF Characteristics	Enable
Touch & Drag AF Settings	Disable	Lens Electronic MF	—
Positioning Method	Relative	Disable after One-Shot	—
Active Touch Area	Right	Focus Ring Rotation	Normal: −+
Relative Sensitivity	0	RF Lens Manual Focus Ring Sensitivity	Varies with rotation speed
Limit AF Methods	All Enabled		

Configure Menu Settings

Set-up Menu Defaults

Record Function+Card/Folder Selection		Auto Rotate	Camera+Computer
Still/Movies Separate	Disable	Add Movie Rotate Information	Disable
Still/Movies Record Options	Standard	Date/Time/Zone	—
Still/Movies Slot	Slot 1	Language	Varies by Country
Folder Name	100EOSR6	Video System	NTSC or PAL
File Numbering	Continuous	Help Text Size	Small
File Name		Mode Guide	Enable
File Name	Preset unique code	Feature Guide	Enable
User Setting 1	IMG_	Beep	Enable
User Setting 2	IMG+Image Size		
Format Card	—	Fine-Tune VF Color Tone	—
Volume		User Interface Magnification	Disable
Shutter Volume	3	HDMI Resolution	Auto
Focused Beep	3	Touch Control	Standard
Touch Sounds	0	Multi Function Lock	—
Self-timer Volume	3	Shutter at Shutdown	Closed
Beep Per Interval Timer Exposure Taken	3	Sensor Cleaning	Off
Headphones		Choose USB Connection App	Photo Import/ Remote Control
Volume	8		
Audio Monitoring	Real-time	Reset Camera	—
Power Saving		Custom Shooting Mode (C1–C3)	—
Screen Dimmer	10 seconds	Battery Information	Unchanged
Screen Off	Disable	Copyright Information	Unchanged
Auto Power Off	30 sec	Manual/Software URL	Unchanged
Viewfinder Off	1 min	Certification Logo Display	Unchanged
Screen/Viewfinder Display	Auto 1	Firmware	Unchanged
Screen Brightness	4		
Viewfinder Brightness	Auto		

Recommended Default Changes

The camera organizes its menu entries into different sections, such as Shooting, Autofocus, Playback, Network, Set-up, Custom Functions, and My Menu. Each section, except for My Menu, has dedicated pages for easy navigation. The pages available may vary depending on the shooting mode you are using. To access menus, simply tap the **MENU button**. Use the Main dial to effortlessly navigate through different menus, while the QCD 1 allows you to easily select and highlight specific menu entries. Press the **SET button** to choose a menu item. Additionally, you have the option to navigate using either the directional controls or the touch screen. Once you have chosen the desired menu item, simply press the **SET button** to make your selection. When you select a menu item, the other options will be hidden, and you'll see a list of options for that item or a submenu screen. Alternatively, a separate settings screen may be displayed for that entry. When navigating the menu options, you can scroll up or down using the QCD 1. Once you've made your selection, simply press **SET**. To exit the menu, just press the **MENU button** again. After making adjustments for a particular type of shooting, it is advisable to save each set of parameters in one of the user slots C1, C2, or C3 in the Set-up 6 menu. Here are some settings you may find helpful to consider. It's important to note that these tables do not represent complete menus. If a specific parameter is not listed, feel free to use any setting you prefer.

Default, All Purpose, Sports: Outdoors, Sports; Indoors

	DEFAULT	ALL PURPOSE	SPORTS: OUTDOORS	SPORTS: INDOORS
SETTINGS				
Exposure Mode	Your choice	Your choice	Tv	Tv
Autofocus Mode	One-Shot	Servo AF	Servo AF	Servo AF
Drive Mode	Single Shooting	Single Shooting	Continuous Shooting	Continuous Shooting
SHOOTING MENUS				
Beep	Enable	Enable	Enable	Enable
Image Review	2 seconds	2 seconds	Off	Off
Metering Mode	Evaluative	Evaluative	Evaluative	Evaluative
Color Space	sRGB	sRGB	sRGB	sRGB
Picture Style	Standard/Auto	Auto	Standard	Standard
ISO Speed	Auto	Auto	800–3200	800–3200
ISO Speed Range	100–102,400	100–12,800	200–3200	200–12,800
Auto ISO Range	100–25,600	100–6400	200–6400	400–12,800
ISO Auto Minimum Shutter Speed	Auto	Auto	1/250	1/250
Long Exposure NR	Off	Disable	Disable	Disable
High ISO Speed NR	Standard	Standard	Standard	Standard
Highlight Tone Priority	Disable	Disable	Disable	Disable
AF MENUS				
AF Assist Beam	Enable	Enable	Disable	Disable
AF Area	Whole Area AF	Whole Area AF	Whole Area AF	Zone AF

Stage Performances, Long Exposure, HDR, Portrait

	STAGE PERFORMANCES	LONG EXPOSURE	HDR	PORTRAIT
SETTINGS				
Exposure Mode	Your choice	Manual/Your choice	One-Shot	One-Shot
Autofocus Mode	One-Shot	One-Shot	One-Shot	Servo AF
Drive Mode	Continuous Shooting	Single Shooting	Continuous Shooting	Continuous Shooting
SHOOTING MENUS				
Beep	Disable	Enable	Enable	Enable
Image Review	Off	Off	Off	2 seconds
Metering Mode	Spot	Center-weighted	Evaluative	Center-weighted
Color Space	Adobe RGB	Adobe RGB	Adobe RGB	Adobe RGB
Picture Style	User—Reduce contrast, add sharpening	Neutral	Standard	Portrait
ISO Speed	800–3200	800–3200	Auto	Auto
ISO Speed Range	100–32,000	100–12,800	200–3200	200–1600
Auto ISO Range	100–12,800	100–6400	200–6400	100–3200
ISO Auto Minimum Shutter Speed	Auto	Auto	1/250	1/250
Long Exposure NR	Disable	Disable	Disable	Disable
High ISO Speed NR	Standard	Standard	Standard	Standard
Highlight Tone Priority	Disable	Disable	Disable	Disable
AF MENUS				
AF Assist Beam	Disable	Disable	Disable	Disable
AF Area	1-point AF	1-point AF	Expand AF	1-point AF

Frequently Asked Questions

1. How do you reset your camera settings to factory defaults?
2. How do you change the default settings in your camera?
3. What are the different recommended settings in your camera?

CHAPTER FOUR
NAILING THE RIGHT EXPOSURE

Overview

This chapter discusses all about exposures including how to adjust exposure with ISO settings, understanding the right exposure, choosing a metering and shooting mode, working with HDR, and others.

Getting a Handle on Exposure

Understanding exposure is essential for capturing great photos. Having the right exposure is crucial for capturing a great photo. Mastering exposure is essential for capturing the intricate details and achieving the perfect balance of tones and colors in your photos. Having proper exposure is crucial to ensure that all important details are visible and not obscured by shadows or washed out by excessive brightness. However, achieving the ideal exposure necessitates a certain level of expertise, whether it is the advanced technology of the camera or the knowledge and skills of the photographer. As a professional, you likely have a good understanding of the traditional "**exposure triangle**." This triangle consists of aperture, shutter speed, and ISO sensitivity, all of which work together to produce the desired exposure. The trio is influenced by the level of illumination present. By making adjustments such as doubling the amount of light, increasing the aperture by one stop, lengthening the shutter speed, or boosting the ISO setting, you can effectively double the exposure. Professionally, you can adjust any of these factors while simultaneously reducing one by a comparable amount to maintain the same exposure.

There are pros and cons to working with any of the three controls. Using different f/stops can have a significant impact on the depth-of-field of your photos. Larger f/stops result in less depth-of-field, while smaller f/stops can increase it. However, it's important to note that using smaller f/stops may also lead to a decrease in sharpness due to a phenomenon known as diffraction. Using shorter shutter speeds is more effective in minimizing the impact of camera or subject movement, whereas longer shutter speeds increase the likelihood of motion blur. Using different ISO settings can impact the level of visual noise and artifacts in your image. Higher ISO settings tend to increase these effects, while lower ISO settings help to minimize them. Exposure plays a crucial role in shaping the overall appearance and atmosphere of an image, in multiple aspects. Having the correct exposure is crucial for capturing a well-composed image. Improper exposure can hide important tones in shadows or overexpose them, resulting in a loss of detail. On the other hand, achieving proper exposure allows you to capture the intricate details in the specific areas you want to capture, while also providing the full spectrum of tones and colors necessary to bring your desired image to life. Mastering the art of achieving the ideal exposure can be quite challenging, as digital sensors have limitations when it comes to capturing the full range of tones. If the range of tones in an image is extensive, encompassing both deep shadows and bright highlights, the sensor may struggle to capture the full spectrum. At times, we have to accept an exposure that captures most, but not all, of the tones in a manner that aligns with our desired photo outcome. When making decisions about your image, it's crucial to determine which details are significant and which ones can be overlooked. To gain a comprehensive understanding of exposure, it is essential to grasp the six fundamental aspects of light that converge to create a captivating image. Begin with a light source, such as the sun, an interior lamp, or the warm glow of a campfire.

Here's a concise overview of the factors that can impact exposure:

- **Light at its source**: Our eyes and cameras, whether film or digital, are highly attuned to the segment of the electromagnetic spectrum known as visible light. The light in question possesses various crucial elements that hold significance in the realm of photography, including color and intensity. The harshness of the light is primarily influenced by the apparent size of the light source as it illuminates the subject. However, when it comes to exposure, the crucial factor of a light source is its intensity. We can directly control the intensity of certain elements, such as an interior light that can be adjusted to be brighter or dimmer. We can also manipulate the intensity of sunlight by using translucent materials that absorb or reflect light, giving us some control over its brightness.
- **Light's duration**: Most light sources are typically considered to be continuous. However, the duration of light can change quickly, allowing for adjustments to the exposure. This is particularly useful when the primary light source in a photograph is intermittent, like an electronic flash.
- **Light reflected, transmitted, or emitted**: After light is emitted from its source, whether it's a steady stream or a quick flash, we can perceive and capture images by capturing the light that bounces off our subjects and reaches the camera lens. This can happen through reflection when light is bounced off an object, transmission when light passes through translucent objects that are illuminated from behind, or emission when light is generated by sources like candles or television screens. When the

amount of light that reaches the lens from the subject varies, it becomes necessary to make adjustments to the exposure.

- **Light passed by the lens**: Only a fraction of the light that enters the lens passes through to the other side. Filters can eliminate a portion of the light before it enters into the lens. The lens barrel contains a diaphragm that can be adjusted to change the aperture size and regulate the amount of light entering the lens. Exposure can be controlled by adjusting the aperture size, either manually or through the camera's auto exposure system. The f/stop refers to the relative size of the aperture.
- **Light passing through the shutter**: When light enters the lens, the sensor's exposure time is controlled by the camera's shutter. It can be as long as 30 seconds (or even longer with the Bulb setting) or as short as 1/8000th of a second.
- **Light is captured by the sensor**, with the precision and expertise of a seasoned professional. Only a portion of the light that reaches the sensor is recorded. Only when a specific threshold is met, information is recorded based on the number of photons reaching a photosite. In the same way, when a pixel in the sensor is exposed to excessive light, it is not properly recorded or, even worse, it affects the neighboring pixels. By adjusting the ISO setting, we can modify the minimum and maximum number of pixels that contribute to image detail. When using higher ISOs, the incoming light is amplified to enhance the sensor's sensitivity.

Exposure settings are typically adjusted using the aperture and shutter speed. If the desired exposure cannot be achieved, the ISO sensitivity can be modified. This allows for the optimal f/stop or shutter speed to be selected, depending on the desired depth-of-field or action stopping. When the camera is set to P (Program) mode, the metering system will automatically select the correct exposure for you. However, you have the option to quickly change to an equivalent exposure by locking the current exposure. To do this, simply hold the shutter release down halfway or press the * button, and then use the Main dial to spin until the desired equivalent exposure combination is displayed. For optimal use of the Program Shift feature, it's important to keep in mind that rotating the dial to the left will increase the depth-of-field or slow down the shutter speed while rotating to the right will reduce the depth-of-field or speed up the shutter. Understanding the importance of adjusting the depth of field and shutter speed is crucial when using Program Shift. When using Aperture-priority (Av) and Shutter-priority (Tv) modes (or Fv mode when manually selecting aperture or shutter speed), you have the flexibility to achieve the same exposure by adjusting either the shutter speed or aperture. In Aperture-priority mode, you can change the aperture and let the camera select the appropriate shutter speed. In Shutter-priority mode, you can adjust the shutter speed and let the camera determine the optimal aperture.

Choosing a Metering Mode

To calculate exposure with precision, it is essential to instruct the camera on the specific area of the frame to measure the light (known as the metering mode) and the appropriate controls to use (such as aperture, shutter speed, or both) to establish the optimal exposure. These are the different exposure modes available: Program (P), Shutter-priority (TV), Aperture-priority (Av), Flexible-priority (Fv), Manual (M), and Scene Intelligent Auto. First, let's know the four metering modes. If you're working with P, Tv, Av, or M exposure modes, you have the option to choose any of the four. However, if you're using Scene Intelligent Auto, Evaluative metering is automatically selected and cannot be altered. When using Live View mode, you have the option to choose between Evaluative and Center-weighted averaging modes.

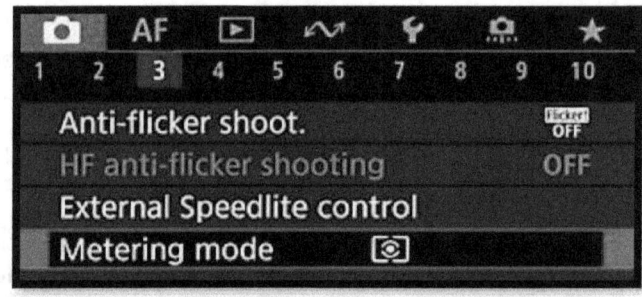

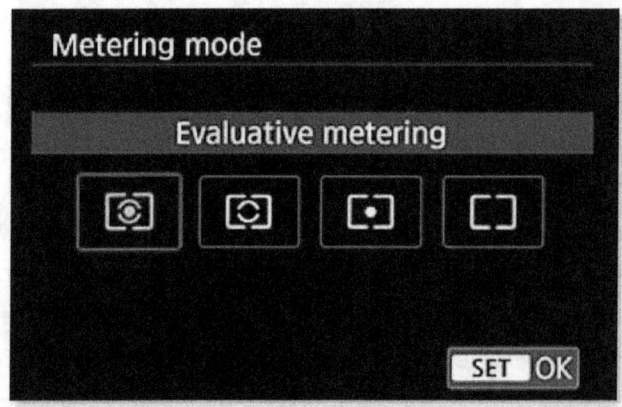

Select a metering mode by accessing the **Q button** and locating the Metering Mode icon, positioned as the fifth box from the top in the left column. Choose the desired mode using the dial and press **SET** to confirm. **Here are the available modes:**

- **Evaluative**: The camera divides the frame into 384 exposure zones, forming a 24 × 16 matrix.

The exposure zones used are connected to the autofocus system in a way that, as the camera assesses the measurements, it places additional importance on the metering zones that indicate precise focus. Using the information provided, the system can make an informed prediction about the type of image you are capturing by analyzing a vast collection of real-life photos stored in the camera's database. For instance, when the upper parts of an image are significantly brighter than the lower parts, the algorithm can infer that the photograph depicts a landscape with a vast expanse of sky. This mode is highly recommended as it provides the most accurate metering for a wide range of pictures. Keep in mind that evaluative metering is occasionally referred to as full-frame averaging. That is not accurate. The camera carefully analyzes the variations in the measured zones and then determines the type of scene it is assessing to calculate the exposure. Two subjects may have identical average illumination, yet the necessary exposures can vary significantly based on the distribution of bright, dark, and mid-tone areas within the scene.

- **Partial**: This mode calculates exposure using approximately 6 percent of the image area, which is a significant portion. The larger yellow circle represents the spot used for this calculation. Use this mode when the background exhibits a significant difference in brightness compared to the subject.
- **Spot**. This mode restricts the reading to a small area in the center of the viewfinder, comprising only approximately 3 percent of the image. This mode can be quite handy when you need to adjust the exposure based on a specific area within the frame. It would be ideal if that area is positioned in the center of the frame. To ensure accurate meter reading, you can either lock exposure by pressing the shutter release halfway or by using the AE lock (*) button. It's important to note that spot metering is not connected to the focus point.

Center-weighted averaging is a method used in photography to calculate the exposure of an image. It takes into account the light in the center of the frame more heavily than the surrounding areas, resulting in a more balanced and professional-looking photograph. When using this mode, the exposure meter prioritizes a zone in the center of the frame to calculate exposure. This is because, in most pictures, the main subject tends to be located in the center. Center-weighting is most effective for capturing portraits, architectural photos, and other images where the primary subject is positioned in the center of the frame, as shown in the example. The light reading primarily focuses on the central part, while also incorporating information from the rest of the frame. When your main subject is in the presence of extremely bright or dark areas, the exposure may not be accurately balanced. Nevertheless, this scheme is effective in various situations when you prefer not to use one of the alternative modes.

Choosing a Shooting Mode

There are five different methods available to select the appropriate shutter speed and aperture: Programme (P), Shutter-priority (Tv), Aperture-priority (Av), and Manual (M). The fifth method, Flexible-Priority (Fv), can replicate the functionality of any of the previous four methods. One additional feature, Scene Intelligent Auto (A+), handles all the exposure calculations on your behalf. To choose one of these modes, simply rotate the Mode dial situated at the top-right side of the R6 II. Ensure that the Shooting/Movie mode switch is set to the still photo mode for accuracy.

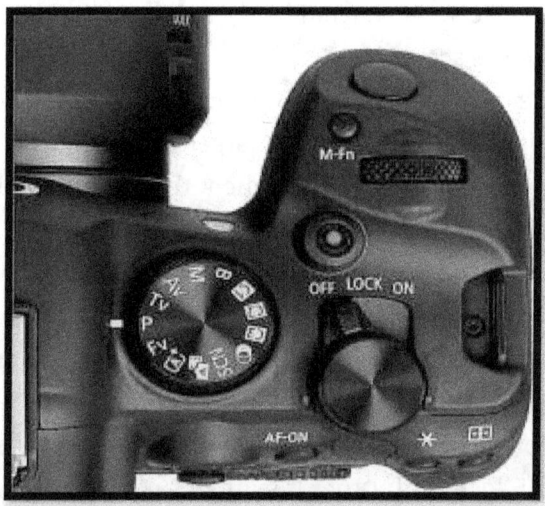

Choosing the most suitable exposure/shooting mode for a specific shooting situation requires considering factors such as the desired depth of field, the intention to capture motion or create motion blur, and the acceptable level of noise in the image. (Recall the exposure triangle mentioned earlier in the chapter.) Each of the camera's exposure methods focuses on different aspects of image capture.

Aperture-Priority Mode

When using Av mode, you can choose the lens opening, while the camera takes care of selecting the appropriate shutter speed. Aperture priority is highly effective when you aim to use a specific lens opening to achieve your desired effect. If you want to achieve maximum depth-of-field in a close-up photo, it would be advisable to use the smallest f/stop available. Alternatively, consider using a wide aperture to create a shallow depth of field, effectively blurring everything except your primary subject. Aperture priority allows you to specify a range of shutter speeds to adapt to different lighting conditions, which may seem contradictory at first. Consider it. If you're shooting a soccer game outdoors with a telephoto lens, it's important to maintain a relatively high shutter speed. However, slight changes in speed due to the sun ducking behind a cloud shouldn't be a major concern. Configure your camera to Av mode and fine-tune the aperture until a shutter speed of approximately 1/1000th second is chosen based on your current ISO setting. When shooting in bright sunlight at ISO 400, you can expect the aperture to be around f/11. With this setting, you can confidently capture the soccer players as they move around the field, ensuring sufficient depth of field. If the lighting conditions happen to change slightly, your camera will automatically adjust the shutter speed to 1/750th or 1/500th second to compensate.

If the shutter speed in the viewfinder or on the Shooting Settings screen is blinking, it means that the camera is unable to choose the right shutter speed for the selected aperture. This could result in overexposure (indicated by the blinking 8000) or underexposure (indicated by the blinking 30 shutter speed) at the current ISO setting. To correct overexposure, consider using a smaller aperture (if possible) or opting for a lower ISO sensitivity. To address underexposure conditions, consider opting for a larger aperture (if available) or increasing the ISO setting.

Shutter-Priority Mode

Shutter-priority (Tv) operates differently compared to Aperture-priority. In this mode, you have the freedom to select your desired shutter speed, while the camera's metering system automatically determines the appropriate f/stop. If you're aiming to capture action photos, you may want to use the fastest shutter speed your camera offers. On the other hand, for certain sports images, adding some blur by using a slow shutter speed can make them more interesting compared to freezing the action completely. Motorsports, track-and-field events, and sports like baseball offer great opportunities for creative use of slower speeds. Shutter-priority mode allows you to have more control over the level of action-freezing capability that your digital camera can provide in different situations. Just as with Av mode, it is possible to select an unsuitable shutter speed. If that's the situation, the aperture of your lens will blink to indicate underexposure or overexposure. To address the issue, you can adjust the shutter speed or ISO settings accordingly. For underexposure, consider selecting a longer shutter speed or increasing the ISO. Conversely, for overexposure, opt for a faster shutter speed or lower ISO setting. Another option is to use Safety Shift, as discussed earlier.

Understanding when to use Shutter-priority:

- **To minimize blurring caused by the movement of the subject**: Increase the shutter speed of the camera to minimize blur caused by moving subjects. The speed at which your subject moves and the level of acceptable blur will determine the exact speed.
- **To achieve a blur effect caused by subject motion**: There are instances where you may desire a subject to appear blurred, such as when capturing the beauty of waterfalls using a camera set for a longer exposure in Shutter-priority mode.
- To achieve a professional-looking effect, you can incorporate blur caused by camera motion while in motion. If you're planning to track a pair of relay runners and to achieve a more polished result, consider using Shutter-priority mode and adjusting the camera settings to 1/60th second. This will allow the background to blur gracefully as you smoothly pan along with the runners. The shutter speed will ensure a crisp image of the athletes.
- **To minimize blurring caused by camera movement while in motion**: In certain scenarios, the camera might be in motion, such as when capturing footage from a moving train or car, and the goal is to reduce any potential blurring caused by the camera's movement. Opting for shutter priority would be a wise decision in this situation.
- **Landscape photography hand-held**: If you are unable to use a tripod for your landscape shots, it is likely that you still desire the highest level of image sharpness. Using shutter-priority mode enables you to set a fast shutter speed to effectively minimize or eliminate any blurring caused by camera shake. Ensure that the ISO setting is adjusted appropriately to allow the camera to automatically select an aperture that provides adequate depth of field.

Program AE Mode

The program mode (P) uses the camera's internal intelligence to automatically determine the optimal f/stop and shutter speed based on a comprehensive database of picture information.

This ensures that the camera selects the most suitable combination of settings for each specific photo. When the ISO setting is not giving the desired exposure, the viewfinder will show blinking indicators for shutter speed or aperture, signaling under or overexposure. Adjusting the ISO allows you to increase or decrease sensitivity as needed. You have the option to override the camera's recommended exposure settings. Use the EV setting feature to adjust the exposure by either increasing or decreasing it from the metered value. One can easily switch from the recommended setting to an alternative setting that achieves the same exposure but with a different combination of f/stop and shutter speed. **To achieve this:**

1. To lock in the current base exposure, you can either press the shutter release halfway or use the AE lock button on the back of the camera. When using the AE lock button, the * indicator will illuminate in the viewfinder to indicate that the exposure has been locked.

2. When the camera is unable to choose the right exposure, the shutter speed and aperture display will start blinking:

- **Underexposure**: The 30-shutter speed indicator will flash, along with the largest aperture of the lens. (The precise number may vary depending on the lens being used.) To address this, you have two options: increase the ISO setting or add extra lighting, like electronic flash.

- **Overexposure**: When using certain lenses, you may notice that the 8000 shutter speed indicator flashes, accompanied by the smallest available f/stop, such as f/16, f/22, or f/32. One way to address this issue is by adjusting the ISO speed to a lower setting. To avoid overexposure, ensure that your scene is well-lit and adjust your camera settings accordingly. Consider using a shutter speed of 1/8000th second and the lowest ISO sensitivity setting (ISO 50 equivalent) for optimal results. If you're capturing images of a blast furnace and encounter an overexposure issue, you have the option to use a neutral-density filter or find a method to decrease the amount of light.

3. After setting the exposure, you have the option to effortlessly adjust the settings by spinning the Main dial. Adjust the dial to the left for a longer shutter speed or smaller aperture, or to the right for a faster shutter speed or larger aperture.

To maintain your adjustment, remember to apply it for each exposure. If you wish to deviate from the recommended settings for the next exposure, you will need to go through the same steps again.

Flexible-Priority Mode

Adapting to flexible priority (Fv) may require some adjustment, especially for experienced photographers who are accustomed to using shooting modes like P, Tv, Av, and Manual (which will be discussed later) as part of their workflow. Using Fv may initially seem counterintuitive, but after a few tries, you'll realize that it is the most intuitive shooting mode of all. With flexible priority, you have complete control over the three legs of the exposure triangle, allowing you to seamlessly switch between all four modes. Essentially, Fv operates similarly to Program AE with Auto ISO enabled. The camera automatically selects the shutter speed, aperture, and ISO setting for you. However, you have the option to manually specify any or all of those three settings, and the camera's shooting mode will seamlessly switch to Av, TV, or Manual. **When the mode is set to Fv:**

- **TV mode**: When using Fv mode, simply rotate the Quick Control dial 2 until you see an orange icon indicating the Main dial next to the shutter speed. Rotate the Main dial to manually select the shutter speed, while the aperture and ISO will still be adjusted automatically. You essentially have TV mode with Auto ISO, just like a professional.
- **Av mode**: When using Fv mode, adjust the Quick Control dial until you see an orange icon next to the aperture. Then, use the Main dial to manually choose the desired f/stop. The camera operates in Av mode with Auto ISO.
- **Manual mode**: When operating in Fv mode, adjust the Quick Control dial to select the desired shutter speed and aperture settings in manual mode. The camera now functions as if it were in Manual exposure mode, with the shutter speed, aperture, and ISO being adjusted automatically. You essentially have Tv mode with Auto ISO.
- **Fixed ISO**: To disable Auto ISO in Fv mode, simply adjust the ISO settings. Rotate the Quick Control dial to highlight the ISO icon and then use the Main dial to select a fixed ISO value that suits your needs.
- **Exposure compensation**: Ensure that you locate the exposure scale at the bottom of the screen and use the Main dial to adjust the exposure compensation as needed.

Manual Exposure Mode

Being a skilled photographer involves understanding the different modes your camera offers and when to use them. This includes relying on automation like Scene Intelligent Auto or P mode, going semi-automatic with TV or Av, and setting exposure manually using M. Many photographers opt to manually set their exposure for most of their shots. This allows them to have full control over the settings and ensure the proper exposure. The camera indicates when the metering system judges the settings to be correct, using the analog exposure scale at the bottom of the display. Having control over exposure settings can be quite useful in certain scenarios. If you're aiming for a more precise effect in your silhouette photo, you may find that the available exposure modes and EV correction features fall short of your expectations.

Adjusting Exposure with ISO Settings

You can also modify the ISO sensitivity setting to adjust exposures. Occasionally, photographers overlook this option, as it is customary to establish the ISO once for a specific shooting session (such as ISO 100 or 200 for outdoor shots in bright sunlight, or ISO 800 for indoor photography) and then disregard it. ISOs higher than ISO 100 or 200 are often regarded unfavorably or as a necessary compromise. Nevertheless, adjusting the ISO can be a legitimate method of fine-tuning exposure settings. The Canon EOS R6 II, in particular, excels at producing satisfactory outcomes even at ISO settings that would result in grainy and unusable images with certain other camera models. When not using Scene Intelligent Auto, the camera allows for manual adjustment of ISO speeds for still images. In video mode, it is necessary to use Auto ISO in all modes except Manual exposure. The Shooting 2 menu provides an entry called ISO Speed Settings, which allows you to customize the available ISO speeds and their usage.

- **ISO speed:** You have the option to select from a range of ISO speeds, including Auto, by using a sliding scale that can be adjusted using the QCD-1, the multi-controller, or the touch screen. Activating Auto is as simple as pressing the INFO button while the scale is visible.
- **The range for stills**: Specify the minimum and maximum ISO sensitivity options, which include **"expanded"** settings like Low (ISO 50 equivalent) and H (ISO 204,800 equivalent), for more precise control.
- **Auto range**: This serves as a reliable safety net for Auto ISO operation. Set the minimum ISO to 100 and the maximum to ISO 102,400, without going beyond. Use this tool to effectively customize the Auto ISO setting according to your preferences.
- **Minimum shutter speed**: You have the option to decide whether the camera should automatically select the slowest shutter speed before Auto ISO is activated. When using a long lens with P and Av modes, it's advisable to increase the ISO sooner. This

will allow the camera to select the appropriate shutter speed. When you set a minimum shutter speed of 1/250th second, the camera will automatically adjust the ISO within the range you've specified with Auto Range to ensure the proper exposure, even if it means using a slower shutter speed in P or Av mode.

There are two modes available in this setting. The camera will automatically determine when the shutter speed is too low in Auto mode. You have the option to adjust this by selecting a slower or faster setting on the scale that is available. Alternatively, can manually choose the desired shutter speed, ranging from 1 second to 1/8000th second.

Dealing with Visual Noise

Visual image noise is a grainy effect that is sometimes used as a special effect. However, it often detracts from the image by reducing detail and adding an "**interesting**" texture. Two factors contribute to the creation of noise in photos: high ISO settings and long exposures. High ISO noise is often noticeable when you increase your camera's sensitivity setting beyond ISO 3200. Noise becomes more apparent in Canon cameras at ISO 6400 and higher, as these cameras are well-known for their excellent ISO noise characteristics. When using the H setting (ISO 102,400 equivalent), noise can be quite bothersome. That's why the lofty sensitivity ratings are disabled by default and need to be activated with ISO expansion. This noise is a result of the amplification required to increase the sensor's sensitivity. Since the sensor has twice as many green pixels as red and blue pixels, areas with red, blue, and magenta tones tend to have worse noise because the green signals require less amplification for detail. While higher ISOs can bring out details in dark areas, they also randomly amplify non-signal information, resulting in noise. During long-time exposures, a phenomenon occurs that can result in increased noise in your photos. This happens because more photons can reach the sensor, allowing for better low-light performance. However, the longer the exposure, the higher the chances of random phantom photons being registered by some pixels. This is often due to the sensor getting warmer over time, which can be mistaken for actual photons. Additionally, CMOS sensors, like the one used in the R6 II, are susceptible to a specific type of noise. Unlike CCD sensors that funnel the entire signal through a single amplifier and conversion circuit, CMOS sensors have millions of individual amplifiers and converters. As a result, they may introduce fixed-pattern noise into the image data due to slight variations in processing between these circuits.

Making EV Changes

At times, you may desire a different level of exposure than what the camera's metering system suggests. You might want to intentionally underexpose to achieve a striking silhouette effect or overexpose for a bright and airy look. Adjusting the exposure compensation is a breeze with the camera's built-in system, which allows you to override the recommended exposure settings in any non-automatic mode except Manual.

There are three methods to modify the exposure value (EV) using the camera:

- **Use the Display/Quick Control dial 1:** To adjust the exposure compensation on the display, simply tap the shutter release halfway and rotate the QCD-1. No need to hold down the shutter release. Rotate to the right to increase exposure, or to the left to decrease exposure. The exposure scale at the bottom of the screen will show you the level of exposure compensation you have set.

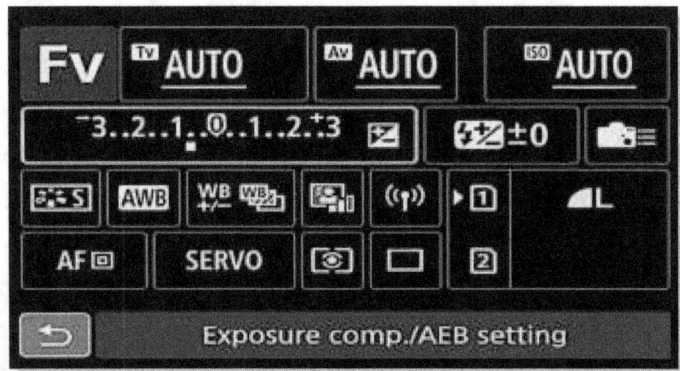

- **Quick Control screen**: When the graphic shooting information screen is displayed, simply press the Q button and go to the exposure scale. Now, carefully rotate the QCD-1. Adjust the rotation to increase or decrease exposure as needed. The exposure scale on the screen will show the level of exposure compensation. Additionally, pressing SET when the scale is highlighted will allow you to access the complete exposure compensation/auto exposure bracketing screen.
- **Shooting 2**: Press the **MENU button** and rotate the Main dial to navigate to the Shooting 2 menu. Give special attention to the Expo. Ensure that the Comp/AEB entry is placed at the top. To access the screen, simply press **SET**. From there, you can adjust the exposure compensation by rotating the QCD-1 or sliding your finger across the

scale. The screen is equipped with clear labels indicating "**Darker**" on the left and "**Brighter**" on the right, ensuring precise adjustments according to your preferences.

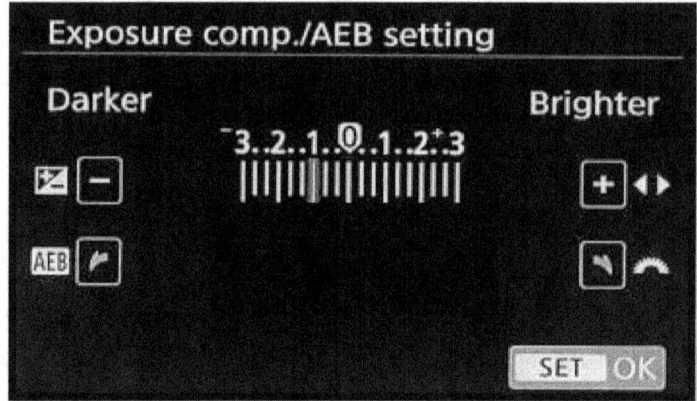

It's worth noting that this method offers a convenient advantage - you can easily set automatic exposure bracketing by simply rotating the Main dial on this screen.

Bracketing Parameters

Bracketing is a technique used by photographers to capture multiple exposures with varying settings, increasing the chances of getting the perfect shot. In the era before digital cameras dominated the scene, it was a common practice among professionals to bracket exposures. This involved capturing a series of three photos at a fixed shutter speed of 1/125th second while adjusting the aperture from f/8 to f/11 to f/16. For enhanced precision, smaller increments were used instead of whole-stop increments. In addition, it was equally typical to maintain a consistent aperture while adjusting the shutter speed. However, in the era before electronic shutters, film cameras frequently offered only shutter speeds in whole increments. When it comes to achieving precise color accuracy in-camera, WB bracketing is occasionally employed. However, auto exposure bracketing (AEB) is the more commonly used technique. When this feature is enabled, the camera captures a sequence of shots with varying exposure values, including one at the standard exposure and others with higher or lower exposure. When using Av mode, the shutter speed will automatically adjust, while in TV mode, the aperture speed will be adjusted.

Number of Exposures

Within the Custom Function 1 menu, you have the option to select the number of bracketed shots. You can choose between 2, 3, 5, or 7 shots:

- **2 shots**: The camera will capture a single image at the base or standard exposure. Another shot is taken, which can either increase or decrease the exposure compared to the original image. Adjust the QCD-1 to the right for increased exposure on the second shot, or to the left for decreased exposure. The level of additional or reduced exposure is determined by the increment you choose.
- **3, 5. 7 shots**: The camera captures a series of images at different exposures, allowing for a range of options to choose from. In the 3-shot setting, the translation is one over/one under. When using the 5-shot setting, it becomes two over/two under. Finally, with the 7-shot option, it results in three over/three under.

Bracketing Sequence

In the Custom Function 1 menu, you will find an option called Bracketing Sequence. This option allows you to specify the order in which the auto exposure bracketing series are exposed. Your decision will be influenced by your personal preferences and the intended use of the bracketed shots. **Here are the available options:**

- **0 − +:** The exposure sequence follows a standard pattern of starting with regular exposure, then decreasing the exposure, and finally increasing it. When using this default value, your camera will capture and save your base exposure first on your memory card. It will then proceed to capture progressively reduced exposure images, followed by shots with increased exposure. If you want to prioritize the standard exposure and have it appear first in each bracket set, while the alternate exposures follow, this order might be more suitable for you.
- **− 0 +:** The sequence consists of decreased exposure, standard exposure, and increased exposure. If you want to combine images using HDR techniques in your image editor or HDR utility, this order is the most logical choice. The bracketed array is stored on your memory card, starting with the most underexposed shot and progressing to the best exposed, and then to the overexposures. It becomes effortless to use all of your bracketed shots in the HDR sequence or to choose specific ones for combination.

- **+ 0 −:** This sequence is the opposite of the previous one, moving from higher exposure to normal exposure and then lower exposure. If you want to showcase your best exposures right at the beginning, this order might be more suitable for you.

Bracketing Auto Cancel

One of the last entries in the Custom Function 1 menu is Bracketing Auto Cancel. When bracketing is activated, the camera will keep capturing bracketed exposures until you manually disable the bracket feature, provided that you have this setting turned off. That is a positive aspect. When shooting a series of bracketed exposures, particularly for HDR, it can be quite handy to have your bracket setting remain "**sticky**" and continue to be active even if you turn off your camera. Many photographers prefer to consistently use bracketing as a professional technique. Most of the time, it is preferable to disable bracketing without having to manually navigate to the Shooting 2 menu. To ensure seamless operation, make sure to enable the Bracketing Auto Cancel setting in the Custom Function 1 menu. This will automatically cancel bracketing when you turn off the camera, change lenses, use the flash, or switch memory cards. When the setting is set to Disable, bracketing will continue until you manually deactivate it or use the flash. Despite the flash still canceling bracketing, your settings will still be retained.

Increment between Exposures

You have the option to select the desired jump size between each of the bracketed exposures. To accomplish that, you will need to visit the Expo. Entry for Comp./AEB can be found in the Shooting 2 menu. You can choose a range of exposure adjustments, from +/− 1/3 to 3 full stops in 1/3-stop increments, simply by rotating the Main dial.

Creating a Bracketed Set

Mastering auto exposure bracketing can be a bit challenging, but it has become more versatile compared to previous models. With the R6 II, you have the flexibility to capture more than just three exposures. You can take up to seven shots, giving you more options to work with. Additionally, you can selectively bracket overexposed or underexposed, which is a highly valuable enhancement.

Simply follow these steps:

1. Provide the number of exposures and the desired sequence. Select the desired number of bracketed exposures and their shooting sequence in the Custom Function 1 menu.

2. Activate the **Expo. Comp. /AEB screen**. Screen for composition and automatic exposure bracketing. Access the **MENU button** and locate the Shooting 2 menu, which contains the Expo option. Option for automatic emergency braking and collision prevention. Press the **SET button** to confirm your selection.

3. Specify the range and increment for the brackets. Adjust the Main dial to expand or narrow the three bars to encompass the range and exposure increment you want to use. With a wider spread, you'll achieve larger increments and a broader range of bracketed shots. You can adjust the bracket range on the Main dial to three stops above or below the standard exposure.

4. Make adjustments to the zero point and standard exposure. Typically, the bracketing is set to zero around the center of the scale, indicating the accurate exposure as measured by the camera. It would be advisable to bias your three bracketed shots towards either overexposure or underexposure, like a professional. Maybe you have concerns about the metered exposure being too dark or too light, and you would prefer the bracketed shots to lean in the opposite direction. Use either QCD to shift the bracket spread towards one end of the scale or the other.

5. Confirm your selection. To access the settings, simply press the **SET button**.

6. Capture your photo sequence. To begin capturing the bracketed sequence, simply press the shutter release. The drive mode you choose will dictate when they are captured.

- Single shooting mode and silent single shooting mode. Ensure that you press the shutter release once for each exposure in the sequence, just like a professional.

- Choose from high-speed continuous, low-speed continuous or silent continuous options. Hold down the shutter release button and all the shots in the sequence will be captured. The camera ceases capturing images once the series has been fully documented.

- Includes 10-second and 2-second self-timer modes for added convenience. Once the necessary pause has passed, all the shots in the sequence will be captured.

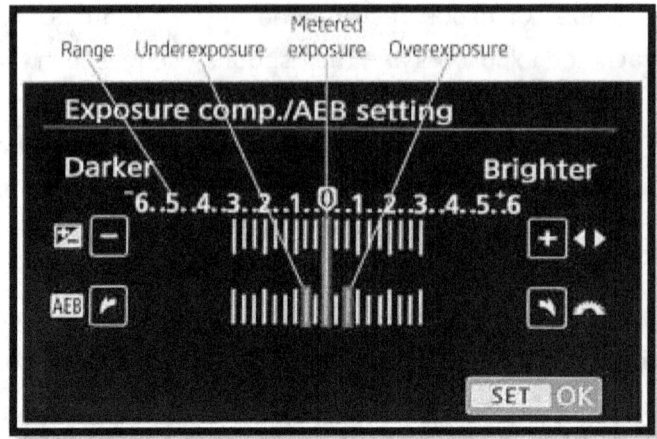

7. Be diligent in monitoring your shots. When capturing images, three indicators will appear on the exposure scale in the viewfinder. Each indicator will flash for each bracketed photo, indicating when the base exposure, underexposure, and overexposure are taken.

8. Disable bracketing once finished. Bracketing remains active throughout the entire shooting process, allowing you to capture a series of bracketed exposures. The bracketing feature will only be disabled if you use the electronic flash, power off the camera, or manually cancel the bracketing from the menu. Even if you have enabled Bracketing Auto Cancel in the Custom Function 1 menu, this remains true. Bracketing is not automatically canceled after each sequence. Instead, the camera conveniently remembers your bracketing settings until you manually cancel them, power down the camera, or start using an electronic flash. It will only cancel the bracketing settings automatically.

Working with HDR

HDR photography gained significant popularity in the past, with numerous books dedicated to this subject. Just like a professional, HDR was often misused and overused, resulting in an abundance of garish and painfully unrealistic images. Imagine capturing the essence of a dimly lit street, where heavy shadows are interrupted by the dazzling glow of street lights and the occasional illuminated shop window. For optimal results, it is recommended to adjust the exposure settings accordingly. To capture the darker areas of the scene, a shutter speed of around 1/60th second at f/2.8 and ISO 200 should be considered. On the other hand, to properly expose the brightly lit areas, a smaller aperture of f/11 and a faster shutter speed of 1/400th second would be more suitable. There is a significant difference of nearly 7 EV steps (equivalent to approximately 7 f/stops) which exceeds the dynamic range capabilities of any digital camera, including the EOS R6 II. As camera sensors continue to improve their dynamic ranges, special techniques such as Active D-Lighting and HDR photography will continue to be essential tools for photographers. You can create in-camera HDR exposures or take HDR photos using the traditional method of capturing separate bracketed exposures.

Using HDR Mode

Here are some expert tips for using the R6 II's impressive built-in feature. These guidelines are also applicable to manually exposed HDR sequences:

- **Consider using a tripod if it is available**: To achieve optimal results, it is recommended to mount the camera on a tripod to minimize any potential camera movement between continuous shots. Nevertheless, the R6 II's anti-shake capabilities offer a significant level of compensation.
- **Moving objects can create ghosts**: There might be some subject motion between shots, resulting in the appearance of "**ghost**" effects. Use the Moving Subjects option in the built-in HDR mode to minimize the impact.
- **Misalignment:** When Auto Image Align is activated, this mode effectively realigns your multiple images during the merging process, even without using a tripod. Nevertheless, it may not achieve flawless results, especially when dealing with intricate patterns that pose a challenge to the camera's processing capabilities. There may be a slight chance of misalignment.
- **Shutter speeds and ISO settings can vary**: The camera adjusts the shutter speed within the selected increment range, even if you're using Tv or M modes and have specified a shutter speed. Adjusting the f/stop during the capture of an HDR photo can impact the focus and potentially the size of the image, making it incompatible with HDR. The R6 II can also automatically adjust the ISO sensitivity to ensure proper exposure and minimize the impact of the camera shake.
- **Unwanted cropping**: In Auto Image Align mode, the processor is capable of shifting each image in any of the four directions. To ensure optimal alignment, the image may need to be slightly cropped to remove any non-image areas. The size of your final image will be slightly smaller compared to images captured in other modes.
- **Weird colors**: Certain types of lighting, such as fluorescent and LED illumination, undergo rapid fluctuations and can cause variations in colors from one shot to another. It may go unnoticed during single shooting, but it becomes more apparent

when using continuous shooting modes, such as HDR mode. The combined images may exhibit unusual color distortions.

- **Limitations**: Images are captured exclusively in JPEG or HEIF format, regardless of whether you have selected RAW or RAW+JPEG. Extended ISO speeds are not supported, the flash does not fire during HDR capture, and Auto Exposure Bracketing is disabled. When Auto Lighting Optimizer is enabled, the camera will automatically disable HDR mode while capturing your HDR images. Once you turn off HDR mode, it will be re-enabled. Uneven exposures can occur in specific lighting conditions, such as fluorescent or LED lighting. In HDR mode, the electronic shutter has a maximum speed of 1/8000th second or slower.

To find HDR Mode in the Shooting 2 menu, press the **SET button.**

The menu is organized into three main entries, each with additional options to choose from:

- **Off**: Disable the setting when HDR images are not desired. By default, this setting will be applied since HDR may not be suitable for every scene. Activate this feature when you have a subject that can gain advantages from a wider range of tones. Next, select an HDR mode, either **Moving Subject or Dynamic Range**, to optimize your settings.

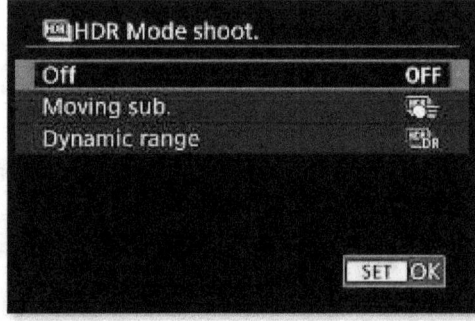

- **Moving subject**: This mode is particularly helpful when dealing with subjects such as humans, animals, or vehicles that are constantly in motion while capturing individual HDR images.
- **Dynamic range**: This mode is perfect for capturing professional-quality images of portraits, landscapes, table-top photography, and other still scenes.

Moving Subjects Mode

The Moving Subject mode is considered the more user-friendly option among the two automatic HDR modes. Simply choose it and press SET. The only available option is Limit Max Brightness, but unfortunately, it is grayed out. It is used exclusively if you possess a monitor that can showcase an expanded brightness range. When using this mode, the R6 II will make adjustments to counter subject motion by employing higher shutter speeds and/or higher ISO sensitivity settings. In darker environments, some noise may be visible due to higher ISO settings. However, it is worth noting that in the past, capturing HDR images of moving subjects posed challenges. Early cameras with built-in HDR modes often struggled to adequately compensate for movement, resulting in frequent ghost images.

Dynamic Range Mode

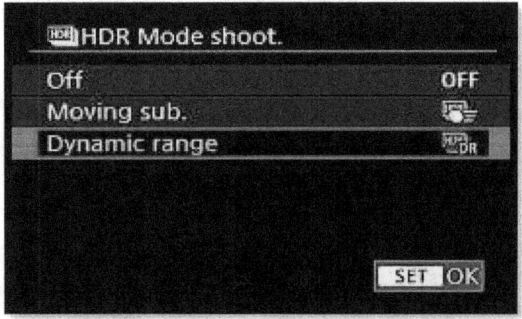

This mode offers a higher level of versatility and customization, enabling you to finely adjust the settings to capture stunning HDR images of stationary subjects, which have long been associated with high-dynamic range photography.

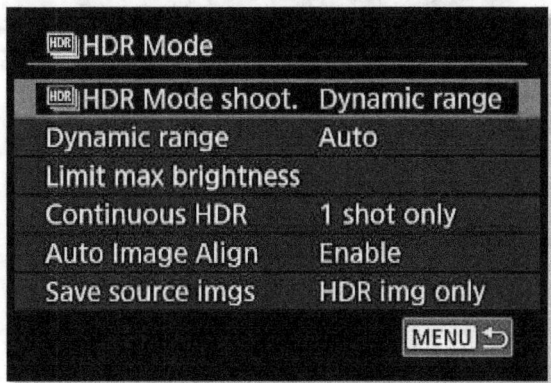

Fixing Exposures with Histograms

To achieve optimal results, it is advisable to ensure proper exposure while capturing photos, thus reducing the need for extensive adjustments during post-processing in your image editor. However, it is important to note that judging exposure solely based on the preview image on your camera's display or the review image in Playback may not always be accurate. Proper lighting conditions are crucial for optimal visibility of the monitor. Additionally, the brightness level you've chosen in the Set-up menu can have a significant impact on the overall image quality. Alternatively, you can use a histogram, a visual representation displayed on the camera's screen that illustrates the distribution of tones captured at different levels of brightness. You can view histograms in real-time on your display while shooting and in the review image during playback. However, note that histograms are only accessible if you have enabled them. To access histograms in shooting mode or playback mode, simply press the INFO button until a screen displaying the histogram is shown. Photographers commonly use an RGB histogram to view the values of red, green, and blue pixels in an image. However, there are other types of histograms available, including CMYK (cyan, magenta, yellow, and black) and HSL/HSV (hue, saturation, and lightness/value), which offer different ways of representing the RGB color space.

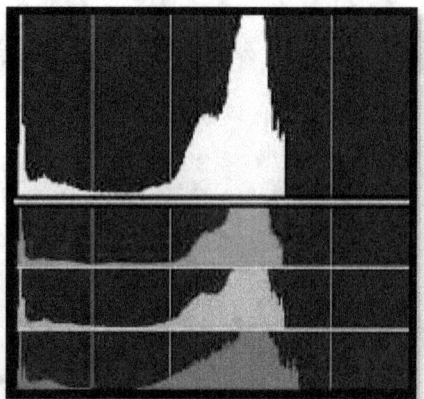

Tonal Range

Understanding histograms is crucial for fine-tuning the tonal range of an image. It allows you to precisely control the distribution of dark and light tones, ranging from absolute darkness to the utmost brightness while encompassing all the intermediate shades. When considering a photo's tonality, it's helpful to imagine it as a black-and-white or grayscale image, even though the tones are captured in three separate color layers: red, green, and blue. Due to the digital nature of your images, the tonal range is not truly continuous. Instead, it is divided into distinct steps that correspond to the different tones that can be captured. The gradient displayed consists of a series of gray shades, starting from pure black on the left and gradually transitioning to pure white on the right. There are a total of 20 gray steps, including the white endpoint. Displayed at the bottom of the chart are the digital values ranging from 0 to 255, which were captured by your sensor for an image with 8 bits per channel. A 24-bit, full-color image is created by combining 8 bits of red, 8 bits of green, and 8 bits of blue. In this color model, black is represented by a value of 0, the brightest white by 255, and the mid-tones are clustered around the 128 markers. The information captured can be more precise, ranging from 0 to 4,094 for an image taken with the camera set to 14 bits per channel for a RAW file.

Black-and-white photos are straightforward to comprehend. Or, at least, that's our assumption. When examining a black-and-white image, it appears as though we are observing a seamless spectrum of shades, ranging from black to white, with all the grays in between. However, that statement is not entirely accurate. In any photo, the blackest black is never truly black. This is because some light is always reflected from the surface of the print. Similarly, when viewed on a screen, the deepest black can only be as dark as the least-reflective area that a computer monitor can produce. Even the lightest areas of a print absorb some light, so they can't achieve a true white. Similarly, when viewing on a computer monitor, the brightness of the display's LCD or LED picture elements limits the whiteness. The continuous set of tones falls short of capturing the complete greyscale tonal range, with its limited range of darker blacks and brighter whites. Understanding the full range of tones is essential for effectively working with images that contain vast areas of gradually changing shades, like the sky, water, or walls. Imagine a photograph capturing a group of campers gathered around a crackling campfire. Due to the direct illumination from the fire, the campers' faces are mostly devoid of shadows. All the different tones of the people around the fire are condensed into the brighter end of the spectrum.

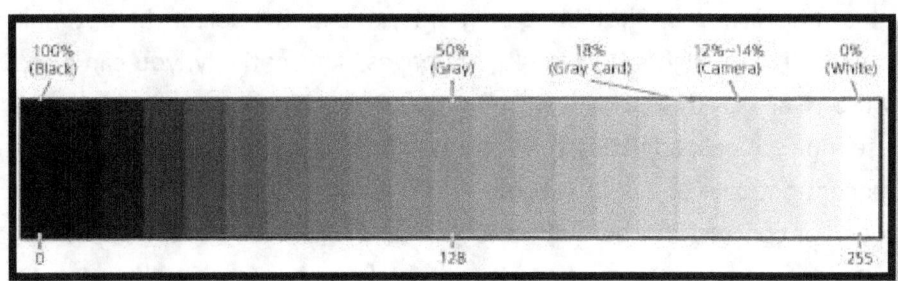

Histogram Basics

The histograms on your camera provide a simplified representation of the pixel distribution across 256 brightness levels, resulting in a visually appealing "**mountain range**" pattern on the graph. When beginning to use histograms, it is recommended to focus on the brightness histogram, even though separate charts may be available for brightness and the red, green, and blue channels. The graph displays the pixel count for each brightness value in the image, ranging from 0 (black) on the left to 255 (white) on the right. The vertical axis represents the pixel count at each level. Histograms are commonly used for exposure adjustments, but they can also provide insights into the image's contrast.

Understanding Histograms

It is crucial to keep in mind that adjusting the exposure on your camera does not alter the contrast of an image when working with the histogram display. As exposure is decreased, the tones gradually shift towards the black end and may even go beyond the scale. Conversely, increasing exposure has the opposite effect. The contrast within the image is adjusted to a level where certain tones become unrepresentable once they exceed the scale. **To adjust the contrast of an image, there are four possible methods:**

- Adjust the camera's contrast setting through the menu system. These adjustments can be found in the Picture Styles options within the Shooting 4 menu of your camera.
- Use the camera's shadow-tone and highlight "**boosters**" to enhance your photos. The Auto Lighting Optimizer and Highlight Tone Priority features are valuable tools for adjusting contrast.
- Adjust the contrast of the scene by using techniques such as incorporating a fill light or reflectors to brighten excessively dark shadows.
- Make adjustments to the contrast in your image editor or RAW file converter for a more professional look. Use features like Levels or Curves in various image editors, such as Photoshop or Photoshop Elements, to expertly select the optimal values for shadows and highlights from multiple images. Alternatively, you can also work with HDR software for this purpose.

Among these four options, adjusting the contrast of the scene is the most preferable choice. Trying to fix contrast by manipulating tonal values is unlikely to provide a flawless solution. Adding a touch of contrast can be quite effective as it allows you to eliminate certain tones and create a more dynamic image. On the other hand, mastering the opposite is quite challenging. Fixing an overly contrasty image can be quite challenging as it is difficult to enhance details that were not captured in the original image. When working with histograms, it is important to ensure that all the tones in an image are evenly distributed across the entire range, without any being cut off at the edges. It is advisable to avoid underexposing your images unless necessary. This is because when you try to recover the underexposed shadows in post-processing, it often leads to an increase in noise, especially when working with RAW files. For optimal results, we recommend you adjust the exposure settings to capture the highlights accurately. However, in situations where it is feasible, it is advisable to use additional lighting techniques such as reflectors or fill flash to illuminate the shadows instead of leaving them significantly underexposed.

Exposing to the Right

Understanding exposing to the right becomes easier when you mentally divide the histogram into fifths, although it's worth noting that the camera's histogram uses quarters instead. Assuming you're shooting in 14-bit RAW, let's keep things simple and work with smaller numbers. Every 14-bit image can capture up to 16,383 distinct tones per channel. Nevertheless, every fifth section of the histogram does not contain 3,277 tones, which is equivalent to one-fifth of 16,383. The highlights on the right-most fifth contribute to approximately half of the captured tones. Progressing to the left, the subsequent fifth denotes a quarter, succeeded by an eighth, and a sixteenth of the total levels. When processing your RAW file, it's important to keep in mind that there are a limited number of tones to recover in the shadows. Boosting or amplifying these tones can lead to an increase in noise. To achieve the desired effect, it is important to carefully adjust the exposure without overexposing the highlights and losing details in the shadows. With approximately 8,000 tones at your disposal in the highlights, you can effectively recover any lost detail in an overexposed RAW image using the Exposure slider in your RAW converter, like the one found in Adobe Camera Raw.

Discovering Basic Zone Modes

Scene Intelligent Auto Mode

At first glance, it may seem surprising to have an exposure mode on a high-end camera like the R6 II that offers very limited user options. This feature essentially simplifies the camera, making it more accessible for casual photographers. Upon closer examination, it becomes evident that Canon's approach is deliberate and calculated. Scene Intelligent Auto is far from being a limited alternative to Program mode. The intelligence behind the mode's nomenclature is crucial. When using P mode, the camera takes care of setting the shutter speed and aperture for you. You can adjust the metering mode, autofocus mode, white balance, and practically every other setting with ease. The camera's Scene Intelligent Auto mode analyzes your scene, determining if your subject is static or moving, and selects the best settings for you without any input required. **The camera offers a range of settings to work with:**

- **ISO speed**: The camera will automatically select the ISO sensitivity.
- **Picture Style:** The camera is set to the A (automatic) Picture Style, which will automatically select the appropriate settings. Be aware that any modifications you have made to the Auto Picture Style will not be taken into account when using Scene Intelligent Auto.
- **White balance**: Adjusting the white balance is essential for achieving professional-looking photos. The white balance is automatically set and cannot be adjusted.
- **Auto Lighting Optimizer**: Consistently engaged in Scene Intelligent Auto mode.
- **Color space**: Converted to sRGB.
- **Autofocus**: When you press the shutter release button halfway, the camera automatically chooses between One-Shot AF and Servo AF. Switching between the two options manually is not possible. The AF point selection is automatically determined, and the AF-assist beam is activated whenever necessary. To enable or disable Eye Detection, simply press the **Q/SET button**, select the **AF Method icon**, and then press the **INFO button**.
- **Metering mode**: Evaluative metering is consistently used. When you switch the Mode dial to A+, a screen will appear. Select OK, and the view displayed on the touch screen will appear as shown in the figure on the right. An icon will be displayed in the upper-left corner to indicate the selected scene mode of the camera, which in this instance is Portrait. Arranged on the left side are icons that allow you to make adjustments using the touch screen.
- **Image quality and size:** Simply tap the icon to effortlessly choose from a range of image size options, including RAW, JPEG, and even Movie Recording Size.
- **Drive mode**: Select from various shooting options by tapping the icon. These include single shooting, three different continuous shooting speeds, self-timer modes with 2 or 10-second delays, and a continuous self-timer mode that captures 2 to 10 shots after the timer ends.
- **Enable or disable the Touch Shutter**: With Touch Shutter enabled, you can simply tap on a person's face or any other subject in the frame to capture a photo.

- **Manual focus**: Furthermore, users have the option to select Manual focus by conveniently toggling the AF/MF switch located on the front of the camera or on the lens barrel (if available).
- **Creative Assist**: You will find the focal length/zoom setting of the lens and a convenient icon to access Creative Assist at the lower-right corner of the screen.

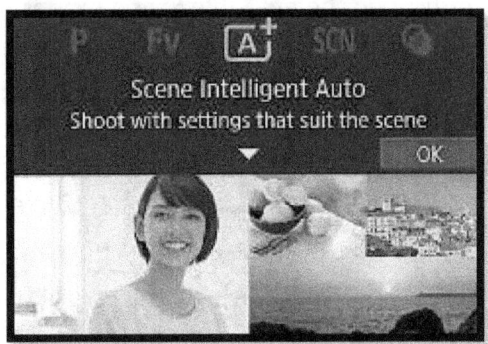

This mode is referred to as Scene Intelligent because the camera can accurately determine if your subject falls into one of its Special Scene categories. It then automatically applies the corresponding Scene mode as if you had manually selected it. A symbol representing the chosen scene will be displayed in the top-left corner of the screen. **Options available in Scene Intelligent Auto mode include:**

- **Manual focus:** To switch to manual focus, simply toggle the AF/MF switch on the lens.
- **Touch focus**: To tap on a person's face or another subject within the frame, simply use the touch screen while Continuous AF is set to Disable in the AF 2 menu.
- **Drive mode**: Use the Quick Control screen to effortlessly select your preferred shooting modes, including single shooting, high-/low-speed continuous shooting, silent single shooting, silent continuous shooting, and 10 sec./2 sec. self-timer modes.
- **Image quality/size**: To choose from your RAW, JPEG, and other image size options, including Movie Recording Size, simply press the **Q button**.

Several shooting menu options can be accessed through the concise four-tab menu system provided in Scene Intelligent Auto mode. Additionally, there are two autofocus menu tabs available.

Special Scene Mode

The SCN position on the Mode dial enables the R6 II's Special Scene mode, offering a diverse selection of 13 subject categories that encompass a wide range of common subjects you may encounter while taking photographs. When the Mode Guide is activated in the Set-up 2 menu, the introductory screen will be displayed. Select a Scene mode by pressing the SET button, as shown in the figure. To cycle through the available Scene modes, simply press the **Q button** and rotate the Main dial when the Mode Guide is disabled. **Here are the options available to you:**

- **Portrait**. This mode typically uses wider f/stops and faster shutter speeds, resulting in beautifully blurred backgrounds and sharp images free from any camera shake. By maintaining pressure on the shutter release, the R6 II effortlessly captures a continuous sequence of photos, allowing you to skillfully capture those fleeting expressions in portrait situations. There is a noticeable emphasis on portraying skin tones and hair in a more professional and flattering manner.

- **Group photo:** For optimal outcomes, it is recommended to use a wide-angle lens to enhance the depth of field. This mode is designed to optimize the sharpness range, allowing you to capture images where everyone in a group, both in the front and in the back, is in focus.

- **Landscape**: The R6 II aims to use smaller f/stops to achieve greater depth-of-field, while also enhancing saturation to produce more vibrant colors. An attached and powered-up external Speedlite will fire, allowing you to capture professional-quality photos without the need for the built-in flash.

- **Panoramic Shot:** By following the on-screen prompts, you can capture a stunning wide-screen panorama by skillfully rotating the camera during the exposure.

- **Sports**: With this mode, the R6 II aims to capture action with precision by using high shutter speeds. It also enables continuous shooting, allowing you to effortlessly capture a quick sequence of pictures with a single press of the shutter release. Additionally, the AI Servo AF ensures that your subject remains in focus even as it moves within the frame.

- **Kids**: This mode uses continuous focusing to track the movement of energetic children, and continuous shooting to capture a continuous stream of still photos. The skin tones are enhanced to appear vibrant and healthy. Position the center AF point in the viewfinder directly on your main subject and gently press the shutter release halfway. The R6 II will adjust its focus to track the child's movement, and you will be notified with a beep when the refocusing occurs. When the camera fails to achieve sharp focus, the focus confirmation indicator in the viewfinder will blink.

- **Panning**: This mode enhances the sense of motion by using a slower shutter speed, resulting in a slight blur as you smoothly rotate the camera to track a moving subject.
- **Close-up**: This mode functions similarly to the Portrait setting, using wider f/stops to create a shallow depth of field and isolate your close-up subjects. Additionally, it uses high shutter speeds to effectively eliminate any camera shake that may be more noticeable when focusing at close distances. If you have your camera mounted on a tripod or are using an image-stabilized (IS) lens, it would be advisable to use the Creative Zone Aperture-priority (Av) mode. This will allow you to specify a smaller f/stop, resulting in greater depth of field.
- **Food**: With this mode, your food pictures will appear vibrant and mouthwatering, thanks to the rich colors and enhanced contrast.
- **Night Portrait**: This mode uses a combination of flash and ambient light to create an image where the main subject is illuminated by the flash, while the background is exposed by the existing light. Using longer exposures in this mode requires the use of a tripod, monopod, or IS lens for optimal results.
- **Handheld Night Scene**: With this mode, the R6 II captures four consecutive shots and merges them to create a perfectly exposed image with a minimized camera shake.
- **HDR backlight control:** The R6 II captures three consecutive shots at varying exposures and merges them to create a single image that exhibits enhanced detail in both the highlights and shadows.
- **Silent shutter**: Capture images with a noiseless shutter. Captures images with minimal noise by using the electronic shutter instead of the mechanical shutter.

Frequently Asked Questions

1. How do you choose a metering mode?
2. How do you choose a shooting mode?
3. How do you make EV changes?
4. How do you adjust exposure with ISO settings?
5. How do you create a bracketed set?
6. How do you work with HDR?
7. How do you fix exposures with histograms?

CHAPTER FIVE
MASTERING THE MYSTERIES OF FOCUS

Overview

Chapter five talks about mastering the focus mode on the Canon EOS R6 Mark II. Additionally, this chapter will teach us how focus mode works, working with the AF system, and the different kinds of AF areas.

Auto or Manual Focus?

With the advancements in autofocus technology, photographers now have the assurance to depend on AF for the majority of their shots. The camera is highly proficient at assessing your scene and swiftly focusing on a suitable subject, ensuring exceptional results for any user. Curiously, the adoption of mirrorless technology has sparked a renewed fascination with traditional manual focus.

Here are five reasons why manual focus is becoming increasingly popular among creative photographers:

- **What you see is what you get (WYSIWYG):** You can expect the same level of sharp focus in the captured image as what you see through the viewfinder or LCD monitor. When you focus manually, you are evaluating the sensor image that will be captured when you press the shutter release, just like a professional. Conventional single-lens reflex (SLR) cameras employ a mirror to redirect the image to a distinct focusing screen (when not in live view mode), which may have a lower resolution, less brightness, and potential misalignment.

- **WYSIWYW**: Mastering manual focus allows you to have complete control over what you capture. Whether it's a stunning macro shot or a captivating portrait, you can precisely choose the plane of focus you desire, instead of relying on the camera's assumptions. Cameras cannot accurately determine the subject you want to be in sharp focus. It cannot currently read your thoughts, at least for now. When the camera is left to its own devices, it tends to choose the nearest object and quickly focus on it, even if it's not the main subject of your photo.

- **Less confusion:** Canon has provided photographers with faster and more precise autofocus systems, offering a wide range of options. However, the abundance of choices can sometimes be overwhelming, even for experienced photographers. If you prefer to avoid the hassle of exploring the various AF options for a particular shot, you can switch to manual focus and capture your image. Rest assured, the camera will consistently achieve optimal focus.

- **Focus aids**: Zooming in on the sensor image while manually focusing allows you to use a helpful feature known as manual focus peaking, or "**outline emphasis**" as Canon calls it. This feature highlights in-focus areas by outlining them with distinct colors. The camera is equipped with a "**focus guide**" feature that assists in determining the level of blurriness in the image and provides guidance on the direction to focus for achieving a crisp and clear image.

- **More lenses**: Every mirrorless camera, including the Canon EOS R-series, had a restricted selection of lenses upon their initial release. Fortunately, the reduced flange-to-sensor distance provides ample space to insert an adapter, enabling the mounting of a wide range of lenses, even those from different manufacturers than Canon. Several third-party optics available are affordable manual focus lenses or lenses designed for different camera platforms, which can only be used in manual focus mode on the R-series models.

How Focus Works

In a nutshell, focus involves fine-tuning the camera to ensure that the desired parts of our subject are sharp and clear. There is the option to let the camera handle the focus automatically or take control by manually adjusting the lens's focus ring. Manual focusing can be challenging due to the limited ability of our eyes and brains to accurately remember the correct focus. Just like a pro, manual focusing requires gently adjusting the focus ring to transition between different levels of focus. With precision and expertise, the small arcs gradually diminish in size until you have pinpointed the exact focal point. What you need is the image that exhibits the highest contrast between the edges of its elements. The autofocus mechanism, similar to other systems in modern cameras, also assesses these changes in sharpness. However, it excels at memorizing the progression, allowing for quicker and more precise autofocus, especially with images that have ample contrast. Regrettably, although the camera's focus system excels at measuring degrees of apparent focus at each focus point in the viewfinder, it cannot definitively determine which object should be in the sharpest focus. Is this object the closest one? Is the subject in the center? Is there something hidden behind the nearest object? Is someone positioned on the side of the picture? Mastering auto focus requires a strategic approach to determine the precise subject to focus on.

Mastering the autofocus system requires a thorough understanding of its inner workings to maximize its potential. Once you have mastered autofocus, you will also become proficient in knowing when to use the manual focus option. The camera collects focus information from the sensors and evaluates it to determine if the desired sharp focus has been achieved. Calculations may be necessary to account for factors such as subject movement and the need for the camera to anticipate the subject's position when the picture is taken. The speed at which the camera evaluates focus and adjusts the lens elements for optimal sharpness directly impacts the autofocus mechanism's speed. In certain shooting scenarios, the R6 II surpasses the speed of the human eye in terms of focus. However, there are instances where even its impressive speed may not be sufficient. For instance, if you encounter difficulties capturing a fast-paced sport with multiple players, you can consider adjusting the autofocus settings. Switching to a different autofocus mode or manually focusing on a specific spot where you anticipate the action can yield better results. For instance, focusing on the goal line or soccer net can help you capture the decisive moments with precision. Autofocus is typically accomplished through two distinct technologies known as contrast-detection autofocus (CDAF) and phase-detection autofocus (PDAF).

Contrast Detection

This mode is known for its precision and is commonly used by professionals. It works best for still subjects and was initially the only autofocus option for mirrorless cameras and dSLRs when shooting in live view and movie modes. With the addition of phase-detection pixels directly on the sensor, contrast detection has been transformed from a primary system into a supplementary tool for designers, resulting in a hybrid system that combines the best of both worlds. **While contrast detection may be slower, it offers both advantages and disadvantages:**

- Compatible with a wider range of image formats. Any subject with defined boundaries is compatible with CDAF.
- Pay attention to any specific point. Contrast detection allows for focusing on any part of the image without the need for dedicated AF sensors. Focus can be easily achieved by selecting the desired part of the sensor image. You can effortlessly move the focus frame to any desired location.
- Possibly more precise. Contrast detection is straightforward and precise. When there is ample light for the camera to analyze the sensor's image, it can accurately detect the point of highest contrast. Nevertheless, a certain level of "hunting" might be

required. When the camera is trying to find the perfect focus, it might need to readjust if it goes too far and then find the right focus again.

Phase Detection

The phase-detection pixels in the sensor split incoming photons arriving from opposite sides of the lens into two parts, forming a pair of images, similar to the rangefinders used for surveying and in rangefinder-focusing cameras like the renowned Leica M series. The dual images are carefully adjusted when out of focus, and then skillfully aligned to achieve sharp focus. This process indicates to the camera when the image pair is "**in phase**" and properly aligned. With the rangefinder approach of phase detection, precise calculations are made to determine the degree and direction of the image's focus error. This is achieved by analyzing the displacement of the split image, which indicates whether the focus is too near or too far. This camera excels at swiftly and accurately capturing images with sharp focus, while also aligning the lines perfectly.

AF Pixel Layout

Thanks to the remarkable flexibility of Dual Pixel technology, Canon has achieved an impressive feat by expanding the AF area to cover almost the entire vertical frame and nearly the entire horizontal area when using RF lenses. When EF-mount lenses are attached using a mount adapter, it is important to note that they may not achieve full coverage. According to Canon, certain lenses may only offer 80 percent horizontal coverage. The extensive coverage of phase-detect pixels offers numerous advantages for mirrorless cameras such as the R6 II. Traditional dSLRs usually have PDAF systems that are not sensor-based. These systems cover a smaller area of the frame and have a limited number of AF points, typically a few hundred at most. In contrast, your camera offers over 1,000 AF points. Canon's PDAF system possesses numerous strengths that were previously associated with contrast-detection AF technology.

- **Compatible with all image formats**: With numerous AF point positions on the sensor, it is highly improbable for the area under examination to lack the necessary edges for achieving precise focus.
- **Focus on any specific point**: With contrast detection, you have the flexibility to examine any position on the sensor. The abundance of AF points on the sensor allows for focusing using any area of the sensor. Additionally, you have the freedom to move the 1-point AF point to your desired location.
- **Just as accurate**: With a generous amount of PDAF points, the accuracy of this device rivals that of contrast detection, all while eliminating any hunting or slowness.

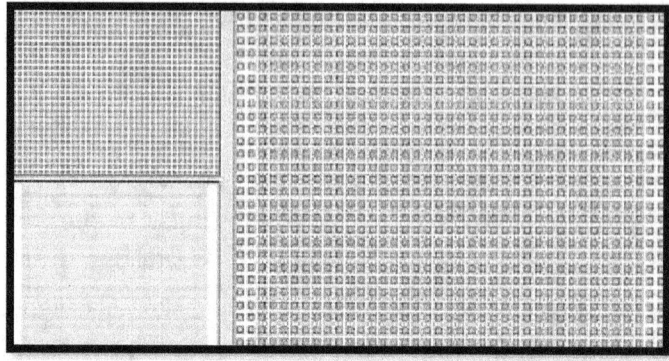

The positions that can be selected using the multi-controller are represented by the green squares located at the bottom left. These also provide complete coverage of the frame. There are a total of 4,897 positions in a large array measuring 83 by 59. These figures do not indicate that your camera has nearly 5,000 phases-detect pixels. The large number and the green squares indicate the available locations for selecting your focus point with 1-point AF. During the AF area selection process, the camera prioritizes the smaller number of sensor sections, which are visually indicated by the blue squares.

Dual Pixel CMOS AF

Having a solid grasp of contrast and phase detection is essential to fully appreciate the impressive capabilities of Canon's Dual Pixel CMOS AF system. When used for both stills and movies, it operates at a significantly faster speed compared to traditional contrast-detection systems. The sensor's pixel array incorporates specialized pixels that enable the use of split-image rangefinder phase-detection autofocus, a feature commonly found in professional PDAF modules. One crucial aspect of the system is its ability to preserve the camera's imaging resolution. Placing AF sensors between the pixels used to capture the image would have resulted in a reduced area for capturing light. It is important to note that CMOS sensors, in contrast to previous CCD sensors, have additional circuitry on board that uses up some of the light-gathering areas. Each photosensitive site is equipped with microlenses that efficiently focus incoming illumination onto the sensor. These microlenses also help correct for any oblique angles from which photons may approach the imager, ensuring optimal image quality.

Using the Dual Pixel CMOS AF system, the photosites can capture both image and autofocus information seamlessly. The camera's pixels are split into two photodiodes, positioned horizontally or vertically for autofocus functionality. Every pair operates as an independent

AF sensor, enabling an advanced integrated circuit to analyze the autofocus data before transmitting it to the digital image processor, which manages both autofocus and image capture. When it comes to the latter, the information from both photodiodes is merged, allowing the sensor pixel to fully use its photosensitive area for capturing the image. With the inclusion of Dual Pixel CMOS AF phase detection, the camera can focus seamlessly, eliminating the frustrating "**hunting**" that often occurs with traditional contrast detection. This smooth focus is crucial for capturing fast-paced action and is especially important when shooting movies, as it prevents any unwanted focus adjustments from being recorded. Movie autofocus tracking has been enhanced, enabling the capture of moving subjects with precision.

Dual Pixel RAW Focus Adjustments

The EOS R6 II offers a fascinating addition to its dual-pixel autofocus approach by allowing users to save Dual Pixel RAW image files. These files include rangefinder-like focus information directly in the RAW files. These files can be further adjusted in the DPRAW Processing entry of the Playback 3 menu. Using Digital Photo Professional, you can manipulate Dual Pixel RAW files to fine-tune focus, adjust bokeh, minimize flare and ghosting effects, and enhance sharpness. It allows for precise adjustments during post-processing. It is crucial to remember that autofocus is only available when using Dual Pixel CMOS AF, and the ability to manipulate files is limited to those captured in Dual Pixel RAW mode. To use Dual Pixel RAW, you need to choose RAW or C RAW or RAW+JPEG/HEIF or C RAW+JPEG/HEIF as your Image Quality. Afterward, you can activate the dual-pixel feature in the Shooting 1 menu. If you wish to shoot multiple exposures, use automatic HDR, the electronic shutter, or One-Touch image quality, DPR is not compatible. The two highest continuous speeds (H+ and H) are currently unavailable.

Circles of Confusion and Focus

It is well known that a greater depth of field allows for a sharper focus on a larger portion of your subject. However, increased depth-of-field can pose a challenge for autofocusing (or manual focusing) as it reduces the contrast between objects at varying distances. This factor goes beyond the technical aspects of lens opening size in phase detection, highlighting the importance of professional expertise. It can be challenging to focus with any type of focus system, whether it's phase detection, contrast detection, or manual focus when the image is dimmer. Mastering the art of photography requires understanding the nuances of different focal lengths. When it comes to focusing, a 200mm focal length offers certain advantages over a 28mm focal length or zoom setting. This is because the longer lens provides a shallower depth of field, making it easier to achieve precise focus. In comparison, a lens with a maximum aperture of f/1.8 will provide a smoother autofocus experience, whether you choose to use autofocus or manual focus. On the other hand, a lens with an f/4 maximum aperture, despite having the same focal length, will have a greater depth of field and a dimmer view, making it slightly more challenging to focus accurately. Another reason why lenses with a maximum aperture smaller than f/5.6 can pose challenges for your autofocus system is the combination of increased depth-of-field and a dimmer image. This makes it more difficult for the phase detection to accurately focus.

Adding to the complexity, numerous subjects fail to maintain their composure. They shift within the frame, causing the need for refocusing even when the camera is sharply focused on the main subject. Occasionally, an unexpected subject may appear in the frame and obstruct your intended subject for photography. It is up to you (or the camera) to decide whether to focus on this new subject or maintain focus on the original subject. Some subjects can be challenging to capture clearly due to a lack of contrast, making it difficult for the autofocus system (or our eyes) to properly focus on them. Plain walls, a bright blue sky, or any other subject matter can be distracting and hinder concentration. If you're feeling a bit overwhelmed by all these focus factors, then you're heading in the right direction. Focus is measured using a circle of confusion, which is a common method used by professionals. A perfect image is made up of countless minuscule points that, in theory, lack any height or width. The point stands out beautifully against its surroundings, creating a perfect contrast. Imagine each point as a shining beacon in a room devoid of light. When a specific point loses focus, its edges lose contrast and it transforms from a sharp point into a small disc with blurred edges. When the blurry disc is sufficiently small, our eye can still perceive it as a point. When the disc reaches a certain size, it appears blurry instead of sharp, indicating that the point is no longer in focus. It is evident that when you enlarge an image, whether by displaying it larger on your computer monitor or by making a large print, the size of each circle of confusion also increases. Getting closer to the image has a similar effect. When viewing an image at different sizes and distances, it's important to note that what may appear sharp in a small print might appear blurry when blown up and examined closely. With a more objective perspective, the situation may regain its clarity.

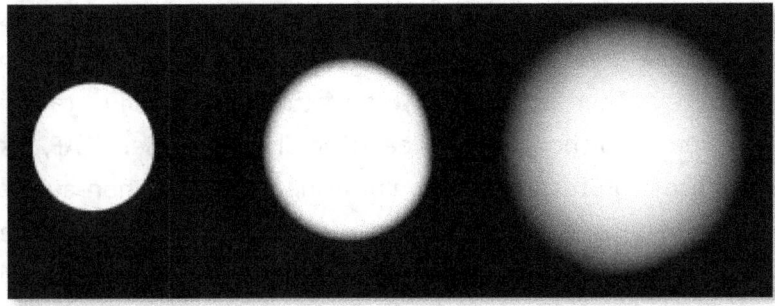

The apparent size of these circles of confusion can also be influenced by the viewer. Certain individuals have a knack for observing details from a specific distance, enabling them to discern smaller circles of confusion compared to those close. In general, though, these differences tend to be minor. Blurry images will appear unclear to most individuals in similar circumstances.

Working with the AF System

Now that you have a solid grasp of the fundamentals of the autofocus system, let's delve into the various settings and options available to you. To consistently achieve precise focus, it is essential to have a thorough understanding of focus modes and focus area selection. By mastering these techniques, you will be able to accurately evaluate a scene and determine where to lock in focus.

AF Operation

The AF Operation focus modes instruct the camera on when to assess and establish focus. Other autofocus features are responsible for determining where the focus should be checked, not this one. Focus modes determine how the camera handles focusing. They can be set to lock in focus when you press the shutter release halfway or use another control like the AF-ON button. Alternatively, they can be set to continuously track your subject and adjust focus accordingly if it's in motion. The camera offers manual focus with the option to magnify up to 10X for precise focusing. It also provides two autofocus modes: One-Shot AF for single autofocus and Servo AF for continuous autofocus. Mastering the selection of autofocus mode and focus points is crucial for achieving professional-level results. Using the incorrect mode for a specific type of photography can result in a series of images that are all sharply focused on the incorrect subject. In still photography mode, the focus will only initiate when you partially depress the shutter release or another defined AF-ON button. This helps to save battery power unless you have activated Preview AF in the AF 3 menu. However, autofocus is not a mindless creature that randomly adjusts your pictures without any input from you once you press the button. There are various settings that you can adjust to regain some level of control. When it comes to choosing between One-Shot AF or Servo AF, it's important to make your decision like a professional. If you're using one of the non-auto modes, simply press the Q button to bring up the Quick Control menu. From there, you can easily navigate to AF Operation, which is the second option from the top in the left column. Rotate the Main dial to switch between One-Shot, AI Focus, or Servo. Ensure that the AF/M switch on the lens is set to AF to adjust the autofocus mode.

One-Shot AF

When using this mode, known as single autofocus, the focus is set once and remains fixed until you fully press the button to capture the picture, or until you release the shutter button without taking a shot. This mode is ideal for subjects that are relatively still. Therefore, for non-action photography, this setting is typically the most suitable option as it reduces the chances of capturing out-of-focus images (although it may sacrifice some spontaneity). One potential downside is that you may not be able to capture a photo until the camera has successfully focused on the subject. During this time, you will be unable to take any pictures until the autofocus mechanism has determined that the current setting is satisfactory.

One-shot AF/single autofocus is sometimes known as focus-priority due to its characteristics. Due to a minor delay in the camera's focus-priority operation, there may be a slight increase in shutter lag. This mode conserves battery power more effectively compared to the other autofocus modes. Once you've achieved sharp focus, the selected focus point in the viewfinder will flash green and the camera will emit a beep, unless you've disabled the Beep option in the Set-up 3 menu. When using Evaluative metering, the exposure will be locked simultaneously. By maintaining a halfway depressed shutter button, you can easily adjust the framing of the image without losing the focus or exposure that has already been set. Another option is to use the AE lock/FE lock button, which allows you to preserve the exposure determined by the center AF point when adjusting your framing. When the camera fails to achieve focus, the focus point will turn orange, preventing the capture of a picture even with full pressure on the shutter release.

Sometimes, you might need to capture a photo in a hurry, without the luxury of time to properly focus by half-pressing the shutter release. If that occurs often, and prioritizing "**capturing the moment**" is more crucial than achieving perfect focus, you have the option to switch from focus-priority to release-priority by accessing the One-Shot AF Release Priority entry in the AF 3 menu. The camera will now capture a photo as soon as the shutter release is fully pressed, regardless of whether the focus is confirmed.

AI Focus

This mode, also known as automatic autofocus, seamlessly transitions between One-Shot AF and Servo AF, depending on the movement of your subject. When you depress the shutter release halfway or shoot continuously, it automatically selects the mode for you.

Servo AF

This mode, commonly referred to as continuous autofocus, is ideal for capturing sports and other fast-moving subjects. It is frequently paired with continuous shooting modes to ensure sharp and accurate images. When the shutter release is partially depressed, the camera will focus on the selected point, whether it's chosen by the camera or manually by you. It will then keep an eye on the subject, making adjustments to the focus if there is any movement from either the subject or yourself. When focus is achieved, the AF point changes to a blue color. There is no audible signal, as it would be disruptive to have a sound every time refocusing happens. As expected, the focus and exposure settings are not finalized until the shutter release is fully pressed to capture the image. With Servo AF, you'll experience minimal shutter lag, allowing you to capture shots instantly when you press the button. Additionally, the autofocus system consumes a significant amount of battery power as it remains active as long as the shutter release button is partially depressed. When using Scene Intelligent Auto mode, the camera seamlessly transitions to Servo AF when it detects any movement from the subject.

Continuous autofocus is commonly known as release-priority, as it has been traditionally used in this manner. When operating in that mode, if you fully depress the shutter release while the system is fine-tuning the focus, the camera will capture an image, even if it is slightly out of focus. With Servo AF, you can take advantage of the advanced predictive AF technology to ensure accurate focus even when your subject is in motion, either moving closer or farther away from the camera at a consistent pace. It uses either the AF point that is automatically chosen or the one you manually select to establish focus. It's worth noting that using release-priority mode minimizes the number of out-of-focus images. This implies that a photograph will be captured even if the camera has not yet confirmed the precise focus. Your image is likely to be sharply focused at the moment of exposure, or at least close enough.

AF Area

The AF area, as defined by Canon, is a valuable feature that allows you to precisely determine the areas of the frame that will be used for autofocus information. There are a total of eight AF area modes available for selecting the initial point or zone of points, each with its variations on additional point deployment if required. You have the option to enable or disable subject tracking for each of these. Simply press the INFO button while selecting an AF method and the R6 II will automatically choose a subject (people, animals, or vehicles) to track and follow.

Spot AF

With this mode, you can focus and direct your attention towards a specific box that is visible on the screen. You can also make precise adjustments to the position of this focus area on the screen. This can be done by using the multi-controller joystick, the Main dial for horizontal movement, or the QCD-1 for up-and-down movement. Before you can move the focus point, make sure to press the AF point selection button.

1-Point AF

In this mode, you can concentrate and direct your attention towards a box that is approximately three times larger than what is shown on the screen. If you prioritize speed while still desiring precise focus location specifications, this option is likely the optimal choice.

Expand AF Area

When operating in this mode, the selected focus point is used in conjunction with the surrounding points. This includes the points directly above, below, and on either side of the selected point, until the manually chosen point reaches the edge of the array and one or more of the additional points move out of view. This mode is ideal for capturing moving objects, as the expanded effective zone enhances the ability to effortlessly track subjects in motion within the frame. When the subject moves outside the area defined by the selected focus point, several surrounding focus points can seamlessly pick up and track the movement. The focus point and expanded point used will be displayed in One-Shot AF mode.

Expand AF Area: Around

This mode functions in a manner akin to the one mentioned earlier, with the distinction that the focusing array encompasses the eight points surrounding the manually chosen point. For subjects with less intricate details at the manually chosen focus point, the surrounding points can enhance your results. This mode is more suitable for larger moving objects, despite sacrificing a small amount of precision.

Flexible Zone AF 1

This method uses a zone-oriented point selection technique, where the AF points are divided into zones, forming a square that covers approximately one-sixth of the frame. When adjusting the focus "**point**" using the controls, you are effectively shifting the zone within the frame from one position to another. If you have a good idea of the general area where your subject will be and want to focus on a specific zone, this mode is highly effective. This mode typically prioritizes the closest subject, resulting in a slightly lower level of accuracy compared to the other autofocus methods. To adjust the zone's position, use the AF point selection button in conjunction with the directional buttons, the Main dial/QCD-1 combination, or the multi-controller.

Whole Area AF

With this mode, the R6 II takes charge of selecting the focus area, using the entire frame. It is highly effective for subjects that are in constant motion, making it challenging to manually select a focus area or zone. When this mode and Subject Tracking are enabled, you can swiftly choose a face or eye by simply tapping the screen.

Subject Tracking

By default, the EOS R6 II uses a range of criteria to precisely focus on a specific subject. The camera tends to prioritize the closest object and considers the movement of the subject, enabling it to anticipate the next focus point. When using One-Shot AF mode, the current focus area is conveniently highlighted in green. On the other hand, if you have the AF operation set to Servo AF, the focus area will be displayed in a cool blue color. To easily view the focus areas in action, simply press the shutter release halfway. It is especially useful when using the Flexible Zone or Whole area AF options, as they encompass a significant portion of the frame.

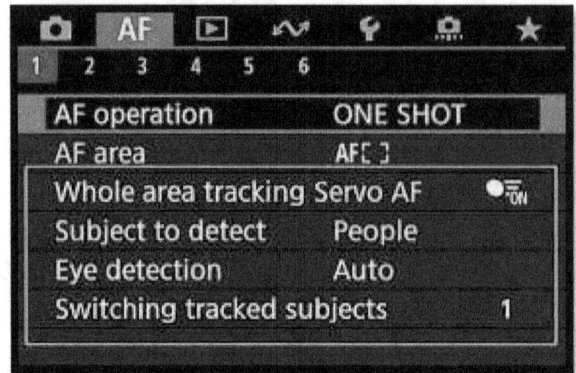

You have several options to choose from, as the AF 1 menu offers four entries specifically dedicated to tracking parameters. Using the Whole area tracking Servo AF, the camera can accurately identify and focus on your subject. However, for optimal results with different types of subjects, it is recommended to explore other AF area modes that are specifically designed for those subjects. That could be true if your subject is positioned in a specific area of the frame and is unlikely to move. With this feature, you have the flexibility to select an AF area specifically designed for stationary subjects. When Servo AF is engaged, the camera seamlessly switches to Whole area AF for optimal performance.

- **On**: Enables Whole area tracking when Servo AF is selected and tracking is enabled. When AF operation is set to One-Shot AF or AI Focus, the specified area in the AF area entry is used.
- **Off**: The specified area for AF will be consistently used for One-Shot, AI Focus, or servo-focus methods.

Subject to detect: Select from the options: People, Animals, Vehicles, or None. The camera can search for specific types of subjects, but you also have the option to manually select the subject to be tracked using the touch screen.

- **People**: The camera prioritizes detecting faces or heads initially, followed by tracking their torso, and finally, other parts of their body. Some faces that are very large or small, partially hidden by a hat, or extremely bright or dark, may not be detected.
- **Animals**: The R6 II is capable of identifying different types of dogs, cats, and birds and attempts to detect their faces or bodies, as long as the subject is close to the camera and facing it. Regardless of the situation, the tracking frame always displays the animal's body. It's worth noting that the camera can also identify people in the frame, although it gives priority to animals.

- **Vehicles**: This setting is perfect for motorsports enthusiasts who are looking to capture the excitement of the action in real-time. The camera scans for both two- and four-wheeled vehicles, as well as pedestrians, with a focus on prioritizing the vehicles. Some vehicles, like bicycles and non-competition motor vehicles such as SUVs, may not be detected. The tracking system may be affected by the dust and dirt that is kicked up during motocross events. While selecting Vehicles, you have the option to activate or deactivate spot detection for key vehicle details like headlights and wheels by pressing the INFO button. Spot detection can be a valuable tool for locating a specific vehicle when there is minimal overlap.
- **None**: By selecting this versatile setting, the R6 II will intelligently track subjects based on the composition you have framed, allowing you to effortlessly capture the moments that matter to you. No tracking frames are being shown. In this mode, it is not possible to detect eyes, even though faces can still be found.

Eye detection: Having keen eyesight is often crucial for capturing a captivating image of a person or animal, whether or not the eyes truly reveal the essence of their soul. Canon offers the feature of enabling eye detection for your convenience. If time is of the essence and capturing any picture is more important than achieving sharp focus, it may be advisable to disable this process. To select an eye using Whole area AF, simply tap the screen.

Switching tracked subjects: This setting controls the speed at which the camera transitions between subjects when the initial tracked subject moves out of the frame or is obstructed by something like a referee running along the sideline. If the subject turns away from the camera or their appearance is altered, such as a standing person crouching down, you may also experience a loss of tracking. When needed, the R6 II can seamlessly transition to a different subject, allowing you to adjust the delay according to your preference. **Here are the options available to you:**
- **Initial priority:** The camera will make every effort to continuously track the initial subject, even in the presence of other subjects.
- **On subject:** The R6 II is designed to track the initial subject and seamlessly switch to other subjects, if needed, with minimal delay.
- **Switch subject:** The camera smoothly transitions to another subject.

Manual Focus

Switching from autofocus to manual focus is a breeze. Just slide the AF/MF switch on your lens to the MF position and take control of setting the focus yourself, like a pro. There are both pros and cons to this approach. Using manual focus mode can extend the lifespan of your batteries, but it also requires more time and effort to focus the camera for each shot, which can be challenging. Canon provides extensive assistance for manual focusing, ensuring a professional level of precision.

Magnified View

For a more professional approach, you have the option to check focus using magnified views of either 5X or 10X. Simply press the Magnify/Reduce button in all modes. If you want to fine-tune the focus plane of your camera, you can also adjust the autofocus modes. To zoom in, simply press the **Magnify/Reduce button** once or twice. Press it a third time to return to the regular view. When using autofocus mode, the magnification is centered on the AF point for Spot AF, 1-point AF, Expand AF area, Expand AF area: Around, and Zone AF Large Zone: Vertical or Large Zone: Horizontal. When you press the shutter button down halfway in Spot AF and 1-point AF, AF is performed in a magnified display. AF is performed after restoring normal display in other modes. When using Servo AF mode, the camera will revert to the regular view to focus. Continuous AF and Movie Servo AF are not accessible when using a magnified view. It can be challenging to maintain focus when there is a shake.

Focus Peaking

Another option is to use MF Peaking in the AF 5 menu, which allows you to enhance the edges of your image by applying a contrasting color. You can also choose the level of peaking to achieve different effects, ranging from high, and medium, to low. Peaking is not visible when using the magnified display.

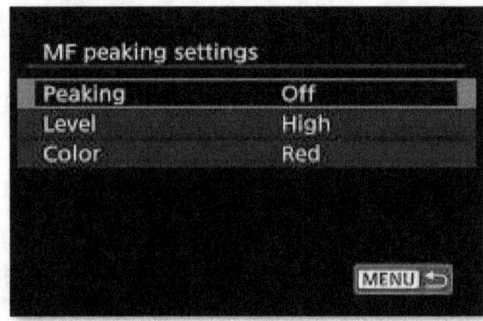

Focus Guide

The Focus Guide, found in the AF 5 menu, is an exceptional tool that can greatly enhance the speed of manual focus. To ensure that your subject is in sharp focus, it is important to adjust the focus ring in arcs of decreasing size.

Fine-Tuning Your Autofocus

Here are the options available to you:

- **Preview AF:** The camera ensures continuous refocusing, even in One-Shot mode, until you press the shutter release halfway. Then, the One-Shot AF mode will lock focus and continue to refocus in Servo AF mode until you fully press the shutter release to capture the image. By using this setting's pre-focus activity, you can enhance the speed of autofocus while capturing images, albeit with a slight impact on battery life. This setting can be located in the AF 3 menu.
- **AF-assist beam firing**: This setting determines the timing for bursts of light emitted by an external electronic flash or the camera's built-in LED. These bursts help create enough contrast to accurately focus on a subject. This entry can be located in the AF 3 menu.
- **Servo AF characteristics:** You can customize the tracking behavior in Servo AF mode using the options in the AF 2 menu. Four preset cases are provided with settings optimized for various shooting scenarios. Another option is Case A (Auto), where the camera can automatically adjust to moving subjects.

You can modify two parameters of the preset cases. Simply select the case you wish to customize and click on the **SET button**. Next, press the **RATE button** and select one of the two adjustments mentioned below. **Press SET one more time and uses the multi-controller to make adjustments:**

- **Tracking sensitivity**: This determines how quickly the AF system switches to a new subject entering the focus area. Your options are −2 (Locked On) to +2 (Responsive). Negative numbers allow you to retain focus on the original subject even if it briefly leaves the area covered by the focus points, making tracking easier. One downside is that in case the camera chooses the incorrect subject, there will be a slight delay before the correct subject is captured. Positive numbers enhance the AF system's ability to swiftly transition to a new subject. Nevertheless, a rapid response may lead to the camera focusing on an unintended subject.

- **Tracking acceleration and deceleration**: This parameter controls the response of the AF system to abrupt changes in speed or stopping. Choose a value between 0 and 2 to indicate the speed of the subjects you are considering. A value of 0 corresponds to subjects that move at a constant speed, while a value of 2 represents subjects that can quickly change their speed. Having lower values can lead to the camera being deceived when a subject that was in motion abruptly stops. This can result in a change in focus to where the subject would have been if it had continued moving. An increased value could potentially lead to focus inconsistencies when dealing with subjects that maintain a constant speed.

When the focus is difficult: Autofocus systems can struggle in low-contrast scenes and dim light levels. It is a common occurrence with long telephotos or lenses that have a relatively small maximum aperture. The Lens Drive When AF Impossible setting (AF 3) allows the camera to choose between continuous focusing attempts or stopping altogether.

Limit AF methods: To optimize your workflow, consider hiding any unused AF methods on the selection screen. This way, you can quickly switch between the ones you frequently use. The 1-point AF mode is always active and cannot be turned off. You can locate these options in the AF 4 entry.

Back-Button Focus

After gaining some experience with your camera, you will inevitably come across the concepts of back focus and back-button focus. At that point, you may start questioning whether they have positive or negative implications. In reality, these two concepts are distinct and frequently mistaken for one another.

Back focus is an undesirable occurrence where a lens consistently focuses on a plane that is situated behind the intended subject. Some of your lenses may have this issue, while others may be free from any defects. If the issue is with a specific lens, rather than a general mis-adjustment affecting all your lenses, it can be resolved. Back-button focus is a technique that allows you to separate the functions of exposure and autofocus. This enables you to lock in exposure while focusing can be adjusted later, or vice versa. Mastering back-button focus may require you to break old habits and develop new finger coordination techniques, but it's worth the effort.

As you may be aware, the standard procedure is to automatically adjust both exposure and focus (if autofocus is enabled) when the shutter release is pressed halfway. When using One-Shot AF mode, the exposure and focus remain locked until you either release the shutter button or press it fully to capture a photo and then release it for the subsequent shot. When using Servo AF mode, the exposure is locked and the focus is set when you press the shutter release halfway. However, if your subject moves while you hold down the shutter button halfway, the system will continue to refocus. The focus is not engaged until the button is fully pressed to capture the image.

Back-button focus effectively decouples or separates the two actions. Retaining the exposure lock feature while pressing the shutter halfway is possible, allowing you to assign autofocus to a separate button. In practice, you have the option to press the shutter button halfway to lock the exposure. This allows you to reframe the image as needed, such as when you're capturing a backlit subject and want to ensure the foreground is properly exposed. You can then reframe it to include a very bright background as well. However, in this particular situation, it is not ideal to have autofocus locked simultaneously.

Certainly, it would be wise to refrain from initiating AF until you feel fully prepared, perhaps while positioned at a sports venue, patiently awaiting the perfect moment to capture a ballplayer in your viewfinder. By using back-button focus, you can precisely lock exposure on the anticipated position of the athlete and effortlessly activate autofocus as soon as your subject enters the frame with a simple press of the AF-ON button. That's where the mastery of new habits and the coordination of mind and fingers come into play. You need to learn which back-button focus techniques work for you, and when to use them. Back-button focus lets you avoid the need to switch from One-Shot AF to Servo AF when your subject begins moving unexpectedly.

You have full autonomy. It's excellent for sports photography, allowing you to activate autofocus with precision based on the action in front of you. It is also effective for static shots. Press and release your designated focus button, then capture a series of shots using the same focus point. The focus will remain unchanged until you press the designated back button once more.

Activating Back-Button Focus

The R6 II has a unique approach to back-button focus compared to other cameras. Unlike them, it doesn't provide the option to assign AF Start exclusively to a button like the AF-ON button. When you activate the AF-ON button, the camera will automatically focus and meter the scene for you. To activate the back-button focus, simply navigate to the Customize Buttons entry in the Custom Functions 3 menu. After activating this feature, you can achieve precise exposure by pressing the shutter release down halfway to lock it and then using the AF-ON button to autofocus whenever you're ready. **Here is a step-by-step guide:**

1. Redefine the shutter release button. In Customize Buttons, highlight the **Shutter Button** entry. Then press the **SET button**.
2. Select the metering start option. When activated, fully depressing the shutter release button meters and locks the exposure, while the autofocus remains unaffected as the shutter is triggered. Press **SET** to confirm.

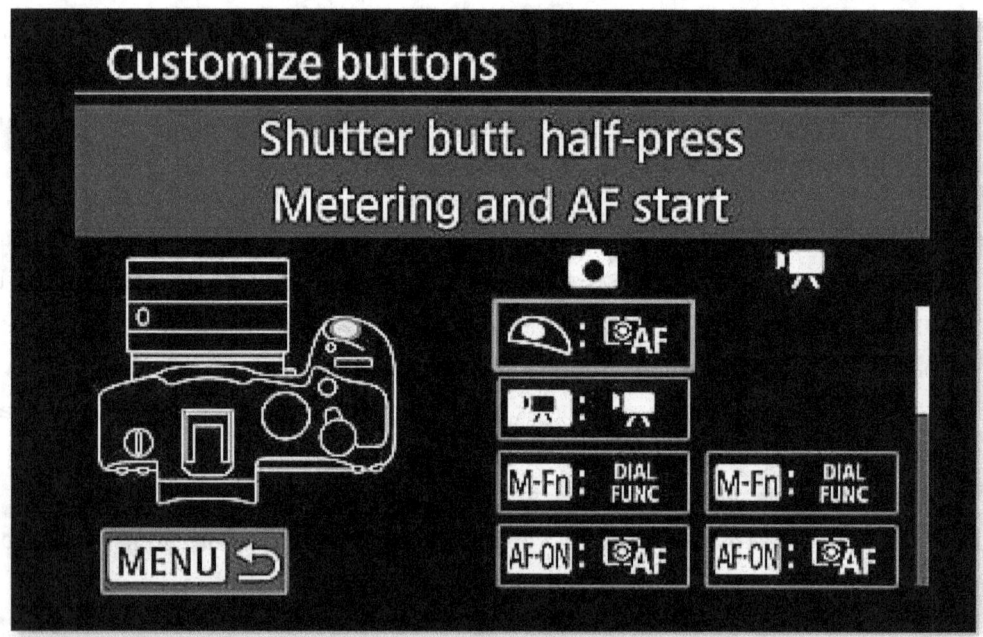

3. Choose the **Back Button**. The default setting for the AF-ON button is satisfactory. When you activate the AF-ON button, autofocus will start and metering will be carried out, constantly updating both until you let go of the button. When the shutter release button is pressed, the camera will perform metering and lock the exposure. To lock the exposure before taking the picture, simply press the AE lock (*) button. As an alternative, you have the option to assign a different button to the Metering and AF Start functions. This allows you to use it for back-button focus if you find it more convenient to access with your thumb.

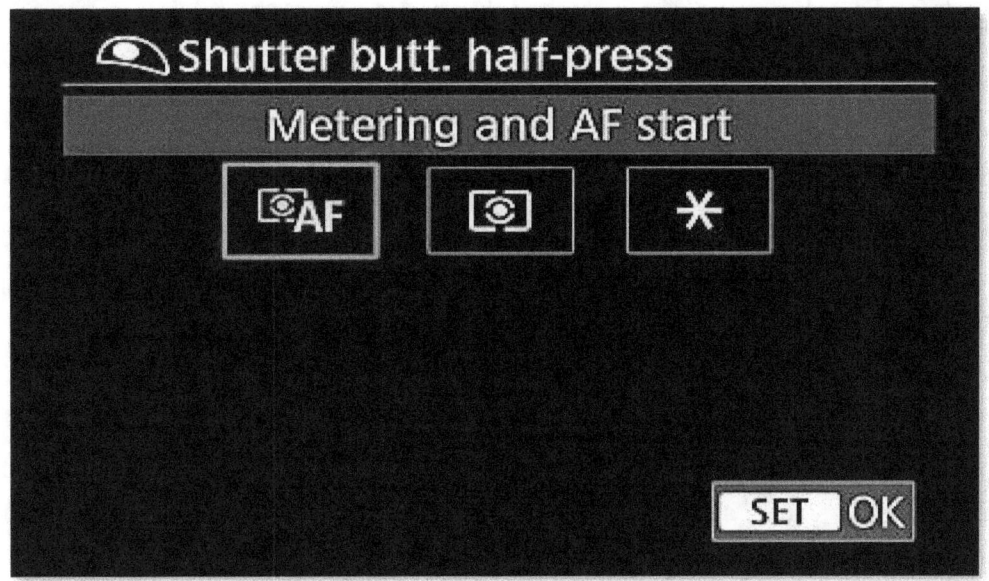

4. Disable continuous focus. For optimal results, it is recommended to use One-Shot AF with back-button focus. Additionally, it is advisable to disable Preview AF in the AF 3 menu.

Frequently Asked Questions

1. How does focus mode work?
2. How do you work with the AF system?
3. How do you use manual focus on the EOS R6 II?
4. How do you fine-tune your autofocus?
5. How do you activate back-button focus?

CHAPTER SIX
ADVANCED TECHNIQUES

Overview

Want to learn about more advanced techniques in the Canon EOS R6 II? This chapter explains the different advanced techniques including continuous shooting, long exposure, shooting panorama, delayed exposures, and a host of other techniques.

Continuous Shooting

Continuous shooting is a valuable feature that allows you to effortlessly capture a series of pictures. Whether you're aiming to capture the perfect moment or create a captivating sequence of images, this function makes it a breeze. With digital cameras, you have the advantage of reusable "**film**," allowing you to easily delete any shots that didn't quite capture the decisive moments and continue shooting.

DRIVE MODE	MECHANICAL SHUTTER	ELECTRONIC 1ST CURTAIN SHUTTER	ELECTRONIC SHUTTER
High-speed continuous+	12 fps	12 fps	40 fps
High-speed continuous	5.5 fps	6.0 fps	20 fps
Low-speed continuous	3.0 fps	3.0 fps	5.0 fps

Enabling flicker control, using Dual Pixel RAW, activating Servo AF, or working with electronic flash may result in a reduction of actual frames per second. Various factors can influence high-speed shooting, such as shooting settings like shutter speed, aperture, autofocus mode, and the type of lens being used. Insufficient battery power can also hinder shooting speeds. Partially pressing the shutter button will show a number, indicating the maximum number of shots you can take with the current quality settings. The number in the viewfinder can be found on the left side of the battery status indicator at the lower right, just above the Possible Shots value. The maximum burst can be found on the LCD screen, positioned to the right of the Possible Shots indicator in the upper left corner. The display indicates a maximum of 99 shots remaining. It's worth noting that the camera may be capable of capturing more shots beyond this limit. However, the number 99 will continue to be displayed until the actual remaining count falls below this value. A "BUSY" indicator will be displayed when the internal buffer reaches its maximum capacity. When the camera's internal buffer becomes full, it will temporarily pause capturing images until enough pictures have been saved to the memory card, enabling shooting to continue. As expected, the number of continuous shots you can take before this occurs will vary depending on the format you select and the write speed of your card. It is advisable to consider using a high-speed memory card.

The limitation on the size of your bursts is due to the buffer. Continuous images are initially stored in the camera's internal memory and then transferred to the memory card as quickly as possible. The camera efficiently processes the RAW data it receives from the digital image processor and converts it to the output format of your choice, be it JPG or RAW/DPRAW, or both. The processed data is then stored in the buffer, waiting transfer to the memory card. This internal buffer is designed to efficiently process photos at a faster rate compared to the memory card. It's worth noting that the speed of different memory cards can vary. According to Canon, the maximum burst when shooting RAW+JPEG Large is estimated to be 85 shots with a standard SDXC card. When capturing JPEG Large images, opting for a smaller file size can be quite advantageous. According to Canon, using a standard card would allow for a maximum burst of approximately 540 shots. For optimal results, it is recommended to use a shutter speed of 1/500th second, the widest aperture of the lens, One-Shot autofocus, and disable image stabilization. When One-Shot AF is enabled, the camera will focus once at the start of the sequence and maintain that focus setting for the remaining shots in the burst. If your subject is in motion, you can use Servo AF instead, which operates at a slightly reduced continuous frame rate.

More Exposure Options

There are various options available to give you precise control over when the exposure is captured, allowing you to experiment with unconventional exposure lengths such as time or bulb exposures.

A Tiny Slice of Time

Electronic flash can freeze action with its incredibly short duration, sometimes as short as 1/50,000th of a second or even less. The camera has impressive shutter speeds that can freeze even the fastest movement, reaching up to 1/8000th second (or 1/16,000th second with the electronic shutter in TV or M mode). Typically, you won't find yourself needing such a fast shutter speed in regular photography. Using an aperture of f/2.8 at ISO 100 outdoors in bright sunlight, a shutter speed of 1/8000th second would be more than sufficient. Even in less-than-optimal lighting conditions, a shutter speed of 1/8000th of a second is more than sufficient for any situation you may come across. For optimal results in capturing sports action, it is recommended to use a shutter speed of 1/2000th second or slower. In fact, in certain sports, a slower shutter speed is preferred to achieve a realistic blur effect, such as capturing the wheels of a racing automobile or motorcycle, or the propeller on a classic aircraft. If you're looking to capture some stunning action-freezing photography without relying on electronic flash, you can use the top shutter speed. **Consider the following factors when delving into the realm of high-speed photography:**

- **Ensure that you have ample lighting**: Using high shutter speeds allows for capturing extremely brief moments and significantly decreases the amount of light that reaches your camera's sensor. To achieve a shutter speed of 1/4000th second with an aperture of f/6.3, an ISO setting of 800 would be required, even in bright daylight. To use a f/stop smaller than f/6.3 or an ISO setting lower than 800, it would be necessary to have a greater amount of light than what is typically available during daylight hours. (This is the reason why electronic flash units are highly effective for high-speed photography when used as the only source of light. They offer the combined benefits of a short shutter speed and the necessary high levels of illumination.)
- **Avoid using high shutter speeds in conjunction with electronic flash:** Using an electronic flash with a high shutter speed may seem like a professional choice. If you wish to effectively capture a fast-moving subject in bright lighting conditions, consider using a short shutter speed during the day and rely on electronic flash as a secondary light source to eliminate any unwanted shadows. Regrettably, in most situations, it is not possible to use flash in low light conditions with a shutter speed exceeding 1/200th second. The camera's focal plane shutter achieves its maximum speed when fully open, allowing for shorter speeds by exposing only a small portion of the sensor at a time as the shutter curtains move across the sensor plane. Consequently, the flash will only illuminate the limited area of the sensor that is visible through the resulting slit.

Working with Short Exposures

Exploring the possibilities of capturing images with brief exposure times can be quite enjoyable. Whether you choose to use the action-stopping capabilities of an external electronic flash or experiment with faster shutter speeds, there are plenty of opportunities to have fun and get creative. **Here are some suggestions to help you begin:**

- **Produce extraordinary images**: High-speed photography can capture subjects in ways that may seem surreal.
- **Capture revealing photos**: Using fast shutter speeds allows you to capture the true essence of a subject, freezing any movement and capturing a meaningful moment in time.

Long Exposures

Longer exposures offer a glimpse into a different realm, revealing the transformative power of capturing familiar scenes over extended periods. During nighttime, capturing long exposures can create captivating light trails from moving objects such as cars or amusement park attractions. With the right techniques, you can capture captivating images even in the darkest of settings, using only the faintest traces of light. Long exposures can make moving objects disappear from photographs, as they don't stay still for long enough to be captured. To achieve this effect during the day, neutral-density filters can be used to reduce the amount of light passing through the lens.

Three Ways to Take Long Exposures

There are three commonly used types of lengthy exposures: timed exposures, bulb exposures, and time exposures. You have the option to choose from all three. To ensure sharp images, it is recommended to use a tripod when using the following techniques due to the extended exposure time.

- **Timed exposures:** These long exposures range from 1 second to 30 seconds, as measured by the camera. To capture a photo within this range, you can use the Manual or TV modes. Adjust the shutter speed to your desired length of time using the Main dial. You have the option to choose from preset speeds such as 1.0, 1.5, 2.0, 3.0, 4.0, 6.0, 8.0, 10.0, 15.0, 20.0, or 30.0 seconds (if you've specified 1/2-stop increments for exposure adjustments). Alternatively, you can select speeds like 1.0, 1.3, 1.6, 2.0, 2.5, 3.2, 4.0, 5.0, 6.0, 8.0, 10.0, 13.0, 15.0, 20.0, 25.0, and 30.0 seconds (if you're using 1/3-stop increments). One of the benefits of timed exposures is that the camera takes care of all the calculations for you. No stopwatch is necessary. When you review your image on the LCD and determine that adjustments are needed, you can fine-tune the exposure with precision by doubling or halving it. One limitation of timed exposures is the maximum duration of 30 seconds for capturing a photo.

- **Bulb exposures**: This type of exposure is commonly referred to as such due to the technique used by photographers in the past. They would manually control the shutter by squeezing and holding an air bulb attached to a tube, providing the necessary force to keep it open. In the world of photography, bulb exposure is a technique where the exposure continues for as long as the shutter release button is held down. Once the button is released, the exposure comes to an end. To achieve a bulb exposure, switch the mode to B. Begin the exposure by pressing the shutter, and end it by pressing the shutter once more.

- **Time exposures**: This feature can be found on certain cameras to achieve extended exposure times. This feature is an improvement on the Bulb exposure function. Set the camera mode to Bulb and find the Bulb Timer setting in the Shooting 7 menu. Press the **SET button**, and on the screen that appears, select the option for Enable. When you press the INFO button, a screen will appear where you can easily adjust the exposure time for up to 99 hours, 59 minutes, and 59 seconds. Long exposures can be incredibly useful in certain situations, especially when capturing continuous star trails. While you won't often require exposures longer than 30 seconds, they can still come in handy. As an illustration, numerous professional photographers capture multiple one-minute exposures (any longer than that, and the star pinpoints become blurred) and subsequently combine them to create a unique type of sky photograph. With this type of Bulb exposure, you have the freedom to press the shutter release button, step away for a few minutes, and return to capture your next shot (assuming your camera remains in place). One drawback of this mode is that exposures need to be timed manually. When using shorter exposures, there is a chance that the vibrations caused by manually opening and closing the shutter may be captured in the photo. When it comes to longer exposures, the period of vibration is typically quite short and rarely a concern. Additionally, photographers can always use a release cable to eliminate any camera shake caused by themselves.

Working with Long Exposures

Given the impressive image quality your camera can achieve with longer exposures, coupled with the multitude of creative possibilities that long-exposure techniques offer, it is highly recommended to engage in some experimentation. To capture high-quality shots, it's important to use a tripod or another stable support. Take some test shots with long exposure noise reduction enabled and disabled. You can find this option in the Shooting 5 menu. This will help you get started on the right foot.

Here are a few suggestions:

- **Render people invisible:** One fascinating aspect of long exposures is the ability to capture stationary subjects in a photograph while swiftly moving objects go unnoticed. It becomes effortless to capture stunning landscape and architectural photos without any people in them, whether it's during the night or even in broad daylight with the help of a neutral-density filter (or multiple filters) to achieve longer exposures. With ISO 100, f/22, and a set of 8X (three-stop) neutral-density filters, you can capture exposures of almost two seconds. If you're aiming to make people disappear in broad daylight, using additional neutral-density filtration or shooting on overcast days would yield even better results. For this to be effective, they will need to walk quickly and at an angle across the camera's field of view, rather than walking directly towards it.

- **Create streaks**: For those aiming to achieve a more polished look, using long exposures with the camera securely mounted on a tripod or monopod can yield captivating streaky effects. There is no need to restrict yourself to indoor photography, though. With just a single 8X ND filter, you can capture stunning shots in broad daylight, using settings like f/22, 1/6th second exposure, and ISO 100.

- **Create light trails**: During nighttime, the movement of car headlights, taillights, and other sources of illumination can create captivating light trails. Hand-holding your camera for longer exposures can add movement and patterns to your trails, eliminating the need for a tripod. To capture stunning fireworks photos, it's best to use a tripod and opt for longer exposure times. This technique allows you to merge multiple bursts into a single, breathtaking image.

Delayed Exposures

Occasionally, it can be advantageous to incorporate a brief delay before capturing an image. If you prefer to be in control, you might find it helpful to have a 10-second delay between pressing the shutter release and the camera taking the picture. Perhaps you'd like to allow some time for a tripod-mounted camera to settle down and minimize any remaining vibration after pressing the release button. This can help enhance the sharpness of your photo, especially when using a slower shutter speed. If you're interested in delving into the realm of time-lapse photography, you may find it intriguing to explore the possibilities. Here are the delayed exposure options available to you.

Self-Timer

The self-timer feature offers both 10-second and 2-second delays, along with a continuous shooting mode that allows you to specify the number of shots to be taken within a 10-second timeframe. To activate the timer, simply use the **Drive option** in the Q menu and rotate the QCD-1 to choose the desired drive modes. To ensure sharp focus on your subjects, remember to press the shutter release button halfway.

If you're capturing a self-portrait, focus on an object at a similar distance and use a focus lock. When you're prepared to capture the image, proceed to fully press the shutter release. The lamp on the front of the camera will blink at a steady pace for eight seconds, specifically when using the 10-second timer, accompanied by a gentle chirping sound from the beeper. Throughout the last two seconds, the beeper emits a faster succession of sounds, while the lamp stays illuminated until the picture is captured.

Time Lapse and Interval Photography

Using Interval Photography

Follow these steps to set up interval timer shooting:

1. Select the Interval Timer option from the Shooting 7 menu.
2. Enable the interval timer. To activate the feature, locate the option labeled "**Enable**" and then press the "**SET**" **button**. A screen appears prompting you to adjust the interval and shots.
3. Select an interval. Emphasize the Interval feature and select the desired time duration between exposures, with a maximum limit of 99 hours, 59 minutes, and 59 seconds. It is important to ensure that the interval is not shorter than the shutter speed. For instance, if the images are being taken at two seconds or longer, setting a one-second interval would not be appropriate. If the camera is unable to capture a scheduled image due to other ongoing tasks, such as saving the previous exposure, the shot will be skipped.

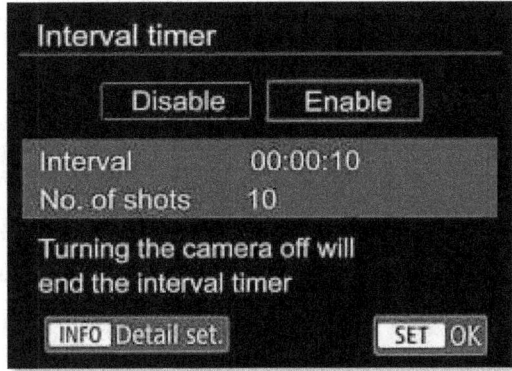

4. Choose the desired number of shots. You can select the desired number of individual shots, ranging from 1 to 99. Photography comes to a halt once the designated number of exposures has been captured. To ensure uninterrupted shooting, select the option to continue capturing photos until manually stopped, the memory card reaches its capacity, or in the unfortunate event of camera theft.

5. Select Ok. The Shooting 6 menu will display the interval and number of shots for you. To determine the total time elapsed, simply multiply the interval by the number of shots. With a maximum elapsed time of nearly 100 hours, it would require over 400 days to capture 99 individual exposures. For optimal results, it is recommended to slightly shorten your sequence.

6. Initiate sequence. Fully depress the shutter release to initiate the capture of your interval sequence.

Star Trails

Star trails are a fantastic use for both long exposures and interval shooting. For capturing stunning shots of the night sky, it's essential to use long exposures and securely mount your camera on a tripod. Due to the Earth's rotation, longer exposures will capture the apparent movement of celestial objects across the sky, resulting in a luminous trail. When employing an extended exposure, the resulting light trails will appear as unbroken streaks, with the focal point being the Polaris in the northern hemisphere and Sigma Octantis in the southern hemisphere, although the latter is not readily visible to the naked eye. By activating Extended Shutter Speeds, you can capture stunning night shots that can last up to 15 minutes. Photographers often opt to capture a series of individual exposures and merge them to create a stunning star trail image. This approach helps avoid issues like excessive noise and sensor overheating that can occur with long exposures. To achieve sharp points for your stars, it is important to ensure that the exposure time is kept short so that any movement in the sky is not noticeable. Thankfully, there is a straightforward formula that can be used to calculate the exposure time, known as the "**500 Rule**." By dividing 500 by the focal length of your lens, you can determine the maximum exposure time (in seconds) before the stars begin to create a blurred trail. With a 50mm lens, the longest exposure would be 10 seconds, calculated by dividing 500 by 50. To capture the full expanse of stars, a broader viewing perspective is typically necessary. Exposures of up to approximately 30 seconds are possible with the 16mm wide-angle setting.

Shooting Panoramas

Now you can effortlessly capture captivating panorama images using your EOS R6 II, just as you have been doing with your smartphone for years. Mastering the technique may take some practice to achieve seamless and precise execution. However, I will share valuable tips and guide you on capturing vertical panoramas with your camera. Accessing the Panorama feature is done through the SCN position on the Mode dial, as it is one of the Special Scene modes. You have the option to choose the direction in which the camera will prompt you to pan: right, left, up, or down. When shooting, it's important to select a direction so that the camera can process the image pieces you've already captured. This allows the camera to efficiently handle the many JPEGs you'll shoot while panning. After capturing your shots, they will be swiftly aligned and stitched together to create a stunning panorama photo. **Once you have chosen a subject, it is important to properly prepare for capturing your panorama. Simply follow these steps:**

1. Choose Panorama. Adjust the Mode dial to the SCN position. When the mode guide is enabled in the Set-up 2 menu, the scene guide will pop up, giving you the option to choose a scene. Simply press **SET** to select Panorama as your Special Scene.

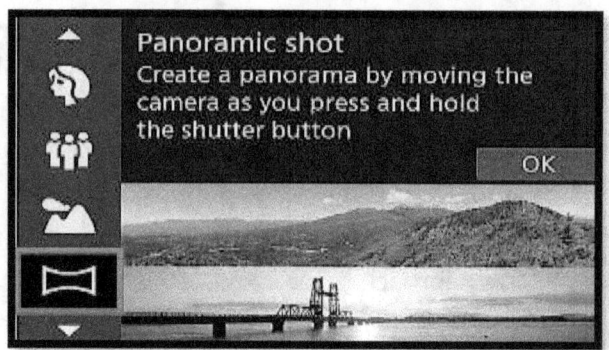

To enable Panorama mode, press the SET button after disabling the mode guide. It's worth noting that regardless of the situation, the next time you rotate the Mode dial to SCN, the previously selected Special Scene will already be selected.

2. **Go to the initial screen:** The initial panorama screen displays the masked area that will be captured while panning. There may be some cropping of the image at the top and bottom. To ensure accurate stitching, it is necessary to include additional pixels above and below the panned area. This accounts for any slight up and down or tilt movements of the hand-held camera as it is rotated. Additional indicators displayed on the screen are:

- **Motion warning**: An icon resembling a waving hand can be seen at the top, indicating that lens stabilization is not active while panning. Only in-body image stabilization will be applied.
- **Horizontal orientation**: Use the horizontal line to align with horizontal features in your subject, enabling you to smoothly rotate the camera without any tilting.
- **Current focus point:** During the panning procedure, the focus point indicates the camera's focal point. The color of the object changes from white to red if the camera cannot focus, and then it switches to green once focus is achieved, signaling that panning can commence.
- **ES icon**: It is important to note that the electronic shutter will be used for capturing individual images.
- **Current focal length**: For optimal results, it is recommended to use wide-angle lenses or zoom settings when capturing panoramas. The current focal length is conveniently displayed in the lower right corner.

3. Select the shooting direction. Continuously press the AF point selection button to navigate through the various shooting directions. A vibration warning screen may appear, similar to the one shown at the lower left in the figure.

4. Take your position. Ensure that your feet are firmly planted, aligning the center of your picture directly in front of you. Ensure that the camera remains close to your body, allowing for a rotation point that is as close to the sensor plane as possible. For optimal results, it is recommended to position the pivot point beneath the center point of the lens. However, using the back of the camera as a reference can be a more convenient approach.

5. Adjust the focus and exposure settings. Ensure that you set the focus and exposure before you begin shooting, as the camera will not make any adjustments once you start capturing.

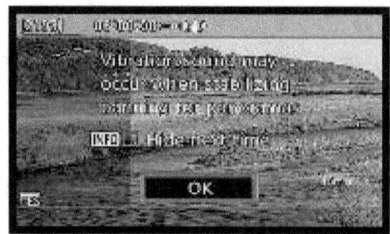

6. Twist and shout. Ensure that your feet are firmly planted and then rotate your body as much as possible towards the desired angle for the start of the exposure. If you opt for the Right option, make sure to twist as much as possible to the right.

7. Shoot and relax. When using the electronic viewfinder, start taking photos and smoothly rotate the camera to pan until you're facing forward again. Use the guides and masked area to expertly frame your image while panning.

8. Keep twisting with precision until you reach the final position. Maintaining a consistent speed is crucial.

9. Monitor your progress. While capturing images, the camera will display a highlighted view of the current area and capture a sequence of overlapping shots. A directional arrow is displayed on the screen to guide your movement.

10. Complete the task with determination and consistency. When the camera detects that you're rotating too slowly or too quickly, it will display a message suggesting that you adjust your speed accordingly to ensure a successful panorama shot. Be rest assured the partial panorama you captured will be preserved.

11. You will end up completely twisted in the opposite direction from where you started. After successfully capturing a panorama, the screen will briefly go blank as the camera seamlessly stitches your exposures together. Once you're done, the final image will be shown on the screen.

12. Take a look at your results. To view the complete panorama, simply press the center button and a scrolling display of the entire shot will be shown.

Frequently Asked Questions

1. How do you work with short exposures?
2. How do you work with long exposures?
3. What are the three ways to take long exposures?
4. How do you shoot panoramas?
5. How do you take continuous shooting?

CHAPTER SEVEN
CHOOSING YOUR LENS ARSENAL

Overview

Chapter seven talks about the various lenses you can adopt using your camera. In addition, it also talks about what lenses can do for your camera and how it works.

Your First Lenses

In the ancient era before the mid-1980s, when technology like zoom and autofocus were yet to be introduced, the process of selecting the initial lens for your camera was quite straightforward. Your choices were limited, leaving you with little to no room for deliberation. Canon cameras, back in the day, were available with a variety of lens options. These included a 50mm f/1.4, a 50mm f/1.8, or for those willing to splurge, a high-performance 50mm f/1.2 lens. It was also an option to purchase a camera as a body alone, although it didn't offer significant savings when a film SLR like the Canon A-1 was priced at $435, including the lens. Today, the options available to you have become more intricate. Canon lenses have evolved to include zoom, autofocus, and frequently, built-in image stabilization (IS) features. As a result, their prices have significantly increased in comparison to the cost of a camera. (Taking inflation into account, the price of the A-1, which was $435, would be equivalent to over $1,000 in today's currency.) Many photographers opt to pair the R6 II with a lens, and a popular choice is the Canon RF 24-105mm f/4L IS USM lens, which was introduced in 2018 and is priced at around $1,300 when bought separately. Alternatively, there is the more budget-friendly option of the Canon RF 24-105mm f/4-7.1 IS, which costs approximately $399.

Despite having a similar focal length range, these two lenses exhibit distinct characteristics:

- This **Canon RF 24-105mm f/4L IS USM lens** stands out with its constant f/4 maximum aperture, which remains consistent throughout the zoom range. It provides fast, precise, and nearly silent autofocusing that is virtually noiseless during video recording. Canon's AF system incorporates both ring-type and STM-focusing motors, showcasing their expertise in professional-grade technology. The optical image stabilization system offers a remarkable five-stop anti-shake compensation. With a rounded 9-blade circular aperture, you can achieve stunning bokeh, creating a beautifully blurred background. Canon's Super Spectra coating effectively minimizes flare and ghost images, ensuring exceptional image quality. This lens can be compared to Canon's renowned EF-mount version, as it shares similar optical specifications. However, it stands out for being noticeably smaller and lighter.

- **Canon RF 24-105mm f/4-7.1 IS lens**: This budget lens offers a variable maximum aperture, giving you an f/4 at the 24mm setting and reducing the amount of light by almost two stops at 105mm. Similar to professional lenses, this lens delivers optimal performance when stopped down by a f/stop or two. This means that when zooming in for indoor portraits, you may find yourself shooting at f/11. Additionally, the camera features a five-stop image stabilizer, allowing for potential compensation with slower shutter speeds. The STM motor in this lens is known for its impressive speed and quiet operation, while the rounded 7-blade diaphragm produces beautiful bokeh. If you're looking to save some money, this optic is a great choice for your first lens. It offers a lot of versatility without breaking the bank.

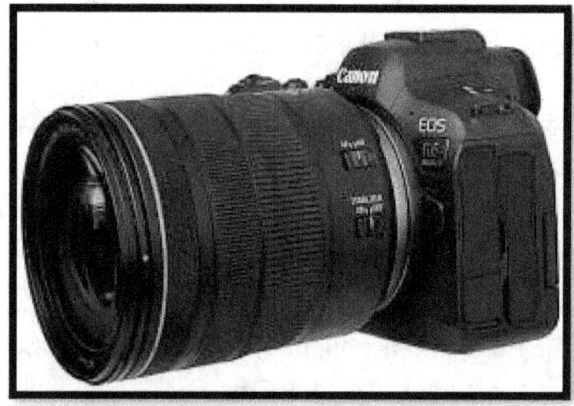

If you are transitioning to a new platform and do not currently possess a lens that is compatible with your R6 II, you have two excellent options to consider: the 24-105mm optic. Photographers who have honed their craft, particularly those who have a fondness for traditional film, often gravitate toward prime lenses. These lenses, with their fixed focal lengths, offer a level of precision and control that professionals appreciate. A popular choice among these photographers is a "normal" lens, such as the RF 50mm f/1.2L USM, which boasts exceptional quality and a price tag of $2,299. For those seeking a more budget-friendly option, the Canon RF 50mm f/1.8 STM lens, priced at $199, provides excellent performance without breaking the bank. Depending on your specific needs, you will have to make a thoughtful decision regarding the lens to purchase or determine the additional lenses required to complete your collection of Canon optics. **When making your initial lens purchases, there are a few important factors to take into account:**

- **Cost of lenses:** If you're looking to stay within a reasonable budget, it would be wise to consider more affordable add-on lenses for your camera.
- **Zoom range**: For optimal versatility, it is recommended to have a lens with a longer zoom range if you only have one. In my opinion, the two 24-105mm lenses would be the most suitable choice for you. However, the remarkable RF 28-70mm f/2L lens has a narrower zoom range and comes with a hefty price tag of $3,000. The RF 24-240mm f/4-6.3 IS USM, priced at $899, boasts the most extensive zoom range out of all the lenses that have been announced.
- **Adequate maximum aperture:** For shooting in low-light conditions, it is recommended to have a lens with an aperture of at least f/3.5 to f/4. It is important to keep an eye on the maximum aperture when the lens is zoomed in to its telephoto end. When using lenses that have a variable maximum aperture, you might find yourself limited to an f/6.3 or f/7.1 as your largest f/stop. It is true that the budget 24-105mm lens and RF 24-240mm f/4-6.3 optic share this characteristic. That's not ideal, but it's something you can usually manage.
- **Image quality**: It is crucial to ensure that your starter lens delivers exceptional image quality, as this will greatly impact the overall perception of your photos.
- **Size**: An excellent choice for a versatile lens that is compact and lightweight. The 24-105mm f/4, my personal favorite, is not exactly small in size.
- **Fast/close focusing:** It is important to have a lens with a fast autofocus system, such as the ultrasonic motor/USM or STM commonly found in many affordable lenses. By focusing at a distance of 12 inches or closer, you can use your standard lens to capture certain macro photography shots.

Canon RF-Mount Lenses

If you are looking to maximize the use of RF-mount optics and have a limited collection of EF/EF-S lenses, it would be wise to keep an eye on Canon's RF "lens road map" and its regular updates. This road map provides a comprehensive list of current and upcoming lenses that are either available or in the development stage. Allow me to offer a concise summary, based on our current knowledge.

Zoom lenses

Zooms are widely favored by photographers due to their versatility in covering various focal lengths. They eliminate the hassle of constantly swapping lenses or adjusting your distance from the subject. Zoom lenses may not always match the sharpness of fixed-focal length lenses, but in many cases, this difference is not readily apparent, especially when the lenses are used at their optimal apertures. It's worth considering that investing in a higher-priced zoom lens can save you money and space in the long run. **Instead of purchasing multiple prime lenses, which can be more costly and take up more room in your camera bag, a single $2,000 zoom lens can serve as a versatile replacement.**

- **RF 14-35mm f/4 L IS USM**: With a price tag of $1,500, this lens may appear expensive at first glance. However, when you consider its counterpart, the premium RF 15-35mm f/2.8L, the cost seems more reasonable. This zoom lens is highly versatile and perfect for capturing stunning landscapes, architectural details, and the beauty of nature.

- The **RF 15-35mm f/2.8L IS USM lens** is a versatile option from Canon's lineup of f/2.8 RF lenses. Priced at $2,300, it is well-suited for a range of photography genres, including landscapes, architecture, and street shooting. With its built-in image stabilization system, this camera offers superior control over camera shake. It's an ideal choice for capturing clear shots in low-light conditions that require longer shutter speeds. The lens features Canon's Nano USM system, which combines USM and STM, motors for swift and silent focusing. With its weather-resistant design, this Canon lens ensures that dust and moisture are kept out even in the most challenging environments. With the 24-70mm f/2.8L and 70-200mm f/2.8L lenses, you have a powerful combination of optics that can capture a wide range of photo opportunities.

- **RF 15-30mm f/4.5-6.3 IS STM lens**: With a more affordable price tag of $550, this optic is a top pick for R6 II owners seeking a wide-angle lens that offers versatility, even if it sacrifices a fast maximum aperture. Impressive features include a 1:2 magnification and an incredibly close minimum focus distance of 5.1 inches.

- The **RF 24-70mm f/2.8L IS USM** is a high-quality lens that comes with a price tag of $2,400. It slightly overlaps the 15-35mm zoom in the 24-35mm range, but it extends to short telephoto at 70mm. With this lens, you can achieve similar results to its wider counterpart, making it a versatile choice for capturing full-length or head-and-shoulders single or group portraits with a flattering perspective. It boasts the hybrid

Nano USM AF system, weather resistance, and image-stabilization features that are present in the other Canon "**trinity**" models.

- **RF 28-70mm f/2L USM:** For those seeking top-notch performance, this lens priced at $3,100 offers a versatile focal length ranging from wide-angle to telephoto and a consistently fast f/2 aperture. This makes it suitable for a wide range of photography genres, including architecture, street photography, indoor sports, and portraiture. This lens has a minimum focusing distance of approximately 1.28 feet and features nine rounded diaphragm blades, resulting in beautiful bokeh effects. Similar to professional RF lenses, this lens features a customizable control ring that allows you to effortlessly adjust exposure settings such as shutter speed, aperture, ISO, and exposure compensation without having to take your hands off the lens. This camera is quite heavy, weighing over three pounds, and its large aperture requires the use of pricey 95mm filters. Image stabilization is not available, which can be a disadvantage in low-light conditions when longer shutter speeds are necessary.

- **RF 24-105mm f/4-7.1 IS**: With a simplified construction of 16 elements in 14 groups, this lens offers excellent value for its price and performs admirably as an all-purpose lens.

- **RF 24-240mm f/4-6.3 IS USM lens**: It covers a wide range of focal lengths, but it may not excel in any particular area. With the optical design flexibility provided by the new RF mount; this lens has the potential to be a standout performer, particularly considering its affordable price of $899. The weight of this lens is 1.65 pounds and it performs at a slower speed (f/6.3) when zoomed to 240mm. Having the built-in IS is quite valuable, even with the presence of in-body stabilization in the R6 II. This is because lenses generally excel at handling pitch movement (tilting up or down) and yaw (rotations from side to side). I will provide a more detailed explanation of image stabilization later in this chapter.

- **RF 70-200mm f/2.8L IS USM**: It is an impressive addition to the RF trinity. It is a highly capable short-to-medium telephoto lens with a constant f/2.8 aperture and a cutting-edge dual-motor Nana USM autofocus mechanism. Similar to other lenses in the trinity, you can make manual focus corrections whenever needed. There are three different IS modes available: the standard single-shot mode, a panning-optimized mode that compensates for up-and-down motion while panning, and a mode that activates stabilization only during the exposure itself to avoid any disruptions while framing a shot. For sports photographers, a rotating tripod collar is a valuable tool, especially when using a monopod or tripod. This high-quality lens comes with a significant price tag of approximately $2,700.

- If you're considering the **RF 70-200mm f/4L IS USM lens**, you might be inclined to find ways to save some money, given that Canon's premium lenses in their top-line trinity come with a hefty price tag of $7,300. If you are willing to work with an f/4 maximum aperture, this lens priced at $1,600 can help you save a significant $1,100. Fortunately, you're not sacrificing much besides the f/stop. This lens is still considered an L lens, equipped with the dual Nano USM autofocus system and 5-stop image stabilization. It can even work together with the in-body image stabilizer to provide an impressive anti-shake capability, which Canon claims to be 7.5 stops.

- **RF 100-400mm f/5.6-8**: This lens is a highly affordable option for RF-mount cameras, offering a medium-to-long telephoto range. With a price tag of $650, this lens is perfect for outdoor photography and delivers exceptional sharpness when stopped down to f/11 or f/16. It offers greater versatility compared to Canon's budget lenses, the 600mm f/11 and 800mm f/11.

- **RF 100-500mm f/4.5-7.1L IS lens**: Canon has swiftly addressed the demand for super-telephoto lenses in the mirrorless camera market by introducing this remarkable lens priced at $2,900. It is also compatible with Canon's Extender RF 1.4x and RF 2x teleconverters, allowing for zoom ranges equivalent to 140-700mm and 200-1000mm with a reduction of one and two f/stops, respectively. The zoom ring offers adjustable settings to customize the lens handling for users seeking different zoom speeds, whether it is fast, slow, or somewhere in between. Additionally, it allows for the option to completely lock the focus ring. With a window in the lens hood, adjusting your polarizer or split/graduated neutral-density filter becomes a breeze, even with the hood attached. This lens weighs a substantial three pounds and has a length of eight inches.

Prime Lenses

Prime lenses are crafted to deliver exceptional sharpness at their fixed focal length, with some even exhibiting remarkable performance when used wide-open. These lenses usually have a faster speed as well. Zoom lenses typically have a maximum aperture of f/2.8 or smaller, whereas prime lenses often offer a faster aperture of f/1.8 or f/1.4. Canon is well-known for its exceptional f/1.2 optics. Professional-grade prime lenses also come with certain optical design considerations. For photographers who are open to working with fixed apertures like f/11, Canon offers impressively compact and budget-friendly RF 600mm f/11 ($799) and RF 800mm F/11 ($999) lenses.

Here are some options:

- **RF 5.2mm f/2.8 L Dual Fisheye 3D VR lens**: If you're questioning the value of this $2,000 lens, it's likely not necessary for you. This revolutionary product is the first of its kind, allowing you to capture stunning stereoscopic 3D 180-degree VR imagery using just one image sensor. This product is designed to create high-resolution virtual reality videos that can be viewed with a headset. It is perfect for immersive entertainment, tourism, training, education, and storytelling purposes. I'm including it for thoroughness, but it's most suitable for full-frame models.

- **RF 16mm f/2.8 STM**: This is a budget-friendly $300 super-compact wide-angle lens that is perfect for capturing stunning shots of interiors, architecture, and street scenes. It is a must-have for photography enthusiasts who appreciate the quality of prime lenses. It narrows down to 5.1 inches for macro work, and vloggers appreciate its wide-angle perspective.

- **RF 24mm f/1.8 Macro IS STM lens**: This lens is well-suited for interior, architecture, and street photography. However, it does come with a higher price tag of $600, which may be a consideration for some. Additionally, the maximum aperture of this lens is twice as fast, enhancing its suitability for low-light situations. It can be adjusted to focus down to 5.5 inches and offers a magnification that is perfect for close-up work.

- **RF 35mm f/1.8 Macro IS STM**: Despite not being an L lens, it boasts several impressive features. With a fast maximum aperture and image stabilization, it excels in capturing stunning low-light street photography. The control ring proves to be particularly handy when it comes to adjusting exposure settings quickly and discreetly during covert photography. With its close focusing capability of approximately 6.7 inches, this macro lens allows for impressive half-life-size reproduction. The STM motor is incredibly precise and operates seamlessly, making it an excellent choice for video applications. This lens is incredibly lightweight, weighing in at only 11 ounces and measuring approximately 3 × 2.5 inches when mounted.

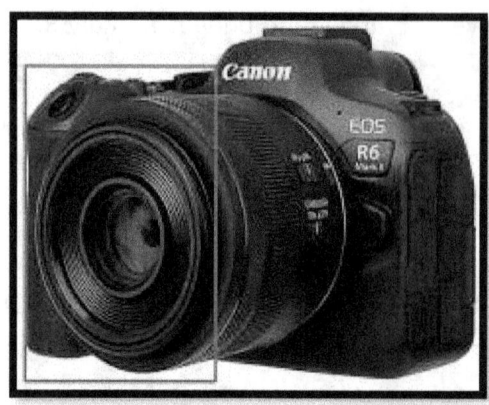

Using Adapted Lenses

Regardless of whether you currently own any Canon lenses, it is important to recognize the benefits of using adapted lenses. It is highly likely that certain lenses, which are considered essential by professional photographers, will take a considerable amount of time to be introduced to the RF system or may come with a significantly high price tag. If you're looking to get the features you need or save some money, considering purchasing an EF lens or exploring the used equipment market for an EF equivalent could be a wise choice. As an illustration, Canon offers a range of tilt-shift lenses (TS-E) with perspective control that can be smoothly adapted to RF-mount configurations. These lenses are designed for manual focus, so there is no need for extensive re-engineering to include autofocus capabilities.

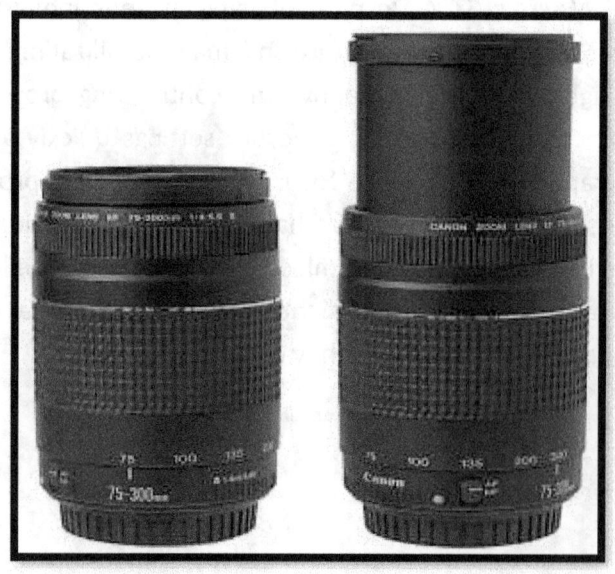

Canon RF-Mount Adapters

Canon has recently unveiled four mount adapters, each offering unique features and capabilities. Here are the options available to you:

- **Mount Adapter EF-EOS R**: This is a budget-friendly option that offers a range of practical features. The camera is incredibly lightweight, weighing only four ounces, yet it is constructed with a durable metal body. Its sleek exterior design perfectly complements EF lenses. The third-party adapters may come with subpar construction and an unattractive appearance. However, this mount adapter is designed to be both dust- and water-resistant. Just like the other mount adapters, it provides all the necessary electrical contacts for seamless compatibility with your EF and EF-S lenses.
- **Control Ring Mount Adapter EF-EOS R**: This adapter is priced at a modest $199. This version is highly recommended as it includes a control ring similar to the one found on RF-mount lenses. Once you experience the convenience of the control ring, it becomes an essential tool you won't want to be without. It weighs just 4.6 ounces, which is only slightly more than the basic adapter.
- **Drop-in Filter Mount Adapter EF-EOS R**: This adapter is available in two options: one with a circular polarizing filter priced at $299, and another with a variable neutral-density (ND) filter priced at $399. You can easily adjust the filter using the thumb wheel on the filter holder to achieve your desired level of polarization or neutral density.

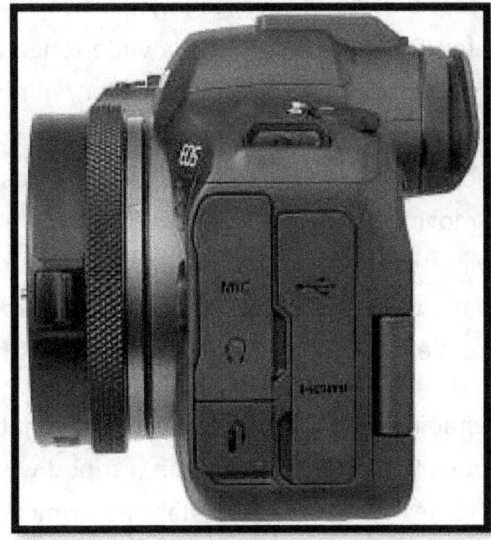

- **Mount Adapter EF-EOS R 0.71x:** This adapter is designed specifically for Canon video cameras, such as the EOS C70 Cinema Camera. Similar to the other three adapters, this version priced at $599 enables the mounting of EF lenses. It also incorporates optical elements that effectively decrease the focal length by 0.71x and enhance the maximum aperture by one stop. With the EF 50mm f/1.2 lens, you can achieve a field of view and exposure settings equivalent to that of a 35mm f/0.95 lens. For R6 II owners, wide-angle lenses are easily accessible, making it a feature that is not typically in high demand.

Canon's cinema models with the RF mount use the Super 35 format, which closely resembles your camera's APS-C mode. For a truly expansive view, cameras of this nature would require a 10mm lens to replicate the perspective of a 16mm lens on a full-frame camera. This adapter offers a field of view that is equivalent to a 24mm focal length. For optimal video shooting, Canon suggests using the adapter with lenses such as the EF 16-35mm f/2.8L III USM (which will give you an impressive 11-25mm f/2 zoom) or the EF 24-70mm f/2.8L II USM (resulting in a versatile 17-85mm f/2 lens).

Image Stabilization and You

An area of concern for the original EOS R and RP was the absence of in-body image stabilization (IBIS), a feature commonly found in mirrorless cameras from other manufacturers. Anti-shake capabilities were only accessible with lenses that had built-in stabilization. Although lens-based IS has its advantages, IBIS also offers its own set of benefits. In-body stabilization allows for IS compatibility with a wide range of lenses, including those that do not have built-in stabilization. Image stabilization/vibration reduction comes in various forms, and Canon excels in all of them. Electronic image stabilization is a technique commonly employed in video cameras. It effectively adjusts the position of pixels from frame to frame, ensuring that non-moving pixels stay fixed while moving elements of the image stay on track. Optical image stabilization is a feature found in numerous EF and RF lenses. It uses specialized lens elements that adjust themselves to compensate for any camera movement. This adjustment is made possible by motion sensors integrated within the lens optics.

Even with advanced image stabilization, it's impossible to eliminate blur caused by moving subjects. However, you'll notice that you'll rely less on a tripod when using longer lenses or shooting with wide-angle lenses in low-light situations compared to before. If you're capturing images in locations that prohibit the use of flash or tripods, the camera's image stabilization feature will prove to be extremely useful.

What Lenses Can Do for You

Here's a comprehensive guide to the various capabilities you can acquire by incorporating a lens into your collection, potentially using an adapter if required.

- **Gain a wider perspective**: For moderate wide-angle-to-medium telephoto shots, a 24-70mm or 28-70mm lens can be a great choice. Now you realize that you're facing a challenge and can't afford to waste any time or miss any important information. Alternatively, if you happen to be positioned just behind the baseline at a high school basketball game, you may desire to capture a captivating shot with a touch of perspective distortion. If you frequently find yourself desiring to capture images with an exceptionally broad field of view, then it is likely that a wider lens will be a valuable addition to your photography gear.

- **Get objects closer**: Using a long focal length enables you to capture distant subjects up close, create images with a narrow depth of field, and avoid the distortion that wide-angle lenses can introduce.

- **Get your camera closer**: Canon lenses like the RF 35mm f/1.8 Macro are known for their ability to focus closer than other lenses, making them a popular choice among professionals. To achieve greater magnification, you should use a dedicated macro lens or extension tubes.

- **Look sharp:** Numerous lenses, especially Canon's L lineup, are highly regarded for their exceptional sharpness and overall image quality. A typical lens should be sharp enough for most uses at the ideal aperture (typically f/8 or f/11), but the top-notch optics are truly exceptional.

- **More speed:** For sports photography, it's important to have a lens with the right focal length and sharpness. However, one thing to keep in mind is that the maximum aperture of your lens may be smaller at longer focal lengths, like f/5.6 or f/6.3 at the far end. Opting for RF-mount lenses with a wide aperture (small f/number) is an excellent decision for capturing stunning low-light photographs, especially when you have the opportunity to be near the action. This is frequently achievable at amateur basketball or volleyball games. There's no need to break the bank; the RF 50mm f/1.8 lens, priced at $200, offers sufficient speed for low-light conditions.

Using Wide-Angle Lenses

Understanding the impact of wide-angle prime lenses and wide zooms on your photography is essential for achieving professional results. **Here's a concise overview of the key points:**

- **More depth-of-field**: When using a wide-angle lens, you can capture an entire scene in your image. The subjects in the photo won't be magnified significantly, resulting in a wide depth of field. When it comes to capturing landscapes, a wide-angle lens can be incredibly useful in expanding the depth of field and ensuring sharpness throughout the scene.
- **Stepping back**: Wide-angle lenses create the illusion of increased distance between you and your subject. They can be quite useful in situations where you want to include a whole group of people in your photo, but face obstacles or limitations.
- **Wider field of view**: Using a wide-angle lens can create the illusion of distance and capture a larger portion of the scene in your photographs.
- **More foreground:** With a wide-angle lens, the foreground is expanded, revealing more of the background objects that are usually hidden from the naked eye. That provides an added emphasis on the area that is nearest to the camera. When it comes to photography, wide-angle lenses can be a great tool for highlighting the foreground, but they can pose challenges when it comes to capturing subjects in the distance.
- **Super-sized subjects**: The way a wide-angle lens highlights objects in the foreground and downplays objects in the background can create a form of size distortion that may be less appealing for certain subjects compared to others. Capture a bed of flowers up close using a 16mm or shorter focal length, and you will appreciate the captivating effect of the nearby blossoms appearing larger in the photo. If you capture an image of a family member using the same lens and distance, you might receive some feedback regarding the prominent nose in the foreground.
- **Perspective distortion:** Understanding perspective distortion is crucial for achieving professional-looking photos. This kind of distortion happens when you tilt the camera in a way that the sensor is no longer perfectly aligned with the vertical plane of your subject. Consequently, certain portions of the subject have been brought nearer to the sensor, while other sections have been pushed farther away. This is what creates the illusion of buildings, flagpoles, or NBA players leaning backward.
- **Smooth and steady cam**: It is more convenient to capture sharp photos without any blurring caused by camera shake when hand-holding a wide-angle lens at slower shutter speeds compared to using a telephoto lens. With the help of image

stabilization, capturing sharp photos at extended shutter speeds and long focal lengths is now a breeze, even without relying on a tripod.

Avoiding Potential Wide-Angle Problems

When using wide-angle lenses, it's important to be aware of certain quirks to ensure you capture the best shots and avoid common pitfalls.

Here is a comprehensive checklist of tips to help you steer clear of common issues:

Issue: Converging lines

For a polished and refined look, it is advisable to ensure that horizontal and vertical lines in landscapes, architecture, and other subjects are precisely aligned with the sides, top, and bottom of the frame. This attention to detail will enhance the overall composition. For optimal results, it is important to avoid tilting the camera to prevent any unwanted perspective distortion. If your subject is quite tall, resembling a towering building, it may be necessary to capture the shot from an elevated position, such as a high level in a parking garage. This will eliminate the need to tilt the lens upwards. When dealing with a shorter subject, such as a small child, it's important to position yourself at a lower level. This allows you to capture the shot without having to tilt the lens downward.

Issue: lines that appear to be bowing outward

Wide-angle lenses can sometimes cause straight lines to appear curved outward, which are known as barrel distortion. This effect is most noticeable at the edges of the frame. Most fisheye (or curvilinear) lenses create this effect as a distinctive feature of the lens, which is more pronounced compared to other types of lenses. To minimize barrel distortion, it's important to frame your photo with some extra space all around. This way, you can easily crop out the edges where the bowing outward is most noticeable, resulting in a more professional-looking picture. The Lens Correction feature is also capable of addressing this issue.

Issue: The presence of light and dark areas is observed when using a polarizing filter

It is important to note that polarizers yield optimal results when the camera is directed 90 degrees away from the sun, while their impact is minimal when the camera is positioned 180 degrees from the sun. At the edges, the polarizing effect tends to be less pronounced, resulting in a lighter tone in the sky in those areas. To achieve optimal results, it is advisable to refrain from using a polarizing filter when capturing images that include the sky with lenses that have a focal length of less than approximately 28mm.

Using Telephoto and Tele-Zoom Lenses

Telephoto lenses can greatly enhance the impact of your photography. Allow me to provide you with the essential information you need to know.

Its advantages:

- **Selective focus**: Long lenses offer a reduced depth of field, providing a narrow range of sharp focus, particularly at wide apertures. This feature is valuable for achieving selective focus and isolating your subject. Master the art of aperture control to achieve either a shallow depth of field or a wider focus range.
- **Getting closer:** Telephoto lenses enable you to capture stunning close-up shots of wildlife, sports action, and candid subjects. Using a professional-grade telephoto lens allows you to effortlessly capture those unforgettable moments while maintaining a respectful distance from the action.
- **Reduced foreground/increased compression**: Telephoto lenses have a contrasting effect compared to wide angles. They diminish the significance of objects in the foreground by compressing everything together. The compressed perspective creates the illusion that objects in the scene are closer than they are. Use this effect as a powerful tool for unleashing your creativity.
- **Accentuates camera shakiness:** Telephoto focal lengths can present a challenge when it comes to camera and photographer stability. The lenses have a larger size and can be a bit challenging to hold steady. Additionally, when supported with one hand halfway down the lens barrel, there might be a slight rocking effect, although it is barely noticeable. When the subject is magnified, even the slightest camera shake becomes more pronounced. It's no surprise that image stabilization is particularly favored by photographers using longer lenses.

Avoiding Telephoto Lens Problems

Most of the challenges presented by telephoto lenses are quite manageable and not overly complicated.

Presented below are the seven most frequently encountered image maladies along with recommended solutions:

Issue: Flat faces in portraits

Using a focal length of 50mm to 85mm can result in more flattering head-and-shoulders portraits of humans. With longer focal lengths, the distance between features such as the nose and ears is compressed, resulting in a wider and flatter appearance of the face. Using a wide-angle lens for a head-and-shoulders portrait can distort the proportions of the face, making the nose appear larger and the ears smaller. To avoid this, it's best to stick to a focal length of around 60mm or less, unless you have no choice but to shoot from a greater distance. When capturing three-quarters or full-length portraits, or group shots, it is advisable to use a wide-angle lens.

Issue: Blurriness caused by camera shake

Ensure that the image stabilization is not turned off, as a longer focal length can magnify the impact of the camera shake. If feasible, consider using a faster shutter speed. This might require adjusting the ISO or using a tripod.

Issue: Color fringes observed

Chromatic aberration is a significant optical issue commonly encountered in telephoto lenses. There are other optical distortions to be aware of, such as spherical aberration, astigmatism, coma, curvature of field, and other similarly complex phenomena. If you want to fix the fringing in your preferred RAW conversion tool, image editor, or the camera's Lens Compensation feature, there are a few options available to you.

Issue: Lines that exhibit a concave curvature

Pincushion distortion is a common occurrence in photos captured with various telephoto lenses. It is characterized by the bowing inward of lines, particularly those near the edges of the frame, resembling the shape of a pincushion. Similar to chromatic aberration, it is possible to partially correct it using tools such as the Lens Correction filter in Photoshop or a similar utility in other software.

Issue: Decreased contrast due to flare

Professional lenses are typically equipped with lens hoods for a specific purpose: to reduce the impact of stray light on the front element, which can result in flare or ghost images of the aperture diaphragm.

Frequently Asked Questions

1. What can lenses do for you?
2. How do you avoid potential wide-angle problems?
3. What are the best Canon RF-Mount lenses to use?
4. How do you avoid telephoto lens problems?
5. How do you use telephoto and tele-zoom lenses?

CHAPTER EIGHT
MASTERING LIGHT

Overview

Chapter eight introduces us to how best we can master light in the Canon EOS R6 Mark II. Additionally, it also talks about available lights and continuous lighting basics.

Light that's Available

Available light refers to the uninterrupted illumination that is consistently present throughout a shooting session. Daylight, moonlight, and the artificial lighting found indoors and outdoors are considered continuous light sources. However, these sources can be temporarily disrupted by factors such as passing clouds, solar eclipses, power outages, or turning off a lamp. Indoor continuous illumination encompasses the existing lights indoors, such as incandescent lamps or overhead fluorescent lights, as well as additional fixtures like photoflood lamps or reflectors that can be used to enhance the lighting on your subject. Continuous lighting provides a constant source of illumination, unlike electronic flash which only lights up our photographs for short periods. Flash or "strobe" light stands out due to its higher intensity compared to continuous lighting, brief duration, and greater portability compared to supplementary incandescent sources. It's a portable light source that can be used anywhere. Every type of illumination has its own set of advantages and disadvantages.

Here's a brief list of advantages and disadvantages:

- **Advantage - Lighting preview—Continuous lighting:** Thanks to the real-time sensor image preview through the viewfinder or LCD screen, you'll have complete control over your lighting. By enabling Exposure Simulation in the Display Simulation menu, you can always anticipate the lighting effect, including color balance, and understand how multiple lights will interact with each other. When the natural light in a scene is ideal for the image you want to capture, it becomes evident right away.
- **Disadvantage - Preview of lighting: electronic flash**: When using electronic flash without a built-in modeling light, it can be challenging to predict the exact effect you'll achieve. It often requires some trial and error, where you review the shot, make adjustments, and reshoot until you achieve the desired look.

- **Advantage: Exposure calculation: continuous lighting:** Calculating exposure for continuous lighting is not an issue for your camera. The constant lighting allows for direct measurement of the light reaching the sensor.
- **Disadvantage – Exposure calculation: electronic flash**: Electronic flash illumination is not measurable by the exposure sensor at the exact moment of exposure, as it only comes into existence when the flash fires. To accurately measure the light, one must use a meter to gauge the intensity of a pre-flash that is triggered just before the main flash. This allows the camera to capture the reflected light through the lens.
- **Advantage and disadvantage – Evenness of illumination_ continuous lighting**: Daylight, among other continuous light sources, offers a well-balanced illumination that evenly lights up the foreground, background, and subject in an image. To achieve a more balanced illumination, it may be necessary to use reflectors or incorporate additional light sources to compensate for shadows.
- **Disadvantage – Evenness of illumination: electronic flash**: Electronic flash units are affected by the inverse square law, which means that as the distance between the light source and the subject increases, the amount of light reaching the subject decreases in proportion to the square of the distance. Put simply, a flash or lamp positioned twelve feet away from a subject will only provide one-quarter of the illumination compared to a source that is six feet away, rather than half as much.
- **Advantage – Action stopping: electronic flash**: Electronic flash has the upper hand when it comes to freezing moving objects in their tracks. When the flash is the primary or sole source of light for the photo, the short duration of electronic flash acts as a high "**shutter speed**." During a flash exposure, the effective exposure time is significantly shorter than the shutter speed you have set. This is because the flash unit reduces the duration of the flash, resulting in a much faster exposure time ranging from 1/1000th to 1/50,000th of a second or even less.

Continuous Lighting Basics

When it comes to continuous lighting, it's important to consider factors such as the color temperature of the light and how accurately it reproduces colors. An essential consideration is the color temperature. Certainly, color temperature considerations apply to more than just continuous light sources. However, the variations in color temperature tend to be more extreme and less predictable compared to electronic flash, which provides a relatively consistent daylight-like illumination.

Living with Color Temperature

From a professional standpoint, color temperature refers to the perceived bluish or reddish hue of the light as detected by the digital camera's sensor. The indoor illumination has a warm and reddish appearance to the sensor. Daylight, on the other hand, appears significantly bluer to the sensor. Our eyes (our brains, actually) are highly adaptable to these variations, allowing white objects to maintain their true color whether viewed indoors or outdoors in full daylight. However, these color temperature variations are indeed genuine, and the sensor remains unaffected. For optimal color accuracy, it is crucial to consider the color temperature when adjusting the color balance (or white balance). This can be done automatically using the camera's intelligent features or manually relying on our expertise and experience.

When making adjustments using the Color Temp, it is important to consider the actual color temperature. You can precisely adjust the color temperatures if you have the information. Additionally, you can adjust and manipulate color balance in terms of blue/amber and magenta/green, as well as bracket white balance. Typically, the Auto setting in the Shooting menu's White Balance entry will effectively calculate the white balance for you. Using an automobile is often a suitable option for various situations. Use the preset values or establish a personalized white balance that aligns with the present shooting conditions as necessary. It is important to note that when shooting RAW, you can adjust the white balance of your image during the import process in software such as Photoshop, Photoshop Elements, or any other image editor that supports Adobe Camera Raw or your preferred RAW converter. Color-balancing filters that can be attached to the front of the lens are particularly beneficial for film cameras. This is because the color balance of film cannot be adjusted as extensively as that of a sensor.

White Balance Bracketing

When using WB bracketing, the camera captures a single shot and subsequently stores multiple JPEG copies, each featuring a distinct color balance. There is no need to take multiple shots because the raw data from the sensor is sufficient to create various versions. Adjust the Main dial or QCD-1 to the right or left to bracket one, two, or three increments in either the blue/amber or magenta/green direction. After setting the blue/amber or magenta/green bias orientations, you can effortlessly adjust the bracket using the multi-controller joystick to enhance bias in either of the two orientations.

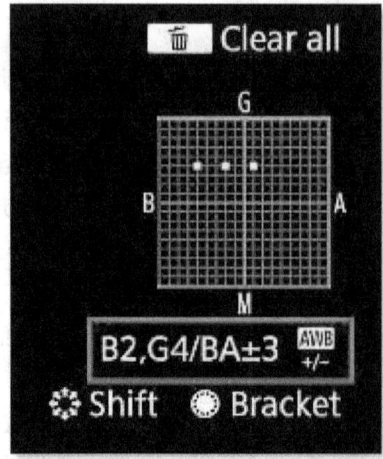

Understanding the naming convention for color temperatures can be a bit confusing at first. The lower numbers represent warmer, more reddish color temperatures, while the higher numbers indicate cooler, bluer color temperatures. It may seem counterintuitive, but 3,400K is warmer than 6,000K. Imagine a radiant red ember juxtaposed with the intense heat of a welder's torch, instead of fire and ice. The confusion comes from physics. Scientists calculate the color temperature from the light emitted by a mythical object called a black body radiator, which absorbs all the radiant energy that strikes it and reflects none at all. When heated, a black body has the remarkable ability to both absorb and emit light flawlessly.

Daylight

The sun produces daylight, while moonlight is simply sunlight that is reflected. Daylight is always present, even when the sun is not visible. When sunlight is direct, it can be bright and harsh. When daylight is scattered by clouds, reflected by surfaces like walls or photo reflectors, or filtered by shade, it can appear significantly less bright and have reduced contrast. The color temperature of daylight can vary significantly. At noon, when the sun is directly overhead, the temperature reaches its peak as the light passes through the atmosphere with minimal filtering. At high noon, the color temperature can reach 6,000K. During different times of the day, the sun's position in the sky changes and the particles in the air have a filtering effect, resulting in a warm illumination of about 5,500K for the majority of the day. During the period starting an hour before dusk and continuing for an hour after sunrise, we can observe the pleasant warm glow of sunlight, even when the color temperature may decrease from 5,000K to 4,500K.

Incandescent/Tungsten/Halogen Light

The term incandescent or tungsten/halogen illumination is typically used to describe the direct descendants of Thomas Edison's original electric lamp. These lights are made up of a glass bulb that either has a vacuum or is filled with a halogen gas. Inside, there is a tungsten filament that gets heated by an electrical current, resulting in the production of photons and heat. Tungsten-halogen lamps are a variation on the basic light bulb, using a more rugged (and longer-lasting) filament that can be heated to a higher temperature, housed in a thicker glass or quartz envelope, and filled with iodine or bromine ("**halogen**") gasses. With a higher temperature, tungsten-halogen lamps can burn at a higher intensity, resulting in a brighter and whiter light. They have also found applications in photographic illumination, in addition to being commonly used for automobile headlamps nowadays.

Fluorescent Light/LEDs

Fluorescent light offers certain benefits in terms of illumination, but it presents certain drawbacks from a photographic perspective. This lamp uses an electrochemical reaction to produce light, prioritizing the emission of visible light overheating, resulting in bulbs that remain cool to the touch. The light produced can vary depending on the phosphor coatings and the type of gas in the tube. The characteristics of the illumination produced by fluorescent bulbs can vary significantly. That's disappointing for photographers. Various types of lamps emit light with different "color temperatures," which cannot be accurately measured in degrees Kelvin since the light is not generated through heating. Additionally, fluorescent lamps have a spectrum of light that is not continuous, resulting in the absence of certain colors. Certain types of tubes may not have all the necessary shades of red or other colors, resulting in fluorescent lamps and other alternative technologies like sodium-vapor illumination producing unflattering human skin tones. Their spectra may not exhibit the warm hues typically associated with healthy skin, instead highlighting the cool tones of blue and green often seen in horror films.

Frequently Asked Questions

1. How do you work with different lighting in EOS R6 Mark II?
2. How do you master available lights?
3. How do you incorporate color temperature to EOS R6 Mark II?

CHAPTER NINE
ELECTRONIC FLASH BASICS

Overview

In this chapter, you will learn the electronic flash basics in the camera including how it works, external Speedlite control, using flash settings, determining exposure, and a whole lot more.

How Electronic Flash Works

An electronic flash is created by a burst of photons that are generated by an electrical charge stored in a capacitor. These photons are then directed through a glass tube filled with xenon gas, which absorbs the energy and produces a short-lived burst of light. For a typical external flash, such as the Speedlite 600EX II-RT, the full burst of light lasts about 1/1000th of a second and provides enough illumination to shoot a subject 12 feet away at f/16 using the ISO 100 setting. Given the brief duration of the burst, when the external flash is the primary source of light, the exposure time becomes quite short, usually ranging from 1/1000th to 1/50,000th of a second. This effectively freezes any moving subject dramatically. These brief bursts can also be repeated, creating multiple-exposure/stroboscopic effects, as explained later in this chapter. The electronic flash is activated precisely when the exposure occurs, while the sensor is completely exposed by the shutter.

Ghost Images

There may not appear to be a significant difference between triggering the flash when the shutter opens or when it starts to close. Whether you opt for first-curtain sync (the default setting) or second-curtain sync (an optional setting), the choice can have a notable impact on your photograph, especially if the ambient light in your scene plays a role in the image. To set either of these sync modes, navigate to the Shooting 3 menu and locate the External Speedlite control section. Within this section, you will find the Flash Function setting option. The control screen for the External Speedlite also provides an option to adjust the balance between ambient light and flash illumination, allowing you to have more control over the overall lighting. When using faster shutter speeds, there is limited time for the ambient light to be captured, unless it is exceptionally bright. The electronic flash will probably be the primary source of illumination, making first-curtain sync or second-curtain sync less significant. Nevertheless, when using slower shutter speeds or in the presence of intense ambient light, notable distinctions arise, especially when capturing moving subjects or when the camera lacks stability. When faced with any of these scenarios, the presence of ambient light will result in a secondary image being captured alongside the flash exposure. If there is any movement, whether from the camera or the subject, this additional image will not align with the flash exposure. When capturing movement, you may notice a faint image that appears like a ghost, sometimes appearing blurred and trailing in front or behind your subject, following the direction of the movement.

Avoiding Sync-Speed Problems

Using a faster shutter speed than the recommended sync speed can lead to potential issues. Timing the electronic flash to synchronize with the fully open shutter is a logical choice when considering the process at hand. When aiming for faster shutter speeds, a technique used is exposing only a portion of the sensor at a time. This is achieved by initiating the movement of the second curtain before the first curtain has fully opened. That efficiently offers a more concise exposure by using a narrow slit that moves across the sensor's surface. When the flash goes off while the first and second curtains are partially blocking the sensor, only the open slit will be exposed. When the picture is taken, only a narrow band would be visible, representing the portion of the sensor that was exposed. When using shutter speeds faster than the sync speed, the second curtain starts moving before the first curtain reaches the bottom of the frame. Consequently, a dynamic slit gradually reveals different sections of the sensor as it glides downwards, allowing for precise exposure.

Determining Exposure

Determining the proper exposure for electronic flash photography requires a higher level of complexity compared to calculating settings for continuous light. Getting the perfect exposure requires more than just knowing the distance to your subject. It's important to consider the autofocus distance that's set before capturing the image. Different objects have varying levels of light reflection at the same distance. Consequently, the camera must accurately gauge the amount of light that is reflected and passes through the lens. However, since the flash cannot be measured until it is triggered, there is no way to obtain a measurement. To achieve the desired outcome, it is recommended to fire the flash multiple times. The first shot consists of a pre-flash which can be analyzed, followed by a main flash that is precisely adjusted to provide the correct exposure. When the main flash is used to trigger off-camera flash units, it can also send coded pulses to convey settings information to the receiver flashes and trigger their firing.

Guide Numbers

Guide numbers, commonly referred to as GN, serve as a convenient method for indicating the strength of an electronic flash. They allow photographers to determine the appropriate f/stop to use based on the shooting distance and ISO setting. Before automatic flash units became widespread, the GN was commonly used for that purpose. A GN is typically provided as a set of measurements in both feet and meters, indicating the range at ISO 100. Take the Canon Speedlite 270EX II, for instance. The 270EX II boasts an impressive GN of 89 at ISO 100. The guide number is specifically for the flash set at the 50mm zoom setting, ensuring optimal coverage for filling the frame when using a 50mm focal length on a full-frame camera body. When the flash is mounted on a "**cropped**" sensor camera like the Canon EOS R7, the effective guide number is only 72. However, if you set the 270EX II to the 28mm zoom position, the light will spread out more to cover the wider area captured at that focal length, resulting in a drop in the unit's guide number to 79. To determine the correct exposure at ISO 100, one would divide the guide number by the distance to obtain the suitable f/stop. (Keep in mind that the shutter speed does not affect the flash exposure. The flash will go off when the shutter is fully open and will last for a shorter duration than the time the shutter remains open.)

Getting Started with Electronic Flash

The accessory flash is an incredibly valuable addition to your equipment. When using Scene Intelligent Auto, P, Av, Tv, Fv, B, or Manual exposure modes, it is important to attach the flash and ensure that it is turned on. **The behavior of the external flash differs based on the exposure mode you are using:**

- **Scene Intelligent Auto**: When enabled, the flash will automatically fire when it is attached and powered up.
- **P:** When using Program mode, the exposure process is completely automated. This allows for subtle fill-flash effects during the day and ensures that your subject is fully illuminated in low-light situations. The camera chooses a shutter speed ranging from 1/60th to the sync speed and adjusts the aperture accordingly.
- **Av**: When using Aperture-priority mode, you have full control over setting the aperture, while the camera automatically selects a suitable shutter speed ranging from 30 seconds to the sync speed. Exercise caution when using this mode, as the camera will use the flash to properly expose the main subject in the foreground while keeping the shutter open for an adequate duration to correctly expose the

background as well. Without the use of an image-stabilized lens, there is a risk of capturing blurry ghost images, even when photographing non-moving subjects with exposures longer than 1/30th second. Additionally, if your camera is not securely mounted on a tripod, blurs may appear in exposures longer than approximately 1/8th second, even if image stabilization is employed.

To disable the use of a slow shutter speed with flash, you can access the Slow Synchro option in the External Speedlite Control entry in the Shooting 2 menu. From there, you can change the default setting (Auto) to either 1/200–1/60sec. Choose either auto or set the shutter speed to 1/200 sec. (fixed). A reminder message will appear, indicating that the electronic first-curtain shutter can be used at a speed of 1/250th second.

- **TV**: When using flash in TV mode, the shutter speed can be adjusted from 30 seconds to 1/200th second. In this mode, the camera automatically selects the appropriate aperture to ensure proper flash exposure. When the shutter speed is set higher than 1/200th second, the camera will automatically adjust it to 1/200th second if you're using the flash. With the electronic first-curtain shutter, you have the option of capturing at 1/250th second.

- **Fv**: With this mode, you have full control over the shutter speed, aperture, and ISO sensitivity. You can choose to adjust them manually or let the camera handle them automatically while taking care of the rest of the parameters. When using flash, the camera will operate like that of a professional. If you opt not to manually adjust the shutter speed or aperture, it will function like Program mode. If you only select a shutter speed, it will mimic TV mode. Similarly, if you solely choose the aperture, it will behave like Av mode. And if you manually adjust both the shutter speed and aperture, it will operate in M mode.

- **M/B:** When using Manual or Bulb exposure modes, you have the control to adjust both the shutter speed and aperture settings. When using a flash, the camera will automatically adjust the shutter speed to the sync speed if you attempt to use a faster speed. With the E-TTL II system, you can expect precise exposure for your main subject at the aperture you've selected, as long as the subject is within the flash's range. When using Bulb mode, the camera's shutter will stay open as long as you keep the release button pressed or activate the remote control.

Flash Exposure Compensation and FE Lock

To lock flash exposure for a subject that is not centered in the frame, you have the option to use the FE lock button (the * button) to secure a precise flash exposure. Ensure that the viewfinder is properly aligned with your desired subject and then press the * button to achieve the correct exposure. The pre-flash is fired and exposure is calculated. The camera retains the accurate exposure setting until the moment you capture an image. To serve as a helpful reminder, the FEL indicator, symbolized by a lightning bolt with an asterisk, can be found in the lower-left corner of the display. To recalculate your flash exposure, simply press the * button once more. Once you are prepared to capture the shot, adjust the composition of your photo and firmly press the shutter to capture the image. You have the option to adjust the exposure manually, eliminating the need to make any adjustments to the flash. When using any of the exposure modes other than Scene Intelligent Auto (such as Program AE, Aperture-priority, Shutter-priority, Flexible-priority, or Manual).

Flash Range

Understanding the external flash's illumination can be influenced by factors such as distance, focal length, and ISO sensitivity setting.

- **Distance**: As the subject moves further away from the camera, the light fall-off becomes more pronounced due to the inverse square law. It's important to remember that when a subject is twice as far away, it only receives one-quarter as much light, equivalent to two f/stops.
- Focal length: A fixed flash only illuminates a specific angle of view, which remains constant. When using a lens that has a wider focal length than the default, it's important to note that the frame may not be fully covered. This can result in dark areas, particularly in the corners. When using longer focal lengths, it's important to note that some of the illumination may not be captured within the area of view, resulting in wastage. This is why certain external flash units, like the 600EX II-RT or EL-1, can automatically adjust their zoom setting to match the lens, ensuring that the flash burst is concentrated on the subject area.
- **ISO setting**: As the ISO sensitivity increases, the sensor captures a greater number of photons. When you increase the sensitivity from ISO 100 to 200, you achieve a similar outcome as when you widen your lens aperture from f/8 to f/5.6.

External Speedlite Control

The External Speedlite control menu in the Shooting 2 menu provides six options, along with the option to Clear Settings.

Flash Firing

This menu entry offers two options: Enable and Disable. It can enable or disable any connected external electronic dedicated flash unit. When the flash is disabled, it will not fire, even if you have an accessory flash connected and powered on. It is important to note that the AF-assist beam can still be used. To disable that as well, you will need to turn it off by accessing the AF-Assist Beam Firing entry in the AF 3 menu.

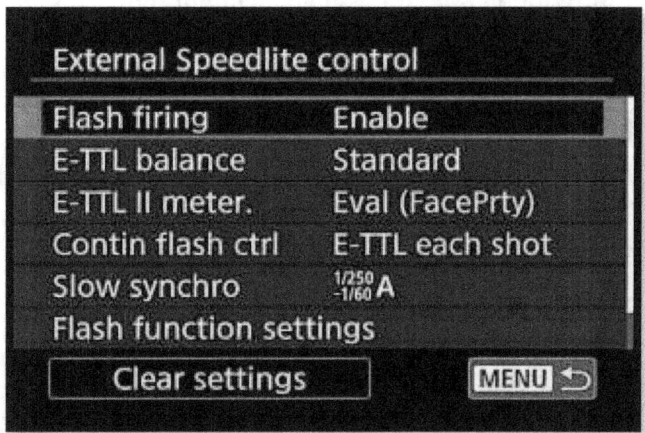

E-TTL II Metering

When using E-TTL II mode, you have the option to choose between Evaluative (Matrix) or Average metering modes for the electronic flash exposure meter. Another option, Evaluative (Face-priority), provides additional exposure emphasis to faces that are detected in a scene. Both types of Evaluative metering analyze specific areas in the scene and compare their measurements to a database of typical scene **"layouts"** to determine exposure. On the other hand, Average metering calculates flash exposure by reading the entire scene.

Continuous Flash Control

When shooting continuously, you have the option to use flash. You can select between two settings: E-TTL Each Shot, which recalculates exposure before every shot, or E-TTL 1st Shot, which uses the exposure determined for the first photo in a sequence for all subsequent shots. Opting for the last option is ideal for achieving the highest continuous shooting speed, especially if you prefer not to recompose between shots.

Slow Synchro

When working in Aperture-priority mode, you have the option to choose the flash synchronization speed. When using flash in Aperture-priority mode, you can set the desired f/stop to be fixed. The exposure can be adjusted by manipulating the output of the electronic flash, unlike non-flash images where the shutter speed is typically adjusted. Understanding the relationship between shutter speed and exposure is crucial for capturing high-quality photographs. The flash primarily determines the main exposure, while the selected shutter speed has a significant impact on the secondary exposure from the ambient light in the scene. The 1/250-30-second Auto option is your best choice under most conditions. The camera will automatically select a shutter speed that effectively balances the flash exposure and the existing ambient light. With the 1/250-1/60 Auto setting, slower shutter speeds are automatically disabled to ensure that there is no blurring caused by camera or subject movement in the secondary exposure. If the flash is not strong enough to illuminate the background, it may appear dark. Using the 1/200th- to 1/250th-second (fixed) setting will greatly minimize the occurrence of blurry images, although it may result in a darker background.

- Automatic exposure settings range from **1/250th** of a second to 30 seconds. The camera automatically adjusts the shutter speed within a range of 30 seconds to 1/200th second (1/250th second with the electronic 1st-curtain shutter). Additionally, high-speed sync (HSS) can be enabled when using the flash.
- Use the auto setting between **1/250 and 1/60**. Shutter speeds ranging from 1/200th to 1/60th second will be used. When working with the electronic 1st-curtain shutter, you have the option to use a top speed of 1/250th second. This setting prevents shutter speeds slower than 1/60th second and comes in handy when you need to prevent blur caused by subject movement or camera shake in the secondary ambient light exposure.
- Shutter speed set at **1/250 sec. (fixed).** For optimal results, it is recommended to use a shutter speed of 1/200th second (or 1/250th second with e-1st curtain shutter) when using flash. When using this setting, you can ensure that the highest flash sync speed is used, reducing the chance of any blurring caused by the secondary ambient light exposure. Similar to a professional approach, when using a fixed 1/200th- or

1/250th-second shutter speed, it's important to note that the background may appear darker. This is because less of the ambient light can be used to balance the exposure. This setting does not allow for HSS in P or Av modes.

Flash Function Settings

This entry grants access to functions that may vary among different flash units. To access this screen, it is necessary to have the Speedlite attached and powered up. This is because the camera needs to identify the flash being used to display the appropriate submenu. The device features six sections for adjusting various settings, including flash mode, wireless functions, zoom head coverage, shutter sync, flash exposure compensation, and flash exposure bracketing.

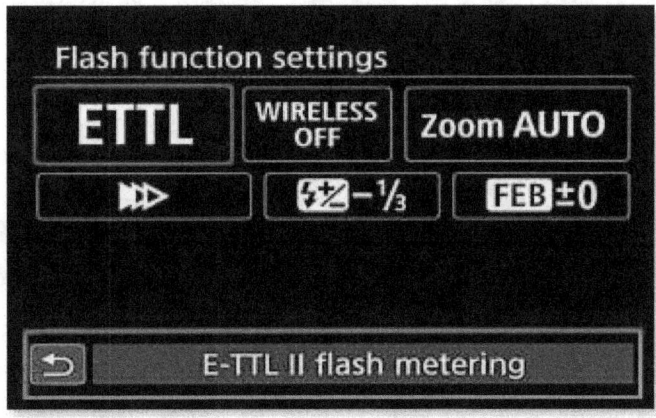

Flash mode. This entry provides multiple options based on the flash modes available on your Speedlite.

- **E-TTL:** The E-TTL II mode is the standard mode used for EX-series Speedlites.
- **M:** With this Manual flash, you can adjust the flash output to your desired level, ranging from full power (1/1) to 1/128th power.
- **MULTI**: This flash is commonly used to create stroboscopic effects.
- **External Auto/External Manual:** Certain flash units are equipped with a metering sensor directly on the flash unit. When you select either of those options, the E-TTL II metering is turned off, and the flash's external sensor is used to measure exposure instead. In most cases, E-TTL II metering is known for its accuracy and is often the preferred choice for various applications. For instance, it works well for balanced fill

flash outdoors or when you need to balance ambient light and flash indoors while using Av or Tv modes.

Zoom: To use a compatible (zoomable) flash, simply choose this option and press the **SET button**. Next, you have the option to adjust the Quick Control dial to select different zoom settings. These include Auto, which allows the flash to automatically adjust its zoom based on the focal length information provided by the camera. Additionally, you can choose from specific zoom settings such as 24mm, 28mm, 35mm, 50mm, 70mm, 80mm, or 105mm (only available with the older 580EX II). For the 600EX II-RT and EL-1 models, you also have the additional zoom options of 135mm and 200mm.

Shutter sync: There are two options available for flash synchronization: first-curtain sync, which triggers the main flash as soon as the shutter is fully open, and second-curtain sync, which delays the firing of the main flash until just before the shutter begins to close. When you have a compatible Canon Speedlite attached, you have the option to select high-speed sync (HSS). This feature enables you to use shutter speeds faster than 1/200th / 1/250th second, giving you more flexibility in capturing fast-moving subjects.

Flash C.Fn Settings

By accessing this menu entry, you will be able to use a screen that grants you the ability to configure various Custom Functions within your camera's flash. The available functions will vary based on the C.Fn settings included in the flash unit. The EL-100 offers a limited selection of Custom Functions compared to the more advanced models like the EX600 II-RT and EL-1, which boast a wide range of 23 Custom Functions each. For adjusting flash Custom Functions, simply rotate the QCD-1 to select the desired C.Fn number, and then press SET. Once more, give the QCD-1 a gentle twist to select one of the available options for that particular function. Afterward, press the **SET button** once more to finalize your selection.

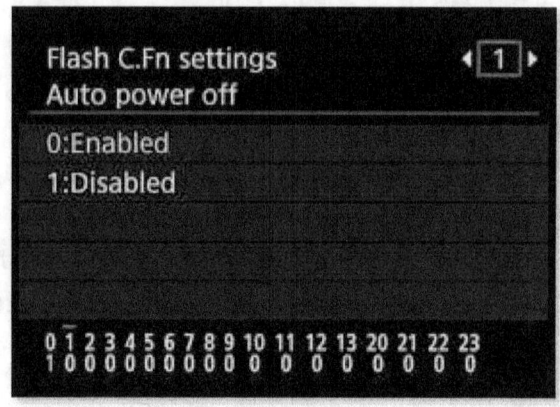

Clear Settings

To reset all flash settings to their factory default values, simply select the menu entry at the bottom of the screen. A prompt will then appear, asking for your confirmation. You have two options: Clear Flash Settings (the settings internal to the camera) and Clear All Speedlite C.Fn's, which will reset all the attached Speedlite's Custom Function settings to their original factory defaults. One exception to note is C.Fn-0: Distance Indicator Display, which will remain unchanged.

Frequently Asked Questions

1. How do you know when an electronic flash is working?
2. How do you avoid sync-speed problems?
3. How do you determine exposure?
4. How do you use external speedlite control?

CHAPTER TEN
WORKING WITH WIRELESS FLASH

Overview

It would be nearly impossible to discuss this camera without talking about how you can work with wireless flash. Here, you will learn the evolution of wireless flash, the elements of wireless flash, and others as well.

Wireless Evolution

Many Canon cameras designed for enthusiasts come equipped with a built-in flash that allows for internal wireless triggering using the on-camera flash. Since the R6 II lacks a built-in flash for wireless triggering, we need to depend on external flash units or additional accessories to remotely activate our Speedlites. Fortunately, the majority of users of this camera are experienced photographers who are typically able to meet the equipment requirements necessary for using wireless capabilities effectively. There are numerous permutations to consider. As an expert, you can use an external flash or the ST-E2 optical transmitter (or ST-E3-RT and ST-E10 radio transmitters) as the sender. You can opt for either a single external "**receiver**" flash or multiple ones. You can also seamlessly control all of your wireless flash units as a unified multi-headed flash, or you can organize them into separate "groups" for individual management. There are various options available for you to choose from when it comes to communicating with your strobes. This includes selecting different "**channels**" or using multiple wireless IDs with radio-controlled units such as the EL-1, EL-5, or 600EX II-RT. These are all aspects that you should consider as you familiarize yourself with the impressive wireless capabilities.

Elements of Wireless Flash

Here are some important concepts to understand about electronic flash and wireless flash.

Flash Combinations

Your attached on-camera external flash can be used independently or, if it can function as a master or controller flash (not all Canon Speedlites have this feature), it can be used in conjunction with other external remote or slave flash units (referred to as receivers by Canon). **Here's a concise overview of the various permutations at your disposal:**

- **On-camera flash used alone:** You can use your on-camera flash as the sole source of illumination when capturing a photo. When operating in this mode, the flash takes on the role of the main light source, while the surrounding ambient light has minimal impact on the final exposure of the photo. Alternatively, the on-camera flash can be used alongside the scene's natural lighting to achieve a harmonious lighting outcome. When using this mode, the flash works in harmony with the ambient light, providing additional illumination without overpowering it. Additionally, the on-camera flash can serve as a "fill" light in situations where the main source of illumination is natural light, like daylight. In this mode, the flash is used to enhance the lighting in areas that are poorly illuminated.
- **On-camera flash used simultaneously with off-camera flash**: Using the off-camera flash as the primary light source and incorporating fill light from the on-camera flash can create captivating effects and enhance the quality of your portraits.
- **On-camera flash used as a trigger only for off-camera flash**: Use the on-camera wireless flash controller to effortlessly control one or multiple Speedlites, allowing you to achieve professional studio lighting effects while ensuring that the flash does not affect the exposure.

Controlling Flash Units

There are various methods for controlling flash units, including direct or wired connections and wireless options. These are the main methods that professionals use:

- **Direct connection**: The on-camera flash is connected directly to the camera and is electronically triggered when a picture is taken. External flash units can be controlled by connecting them to a camera using a dedicated flash cord, like the Canon OC-E3 EOS Dedicated TTL off-camera shoe cord.
- **Dedicated wireless optical signals**: When using this mode, external flash units establish communication with the camera by using a pre-flash. This pre-flash is used to calculate the exposure before the actual flash burst occurs a moment later. The pre-flashes can wirelessly transmit data from the camera to the flash unit, allowing for precise control over the burst duration to achieve the desired exposure. In addition, the pulses can be used to fine-tune the zoom head position, provided that the flash supports this functionality. When it comes to Canon flash units, the pre-flash information is transmitted and received as visible light.
- **Dedicated wireless infrared signals:** Certain devices, like the Canon ST-E2 Speedlite Transmitter, can communicate with specialized flash units using infrared signals,

similar to how a remote control operates your television. (Similar to a professional, the IR signal may slightly bounce around the room, but for optimal communication, a line-of-sight connection is generally required.)

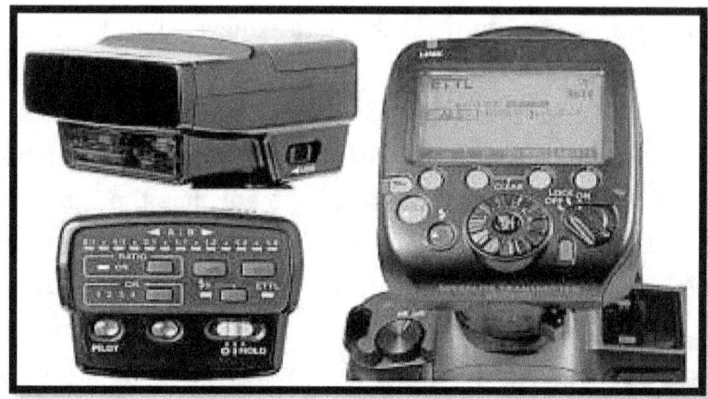

Why Use Wireless Flash?

Canon's wireless flash system offers numerous advantages, allowing you to use directional lighting to enhance detail and highlight specific elements within the frame. It also allows for the operation of multiple strobes. With models such as the popular 580EX II, you can control up to four flash units in each of three groups, totaling twelve units in all (although it's unlikely that most of us will own 12 Canon Speedlites). By using the EL-1, 600EX-RT/600EX II-RT, and 430EX III-RT, you gain the ability to expertly control a multitude of flash units through both optical transmission and radio control.

Optically, you can control numerous flash units, while with radio control; you can manage up to 15 Speedlites, divided into five distinct groups. You can create intricate portrait or location lighting setups. With the two top Canon Speedlites, you can achieve a level of lighting that rivals that of a professional studio. These shoe-mount flashes emit a powerful amount of light, allowing you to capture high-quality images. Naturally, the price of these top-of-the-line Speedlites is comparable to, or even higher than, certain studio monolights. However, the Canon battery-powered units offer greater portability and eliminate the need for an external AC or DC power source.

Key Wireless Concepts

Before diving into wireless flash photography, it's crucial to grasp three essential concepts: channels, groups, and flash ratios. **Here is a detailed explanation of each:**

- **Channels**: Canon's wireless flash system provides users with the option to select from four different channels for communication between the flash units. For those with expertise in aviation, amateur radio, or radio scanning, the channels can be likened to separate communication frequencies. In the case of optical transmission, the channels are labeled 1, 2, 3, and 4, and each flash must be allocated to a specific channel. Additionally, it is important to assign each of the flash units you are working with to the same channel. This ensures that the receiver Speedlites will only respond to a sender flash that is on the same channel.

When using the EL-1, 600EX-RT, or 430EX III-RT in radio control mode, or the ST-E3-RT and ST-E10 transmitters, you have access to a total of 15 channels. Additionally, there is an Auto setting that enables the flash to automatically choose a channel. Furthermore, you have the option to designate a four-digit Wireless Radio ID to further distinguish the communication channel used by your flashes.

- **Groups**: Canon's wireless flash system allows you to easily assign multiple flash units to different groups. With earlier Speedlites like the 580EX II, or newer models like the EL-100, you can have up to three groups labeled A, B, and C.

Using the EL-1, EL-5, 600EX-RT, 430EX III-RT, and ST-E3-RT/ST-E10 transmitters, you can control up to five groups (A, B, C, D, and E) and connect as many as 15 flash units. All the flashes in all the groups use the identical channel and respond to the sender controller in unison. However, it is possible to adjust the output levels of each group individually. In a professional setting, Speedlites in Group A can be used as the primary light source, while Speedlites in Group B can be adjusted to provide a softer illumination and act as a fill light. Being able to adjust the output of all the units within a given group simultaneously is incredibly convenient. You can effortlessly create various lighting styles to enhance your portraits and other photographs.

Which Flashes Can Be Operated Wirelessly?

One function of a Speedlite is to have two different modes. This device functions as a sender flash, capable of triggering other compatible Canon units on the same channel. Alternatively, a Speedlite can be wirelessly triggered as a receiver unit, activated by a sender, allowing for complete control over exposure using the camera's eTTL flash system. Triggering the second function is a breeze. A wide range of Canon shoe-mount flash units, both current and recent models, can be wirelessly triggered. This includes the EL-1, 600EX-RT, 580EX II, 470EX AI, 430EX II, 430EX III, 430EX III-RT, EL-100, 320EX, and 270EX II. Furthermore, certain Speed-lites possess the capability to function as a transmitting flash.

Here's a brief overview of the current flash capabilities:

- **Canon Speedlite EL-1 or the 600EX-RT/600EX II-RT:** These high-quality flashes can act as a sender flash when connected to any Canon EOS model. They can be triggered wirelessly by another sender flash, like a compatible EOS model, another EL-1, 600EX-RT/600EX II-RT, 580EX II, or the ST-E2/ST-E3-RT transmitters.
- **Canon Speedlite EL-5:** This flash can operate as a transmitter (in radio mode exclusively) and as a receiver when using both optical and radio technology.
- **Canon Speedlite 580EX II:** This flash can serve as a sender flash when connected to a Canon EOS model. It can be wirelessly triggered by an optical transmission from another compatible EOS camera, such as the 580EX II, 600EX-RT, 600EX II-RT, 430EX III-RT, or the ST-E2 transmitter. The ST-E3-RT transmitter operates exclusively in radio mode.
- **Canon Speedlite 470EX AI:** When used off-camera, this flash can only function as an optical receiver. It is not capable of functioning as a sender.
- **Canon Speedlite 430EX III:** This version, which is similar to the radio-compatible one mentioned later, is unable to transmit signals but can serve as a receiver when used with optical triggering technology.
- **Canon Speedlite 430EX III-RT**: This flash can operate as a transmitter (in radio mode exclusively) and as a receiver when using both optical and radio technologies.
- **Canon Speedlite 430EX II:** This flash model is no longer in production and is not capable of operating as a standalone sender. However, it can be wirelessly activated by a sender flash, such as a compatible EOS camera, a Speedlite 600EX-RT/580EX II, or the ST-E2 transmitters.
- **Canon Speedlite 320EX:** This is capable of wireless triggering when paired with a sender flash, such as a compatible EOS camera, a 600EX-RT/600EX II-RT, 580EX II, or the ST-E2 transmitter.
- **Canon Speedlite 270EX II**: This flash can be triggered wirelessly by a compatible camera's sender flash, such as the 600EX-RT/600EX II-RT, 580EX II, or the ST-E2 transmitter in optical mode.

- **Canon Speedlite EL-100:** This flash can be triggered wirelessly by a compatible camera's sender flash, such as the 600EX-RT/600EX II-RT, 580EX II, or the ST-E2 transmitter in optical mode. Additionally, it can also serve as a sender to trigger other flashes.

Any combination of compatible flash units can be used in your wireless setup. For optimal results, you have the option to use a variety of compatible devices as a sender, such as the 600EX-RT/600EX II-RT, 580EX II, 430EX III-RT, EL-100, or ST-E2/ST-E3-RT/ST-E10. Additionally, you can pair these with any number of 600EX-RT, 580EX II, 470EX AI, 430EX III, 430EX III-RT, EL-100, 430EX II, 320EX, or 270EX II units.

Setting up a Sender/Controller Flash

To work with wireless flash, start by setting up one unit as the sender, either a flash or a controller. Various Speedlite models such as the Speedlite EL-100, 580EX, 580EX II, EL-1, EL-5, or 600EX-RT/600EX II-RT can be mounted onto your camera. These Speedlites can function as sender units, allowing you to transmit E-TTL II optical signals to one or more off-camera Speedlite receiver units. The sender unit can be configured to disable its flash output, allowing it to control the remote units using pre-flash without adding any additional illumination to the exposure. This technique is beneficial for images where you aim to avoid any noticeable flash illumination from the camera position.

Using a Speedlite as an Optical Sender

Here is a step-by-step guide on how to set up and use compatible Speedlites as a camera-mounted sender unit for automatic exposure. The EL-100 is configured as a sender using the Flash Function settings instead of the Flash controls. When you enable the Wireless functions, you will have access to adjustments for Channel, Group, and Flash Ratio.

EL-1

1. Use the joystick on the flash to the left to select flash functions.
2. Use the joystick or rotate the Select dial to highlight the Optical sender (indicated by a lightning bolt symbol on the flash LCD).
3. Ensure proper confirmation by pressing the joystick in a vertical direction.
4. Use the menu system to efficiently manage and customize the RATIO, output, and various other options on both the sender and receiver units.

580EX

1. Move the wireless switch located near the base of the unit to the SENDER position.
2. Use the **MODE button** to navigate between the ETTL, M, and Multi modes.
3. To cycle through the available options, simply press the **ZOOM button multiple times**. The options include Flash Zoom, RATIO, CH., and flash emitter ON/OFF. Use the Select dial and **Select/SET button** to make adjustments to these options.
4. Use the **Select/SET button** to effortlessly choose and verify the output power settings in Manual and Multi modes, or to use FEC or FEB while operating in ETTL mode.

Using the Speedlite 430EX III-RT as Radio Sender

The Speedlite 430EX III-RT can function as a radio sender unit, allowing it to remotely trigger another 430EX III-RT or a 600EX-RT flash. **Simply follow these steps:**

1. Use the left directional key on the Select dial.
2. Adjust the Select dial until SENDER is displayed on the LCD screen.
3. Press the Select button located at the center of the Select dial.
4. Make sure to set any 600EX-RT or 430EX III-RT units that will be used as receivers to the Receiver mode.
   - To activate radio wireless receiver mode on the 600EX-RT, simply press the Wireless button until the LCD panel confirms the change.
   - To operate the 430EX III-RT receivers, use the left directional key and rotate the Select dial until the Receiver is displayed on the LCD. Next, simply press the Select button to confirm.
5. Perform Step 4 for any extra receiver units.
6. During communication between the sender and receivers, the LINK lamps on all units will illuminate in a green color.

Setting up a Receiver Flash

Working wirelessly allows for seamless control and synchronization of one or more receiver flash units using a sender flash/controller trigger. After defining your sender flash, the next step is to switch your remaining Speedlites into receiver mode, just like a professional. Each Canon Speedlite has its unique way of doing that.

- **Speedlite EL-1**: Follow the instructions provided to operate the joystick on the flash and select either Optical Receiver or Wireless Receiver.

- **Speedlite 600EX-RT/600EX II-RT**: Continuously press the Wireless button until the LCD panel displays that the unit is in optical wireless receiver mode or radio wireless receiver mode. When operating in this mode, the 600EX-RT flash is designated a flash mode by the transmitting device, such as the flash or ST-E2 or ST-E3-RT.
- **Speedlite 580EX II**: Hold down the **ZOOM button** until the wireless setting options pop up. Use the **Select dial** and **Select/SET button** to choose and verify that the wireless function is enabled and set to receiver mode.
- **Speedlite 430EX III/430EX III-RT:** Simply press the left directional key and use the Select dial to navigate to the Receiver option on the LCD. Next, simply press the Select button to confirm.
- **Speedlite 430EX II**: Hold down the **ZOOM button** for at least two seconds until the wireless setting options appear. Use the **Select dial** and **Select/SET button** to choose and verify that wireless is enabled and set to receiver mode.
- **Speedlite 320EX:** The flash features a convenient On/Off/Receiver switch located at the lower left of the back panel. When operating in Receiver mode, you have the option to configure the flash's C.Fn-10 setting to automatically power down after a period of inactivity, either 10 or 60 minutes. That can assist in conserving the batteries of the 320EX. The C.Fn-11 setting of the unit can be adjusted to enable the sender transmitter to activate a dormant 320EX within a selected time frame of either 1 hour or 8 hours. It is important to keep in mind that the C.Fn settings for the 320EX and 270EX II can only be adjusted when the Speedlites are attached to the camera via the hot shoe.
- **Speedlite EL-100:** Using this flash as a remote is incredibly simple. Ensure that the Receiver switch on the back of the unit is set to the same channel as the sender. Then, adjust the Mode dial to the appropriate Group, typically A.

Frequently Asked Questions

1. How do you set up a sender/controller flash?
2. How do you set up a receiver flash?
3. Which flashes can be operated wirelessly?
4. How do you use a speedlite as an optical sender?
5. How do you control flash units?

CHAPTER ELEVEN
CUSTOMIZING WITH THE SHOOTING MENU

Overview

This chapter is more like a breath of fresh air. Additionally, this chapter takes us on a rollercoaster ride to discovering the anatomy of the menus in this camera including customizing the shooting menu and its options.

Anatomy of the Menus

The menus are organized into seven main tabs: Shooting, Autofocus, Playback, Wireless, Set-up, Custom Functions, and My Menu. Every tab is comprised of multiple individual pages, where each page's listings are displayed on a separate screen without the need for scrolling. The tabs have different colors assigned to them for easy identification. The colors are: red for Shooting, magenta for Autofocus, blue for Playback, violet for wireless, amber/yellow for Set-up, brown for Custom Functions, and green for My Menu. The icon of the currently selected menu tab appears white against a background that matches its color code. A lineup right below displays the available page numbers. The number on the current screen is highlighted. The inactive menus are displayed in a gray and dimmed state.

The menus are user-friendly as well. Simply press the MENU button and use these controls:

- **Jump between tabs**: Master the art of navigating between main tabs by smoothly rotating the QCD-2. Highlighting will always shift from the current page on the current tab to the most recently visited page and the most recently accessed entry of the next main tab. As an illustration, when you select an entry on the Shooting 3 page and turn the QCD-2 to the right, you will be taken to the last page you accessed in the AF (autofocus) menu, with the specific entry you last used on that page highlighted. Turn the QCD-2 to the left to go back to your previous location and entry in the Shooting 3 menu.

- **Move from page to page**: To navigate seamlessly from page to page, simply rotate the Main dial or use the multi-controller joystick to move left or right. For instance, when navigating the AF 3 menu, you can smoothly progress to AF 4, and AF 5, and then seamlessly transition to Playback 1, Playback 2, and so on. Turn to the left to change the direction of your movement. The forward and reverse movement also wraps around, and you can find the Shooting 1 menu right after the last entry in My Menu. Just like a pro, the most recently used entry on each page visited is highlighted. This is incredibly convenient if you frequently use specific entries.

- **Scroll among page entries**: To navigate through the entries on a page, simply rotate the QCD-1 or use the multi-controller joystick to scroll up or down.

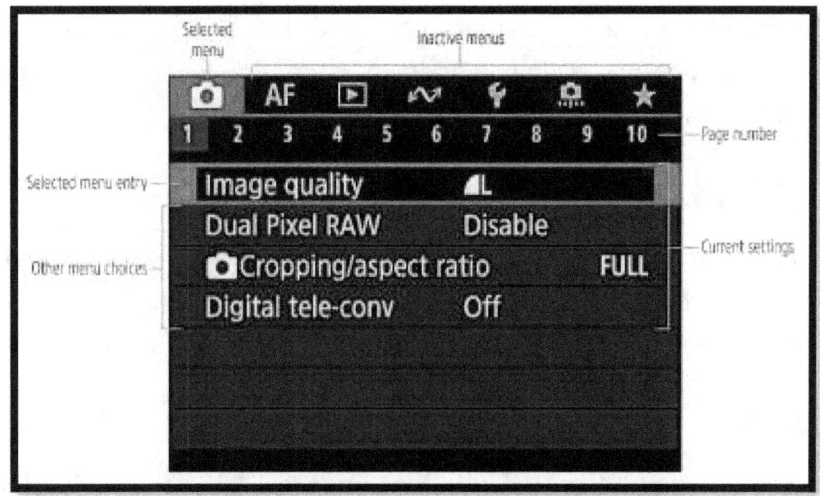

Here are some important things to keep in mind as you navigate the menus:

- **Menu tabs:** The active menu will be highlighted in the top row of the menu screen, as mentioned before. The numbers within the tab indicate the different set-up options available, allowing you to easily navigate between Set-up 1, Set-up 2, Set-up 3, and other tabs. It's important to keep in mind that the red camera icons indicate the options for still and movie shooting. The blue right-pointing triangles represent the playback options. The yellow wrench icons indicate the set-up options. The brown camera icons represent the Custom Functions. Lastly, the green star represents the personalized menus that are defined specifically for you, the star of the show.
- **Selected menu item**: When a menu entry is selected within a tab, it will be distinguished by a black background and a surrounding box that matches its color code.
- **Other menu options:** All the other menu items displayed on the screen will feature a dark gray background.
- **Current settings**: The visible menu items are displayed in the right-hand column, and will remain there until a menu entry is selected by pressing the **SET key**. The current

settings do not align properly with certain menu entries that serve as functions, such as the Protect Images or Print options in the Playback 1 and 2 screens. As a result, the right column remains empty.

Once you have positioned the menu highlighting the desired menu item, simply press the **SET button** to make your selection. When you select a menu item, the other options will be hidden, and you will see a list of choices or a submenu screen. Alternatively, a separate settings screen may be displayed for that entry. With the QCD-1, you can easily navigate through the menu options by scrolling up or down. To confirm your selection, press **SET**, and then press the **MENU** button once more to exit.

Shooting Menu Options

The Shooting menu options are typically the ones you access after the most frequently used ones. It is important to make adjustments as you start a shooting session or transition between different subjects. Canon simplifies the process of accessing these changes.

Image Quality

- **Options:** Resolution: Large (default), Medium, Small 1, Small 2; JPEG/HEIF Compression: Fine (default), Normal; JPEG/HEIF (default), RAW, or RAW+JPEG
- **RECOMMENDATIONS:** Resolution: Large; JPEG Compression: Fine; RAW+JPEG/HEIF

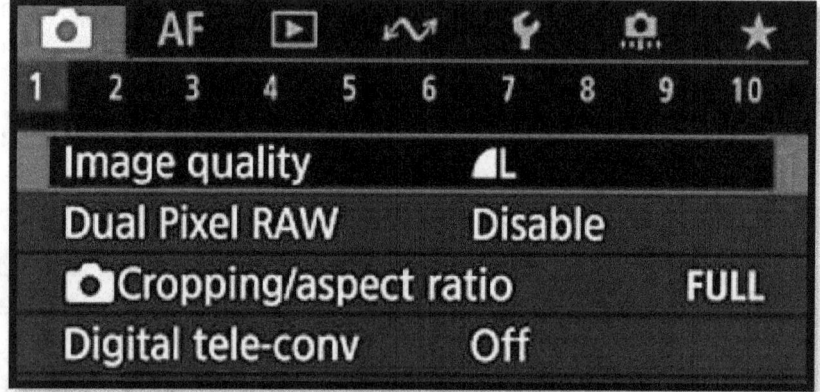

This entry is the first one in the Shooting 1 menu. You have the option to select the image quality settings for file storage.

When choosing a quality setting, you have several options available:

- **Resolution**: The number of pixels captured determines the absolute resolution of the photos you capture. Choose from a range of options for image resolution: Large/RAW/C-RAW at 6000 × 4000 pixels (24MP), Medium at 3984 × 2656 pixels (11MP), Small 1 at 2976 × 1984 pixels (5.9MP), and Small 2 at 2400 × 1600 pixels (3.8MP).

- **JPEG/HEIF compression**: The camera uses compression to efficiently reduce the size of image files, enabling you to store a greater number of photos on your memory card. You have the option to choose between Fine compression and Normal compression, which slightly reduces the image quality. These symbols serve as a helpful reminder that Fine compression (depicted by a quarter-circle) yields the smoothest outcomes, whereas Normal compression (indicated by a stair-step icon) produces more jagged images. The Small 2 (S2) file option does not display a quality option icon, although it is set to Fine quality.

- **JPEG/HEIF, RAW, or both options**: You have the option to store either JPEG/HEIF versions of the images you capture or save your photos as uncompressed, loss-free RAW files. However, it's important to note that RAW files take up approximately four times more space on your memory card. Alternatively, you have the option to store both simultaneously while capturing the shots. Photographers often choose to save both a JPEG and a RAW file. This way, they have a ready-to-use JPEG or HEIF version, as well as the original RAW file for future image processing. You will have two distinct versions of the file: one with a JPG extension and another with the CR3 extension, which indicates a Canon RAW file. To select the desired combination, navigate through the menus, locate the Image Quality option, and then press the **SET button**.

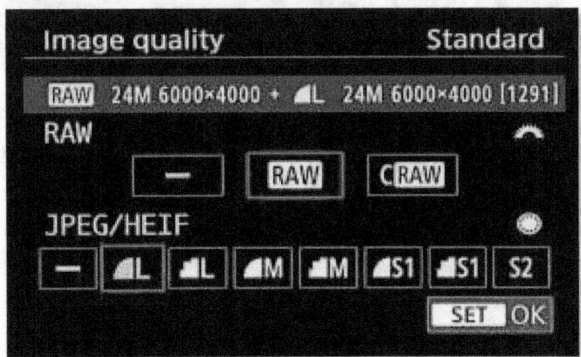

Dual Pixel RAW

- **Options:** Enable, Disable (default)
- **RECOMMENDATIONS:** Disable unless this special format is needed

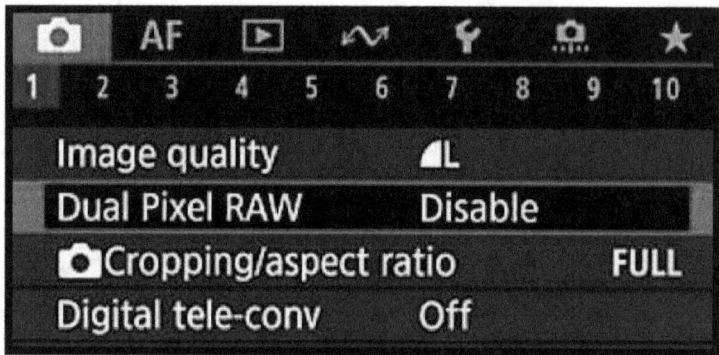

Dual Pixel RAW is a unique RAW format that allows for precise adjustments to the focus plane, enhancing bokeh effects, and correcting ghosting and flare in an image editor. Advanced users can take advantage of Dual Pixel RAW files to recover up to one extra stop in the highlights and make adjustments to virtual lighting. The camera effectively saves two distinct RAW files: one that includes information from both sets of pixels (Sets A+B) and another that only contains the pixels in Set B. This allows the software to process each subset independently.

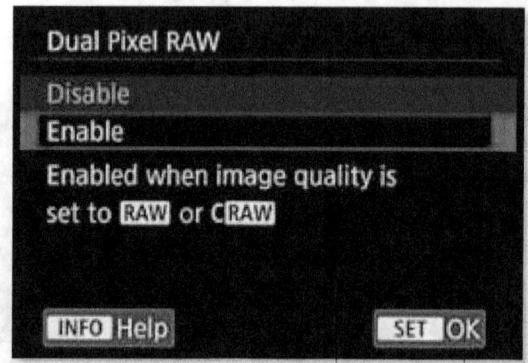

To utilize Dual Pixel RAW, you need to choose RAW, C RAW, or RAW+JPEG as your Image Quality and activate the Dual Pixel feature. Unfortunately, this feature is not accessible when attempting to capture multiple exposures, use automatic HDR, or adjust image quality with just one touch. Using larger lens apertures enhances the extent and impact of available corrections, while continuous shooting may experience a decrease in speed when using DPR. Sadly, high-speed continuous shooting is not available.

HDR Shooting [HDR PQ]

- **Options:** Disable (default), Enable
- **RECOMMENDATIONS:** N/A

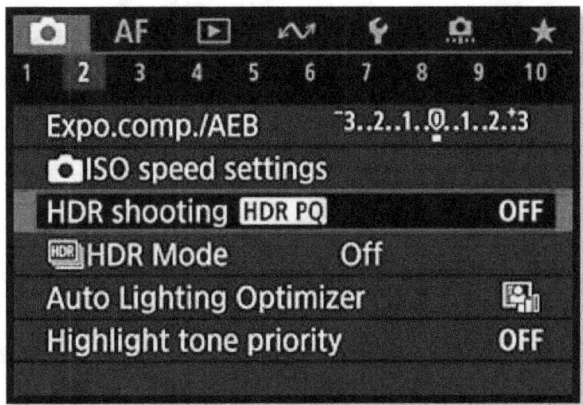

This entry allows for the capture of high dynamic range (HDR) images in HEIF and RAW formats that adhere to the Perceptual Quantization (PQ) specification. When HDR Shooting is enabled, you won't be able to use expanded ISO speeds (L or H). PQ is a non-linear electro-optical transfer function that lets you display HDR images using technical language.

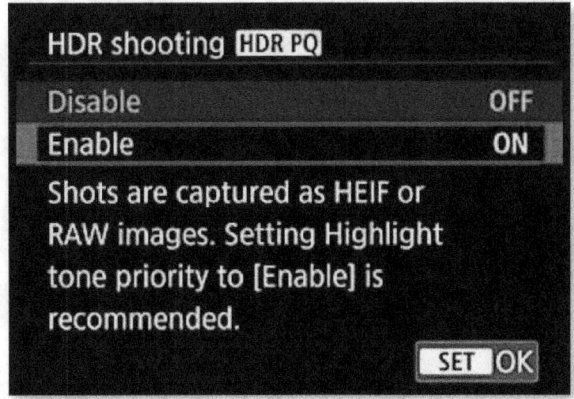

To view HDR images with utmost accuracy, it is recommended to use an HDR-compatible monitor. It's worth noting that certain scenes might appear differently when viewed on a non-

HDR-compliant monitor or through the camera. It is recommended by Canon to enable Highlight Tone Priority when HDR capture is enabled.

ISO Speed Settings

- **Options:** ISO Speed, ISO Speed Range, Auto Range, Minimum Shutter Speed
- **RECOMMENDATIONS:** N/A

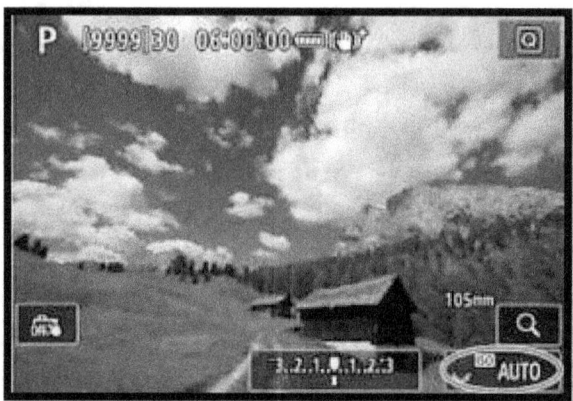

Use this entry to effortlessly choose a precise ISO speed for still photography through a conventional menu, offering a seamless alternative to the Quick Control menu.

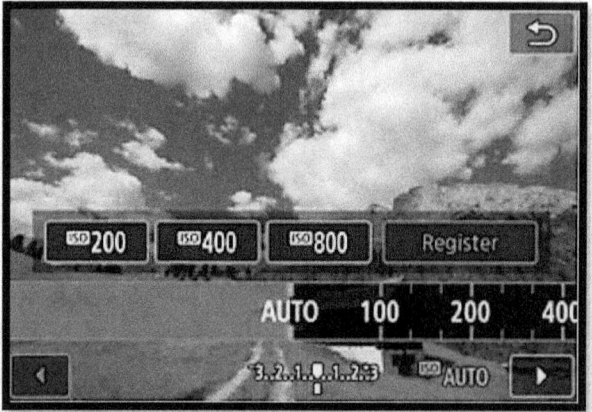

Alternatively, you can also restrict the range of ISO settings and shutter speeds that the camera automatically selects. ISO is automatically set in Basic Zone modes such as Scene Intelligent Auto.

Highlight Tone Priority

- **Options:** Disable/OFF (default), Enable D+, Enhanced D+2
- **RECOMMENDATIONS:** Choose Disable

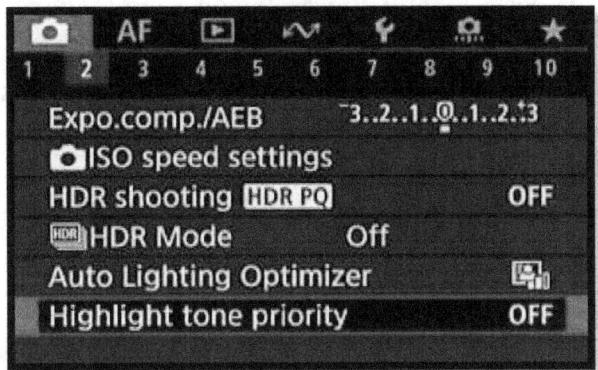

This setting enhances the tones in an image, emphasizing the middle grays and brightest highlights. As a result, the dynamic range of the image is expanded, although some shadow detail may be sacrificed. Activating this option is recommended for capturing subjects with significant detail in the highlights and less detail in shadow areas. Tones will be carefully maintained to bring out the highlights while allowing the shadows to deepen, which may result in a slight increase in noise levels. For optimal results, consider using Highlight Tone Priority when capturing vibrant beach or snow scenes, particularly during midday when shadows are minimal. Note that the Highlight Tone Priority feature is not accessible when the HDR Mode is set to Moving Subject or Dynamic Range.

Here are the options available to you:

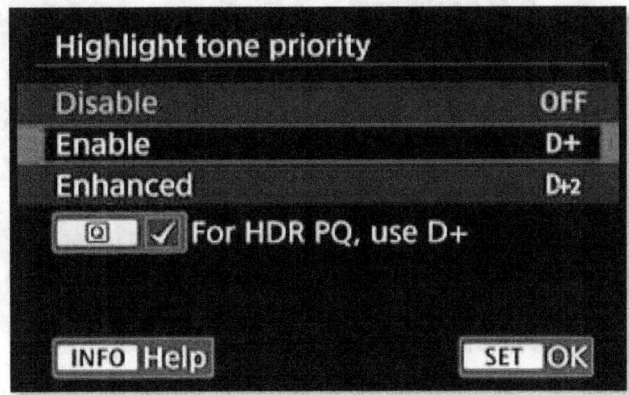

- **Disable/OFF**: The standard dynamic range is used.
- **Enable D+:** Areas of emphasis are given increased tonal values, while the tones for shadow areas are decreased. The ISO 100 sensitivity setting is not available, and you can only choose ISO 200 and higher settings. The L and H ISO speeds have been disabled. One can easily identify the implementation of this restriction by observing the D+ icon displayed in the viewfinder, ISO Selection screen, and shooting information display for a specific image. The camera's manipulation of the image can result in a slight increase in image noise. For optimal results in HDR photography, it is advised to use the D+ setting. To enable or disable this setting in the corresponding mode, simply press the Q button and mark the option in the Highlight Tone Priority screen.
- **Enhanced D+2**: Implementing a more assertive approach to preserving overexposed highlights. Exercise caution when using this tool, as it has the potential to significantly alter your images. This feature is not accessible during movie recording.

Note:

- There may be a slight increase in noise.
- The ISO range begins at ISO 200. You are unable to adjust the ISO speeds beyond their default settings.
- Results in certain scenes may not appear as anticipated with [**Enhanced**].

Anti-Flicker Shooting

- **Options:** Enable, Disable (default)
- **RECOMMENDATIONS:** Disable, unless shooting under a flickering light source

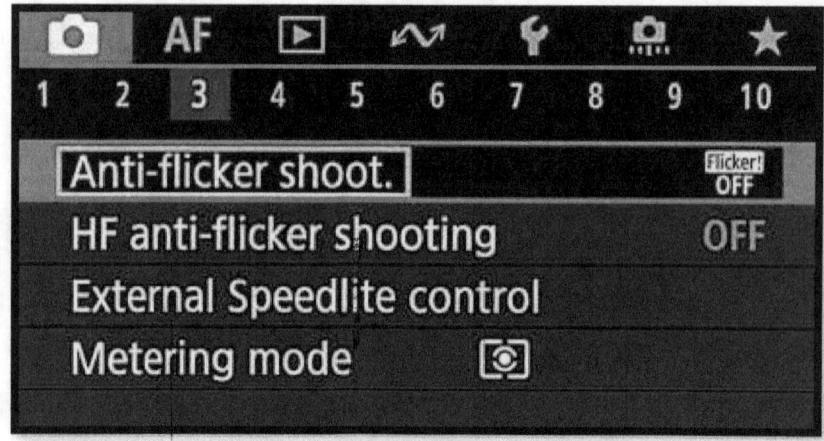

This menu item is the inaugural addition to the Shooting 3 menu. Many inexperienced sports photographers often inquire about the reasons behind the inconsistent exposure, unpredictable color variations, or banding in shots taken in specific gymnasiums or arenas. Some types of artificial lighting have a blinking cycle that is undetectable to the human eye but can be captured by a camera. When activated, this feature can detect the blinking frequency of the light source and capture the image at the optimal moment to minimize any flickering impact on the final picture. This feature is not compatible with live view or movie shooting. When using this setting for sports and other fast-paced activities, you may notice a slight delay in the shutter release time and a decrease in continuous shooting speed. However, these trade-offs are necessary to capture the perfect moment like a professional. Results can vary when using P or Av modes, as the shutter speed may change between shots to ensure proper exposure. It is recommended to use Tv or M mode to ensure a constant shutter speed.

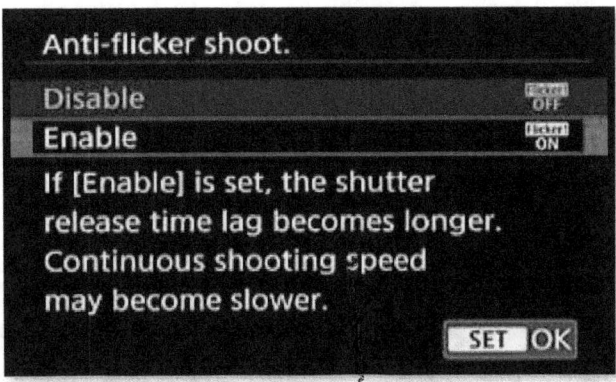

To detect flicker manually, you can enable this feature and follow these steps: press the **Q button**, select **Anti-Flicker Shooting** from the Quick Control menu, and then press the **INFO button**. You will be informed by the camera if a flicker has been detected. Disabling Anti-Flicker is recommended when using Basic Zone modes. However, it may not perform optimally in situations involving dark backgrounds, bright lights within the image area, wireless flash usage, and other shooting conditions. It is advisable to capture some test shots to assess the effectiveness of the feature under the specific light source you are using.

High-Frequency Anti-Flicker Shooting

- **Options:** Enable, Disable (default); Manual Setting, Auto Detecting

- **RECOMMENDATIONS:** Disable, unless shooting under a flickering high-frequency light source

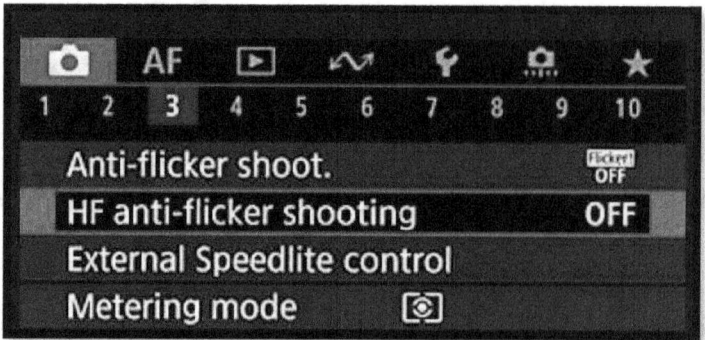

Traditional incandescent lights, operating on 60 Hz circuits, exhibit a flickering effect at a rate of 100 to 120 cycles per second. However, their brightness only varies by approximately 10 percent. Typically, such a situation does not usually lead to any discomfort or have an impact on photography. The movie display does not get updated when there is automatic detection of high-frequency flickering during the HDMI output of 4K movies.

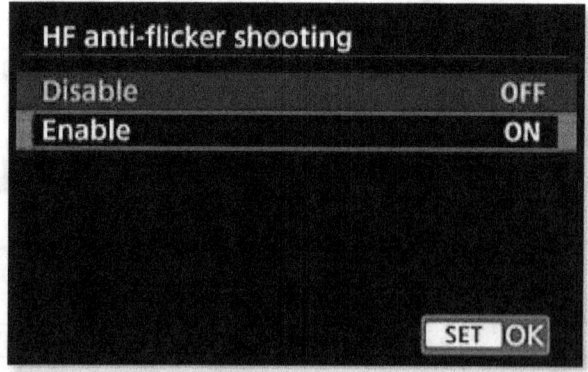

Different types of artificial illumination can sometimes cause banding due to variations in intensity. However, the Anti-Flicker Shooting entry mentioned earlier effectively addresses this issue. However, newer types of lighting, such as high-quality LED lamps, may exhibit flickering at lower intensities and higher frequencies, necessitating more advanced correction techniques. With this setting, you can adjust the shutter speed to perfectly synchronize with the flickering light sources, effectively minimizing or eliminating any unwanted banding effects. There are two choices available to you.

Simply follow these steps:

For Auto Detecting:

1. Select the shooting mode. Adjust the Mode dial to either M or Tv, which will give you the ability to manually set the shutter speed.
2. Choose the appropriate shutter speed. Select the shutter speed that suits your needs. The Auto Detecting feature will accurately calculate a speed that closely matches the desired setting.
3. Select the Auto Detecting option. The camera is capable of automatically detecting flickering within a range of 50.0 to 2011.2 Hz.

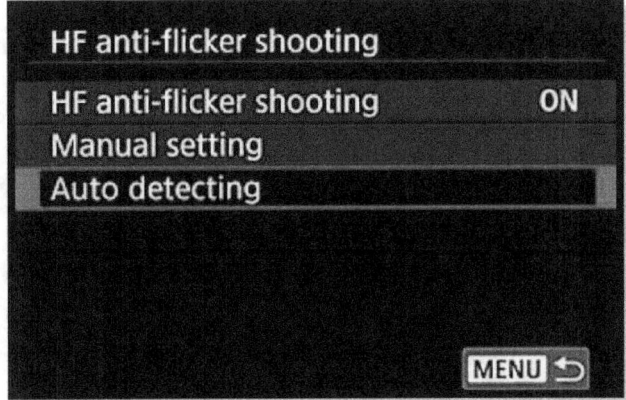

4. Ensure a stable grip on the camera. A message will be displayed. To ensure accurate frequency detection, it is important to maintain a steady grip on the camera. Select OK to continue.

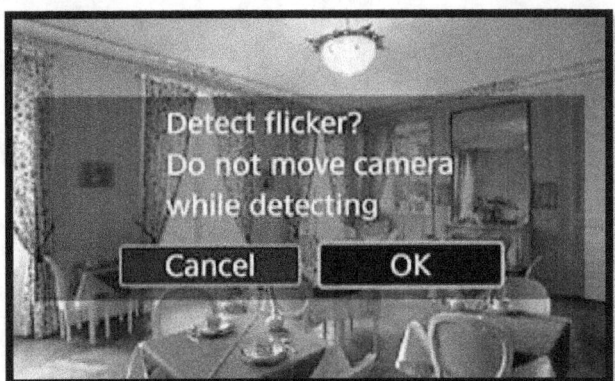

5. The camera is searching for any flicker. The screen will show a message: Detecting.
6. No flicker was detected. If this display is shown, the light source remains steady, allowing you to exit and explore the alternatives listed below.
7. Discovered xxxx.hz flicker. When this display appears, the camera will provide a suggestion, like adjusting the shutter speed to 1/1002.1.
8. Indicate your decision regarding the selection. To confirm, you have the option to highlight "**No**," select the default option "**Yes**," or choose the third option "**Yes** (Move to Tv Settings)."

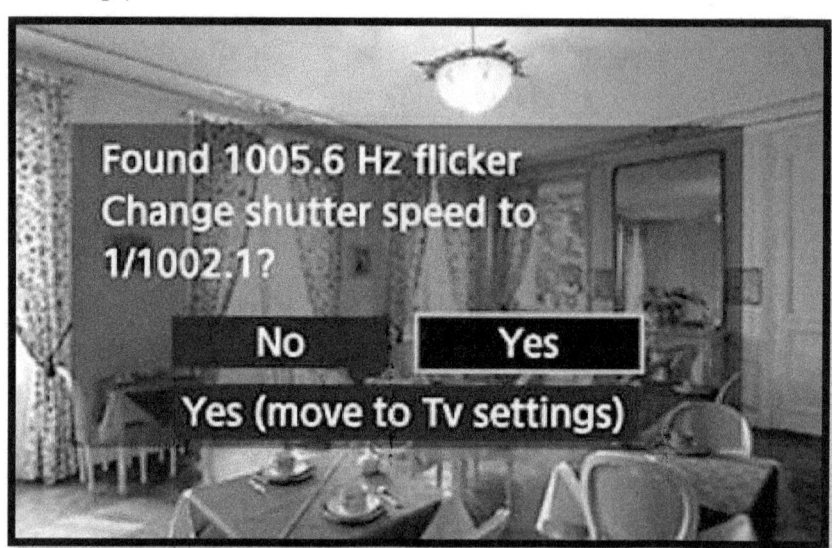

If the Auto Detecting feature fails to detect any flickering or if the suggested shutter speed still results in banding, you can attempt to use the auto-detect feature once more. With some persistence, success can be achieved on subsequent attempts. For a more polished result, consider rotating the camera about 90 degrees and giving it another shot. Flicker detection can be challenging in certain situations, such as scenes with repetitive patterns, extremely bright or dark scenes, moving subjects, flashing light sources, and lower-frequency flickering. Adjusting the camera angle can enhance the accuracy of auto-detection.

Custom White Balance

- **Options:** White balance setting
- **RECOMMENDATIONS:** N/A

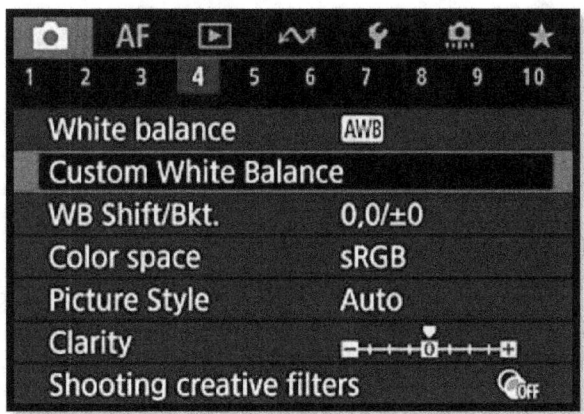

If the automatic white balance or any of the preset settings (Daylight, Shade, Cloudy, Tungsten, White Fluorescent, or Flash) do not meet your needs, you have the option to manually adjust the white balance using this menu feature. Once you've set your preferences, they will be automatically applied whenever you choose the Custom option in the White Balance menu. For optimal color balance in the prevailing lighting environment, adjust the white balance by manually focusing on a plain white or gray object, such as a card or wall, ensuring that the object occupies the spot metering circle at the center of the viewfinder. Next, capture an image.

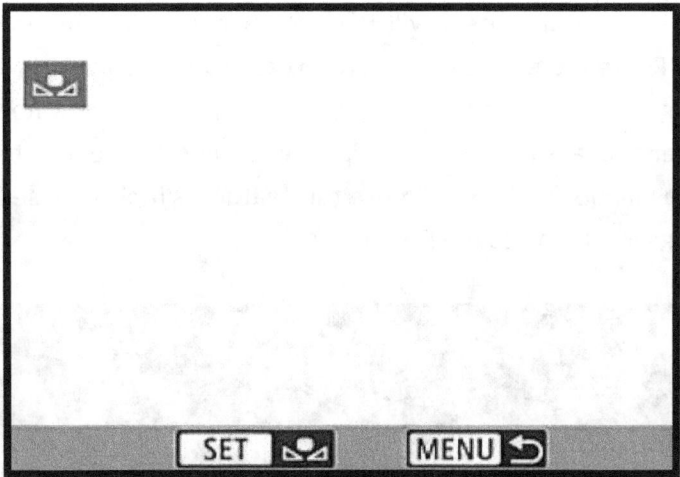

After that, locate the **MENU button** and choose **Custom White Balance** from the Shooting 4 menu. Adjust the QCD-1 until the reference image you recently captured is visible, and then select **SET** to save the white balance of the image as your Custom setting.

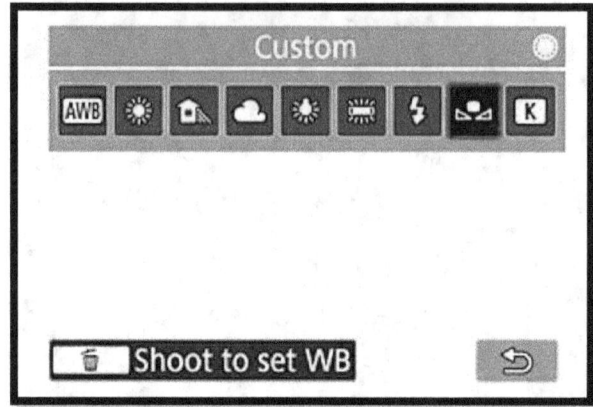

Only the appropriate images for setting a custom white balance will be displayed on the screen. Images set to custom white balance are designated by a unique icon and cannot be deleted, although they can be substituted with a new custom white balance image.

Dust Delete Data

- **Options:** Store Delete Data
- **RECOMMENDATIONS:** N/A

With this menu option, you can capture an image of any dust or particles that might be sticking to your sensor. Your photos will have the location information added to them, allowing the Digital Photo Professional software to easily detect and remove any dust present in your images. It is advisable to periodically capture a Dust Delete Data photo to serve as your last line of defense against sensor dust. Upon accessing this menu entry, the date of your most recent update will be presented. To use this feature, simply choose **Dust Delete Data**, confirm by selecting OK, and press the SET button.

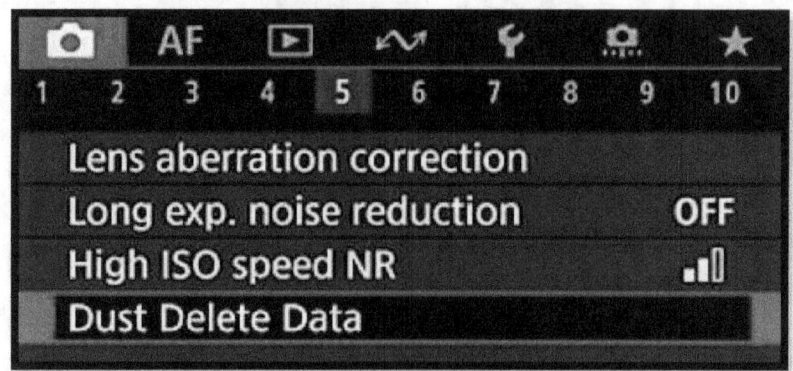

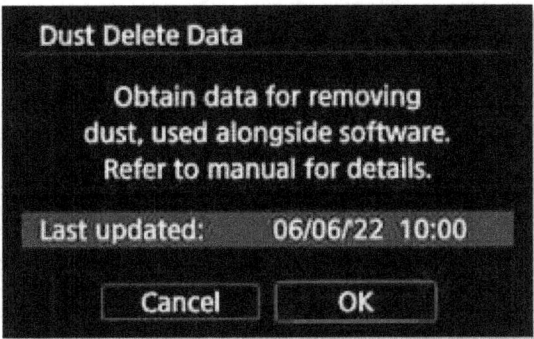

The camera will begin by conducting a self-cleaning procedure, using ultrasonic vibration to clean the low-pass filter located on top of the sensor. Next, you will be prompted to press the shutter button.

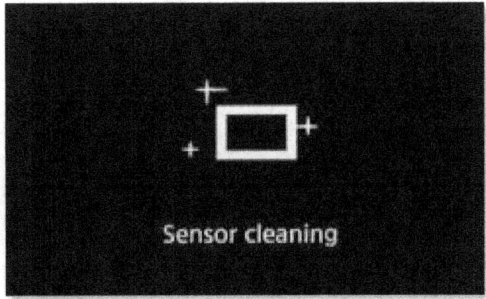

Ensure that the camera is directed towards a solid-white card and adjust the lens to manual focus. Rotate the focus ring until it reaches the infinity setting. When you activate the shutter release, the camera captures an image of the card using aperture priority and f/22. This setting ensures sufficient depth-of-field to sharply capture the dust in the image.

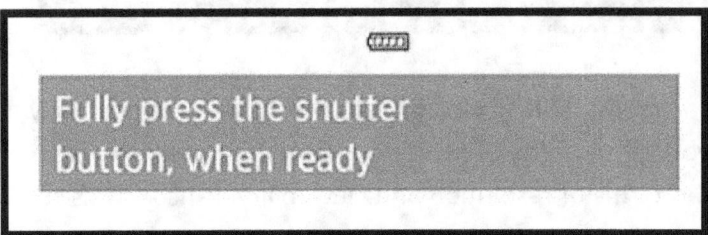

The image is not saved to your memory card, but instead, it is stored in a dedicated memory area within the camera. At last, a screen displaying the obtained data appears.

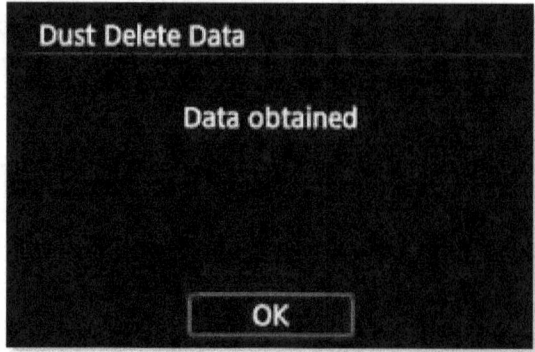

The Dust Delete Data information remains stored in the camera until you refresh it by capturing a new "**picture**." This information is then automatically included in every image file.

OVF Sim View Assist

- **Options:** On, Off (default)
- **RECOMMENDATIONS:** Choose the Off option.

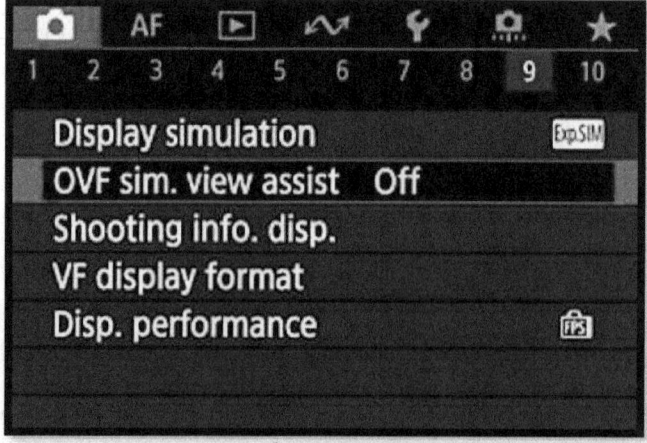

If you long for the nostalgic "**optical viewfinder experience**," this feature will seamlessly bring it back to life for you. In the world of mirrorless cameras, the electronic viewfinder has made significant strides in terms of resolution and viewability. It now rivals the big, bright optical viewfinders found in digital (and film) SLR cameras. The Canon EOS R6 II uses the enhanced dynamic range of the OLED viewfinder to its advantage. This feature, first introduced in the high-end EOS R3, automatically adjusts the brightness of the scene displayed through the EVF. As a result, you can preview the scene in a way that closely resembles what you would see through a traditional optical viewfinder unless you have made significant exposure compensation adjustments. When using this feature, Display Simulation is disabled, resulting in brighter highlights and shadows compared to the midtones in your scene. This is achieved through an adjusted, more linear tone curve.

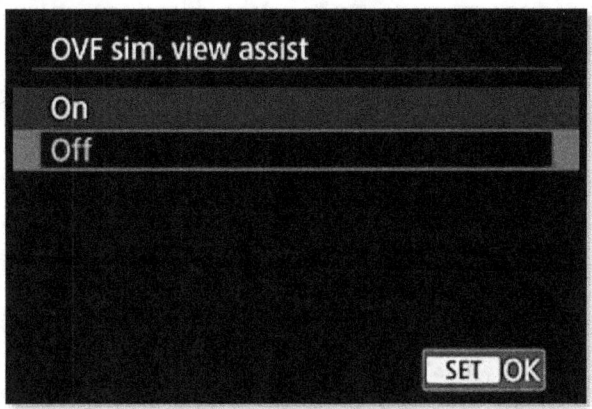

Without using OVF simulation, the EVF preview takes on a similar appearance to the JPEG version, exhibiting a narrower dynamic range and heightened contrast due to the implementation of an S-shaped tone curve. If you have a preference for the optical viewfinder aesthetic, you can try enabling the OVF simulation to see if it meets your requirements. It's important to keep in mind that when you're using an external monitor via the HDMI port, the simulation feature is disabled for both the EVF and LCD screen.

Note:

- Enabling this feature will disable the display simulation for shooting.
- When the optical viewfinder simulation is enabled, the display will show the HDR shooting feature.
- When shooting with Creative filters, the creative filter display is used, regardless of whether this feature is set to "**On**".
- The image brightness is more likely to change before and after using One-Shot AF when it is set to [On] compare to when it is set to [Off].
- The simulation of an optical viewfinder is not utilized when displaying content on external monitors, whether it is on a separate monitor or on the camera screen.
- In certain cases, the use of optical viewfinder simulation may not be available on the display, depending on the settings of the screens.

- In certain situations, the display may not have the appearance of an optical viewfinder.
- During continuous shooting, the display appearance may vary depending on the drive and shutter modes used.

High-Speed Display

- **Options:** Enable, Disable (Default)
- **RECOMMENDATIONS:** Enable

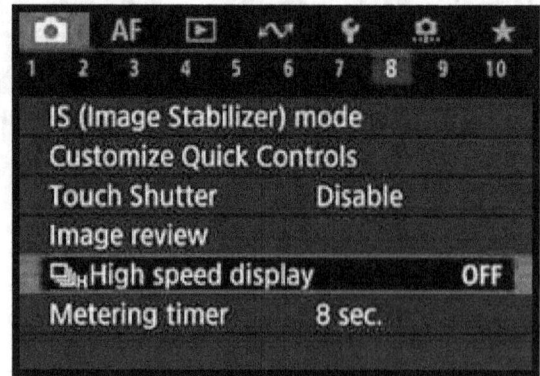

This function enables a high-speed display that is highly responsive, seamlessly transitioning between the captured image and the live view. It is always engaged when working with the electronic shutter. This tool is especially beneficial for sports photographers who need to capture fast-paced action.

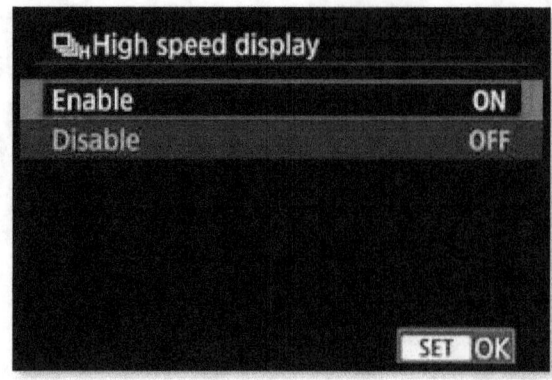

High ISO Speed Noise Reduction

- **Options:** Disable, Low, Standard (default), High, Multi Shot Noise Reduction
- **RECOMMENDATIONS:** Low, with further noise reduction as required in an image editor

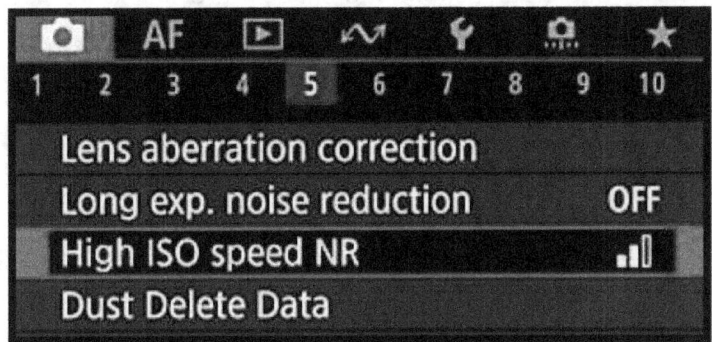

Another type of noise is caused by using higher ISO settings. With this feature, you can fine-tune the level of noise reduction applied. This is a valuable option as noise reduction can sometimes sacrifice detail while reducing noise. You have the option to choose between Standard, Low, or High noise reduction settings, or you can choose to disable noise reduction altogether. When using lower ISO values, the noise reduction feature can effectively enhance the look of shadow areas while leaving the highlights untouched. On the other hand, when shooting with higher ISO settings, the noise reduction is applied to the entire photo for a smoother result. It's important to keep in mind that selecting the High option will result in a noticeable decrease in the maximum number of continuous shots. This is due to the additional processing time required for the images.

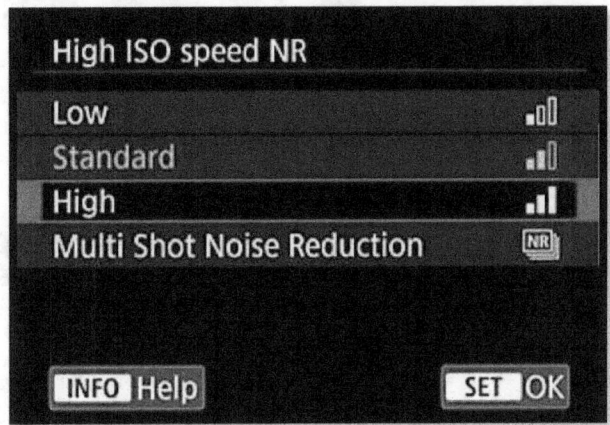

Here are the options available to you:

- **Disable**: No further noise reduction will be implemented.
- **Low**: Noise reduction is applied more sparingly. By implementing this technique, you can enhance the grainy aesthetic while retaining intricate details in the image.
- **Standard**: Noise reduction is applied to shadow areas at lower ISO values, while at higher ISO settings, it affects the entire image.
- **High**: A more aggressive noise reduction technique is employed, sacrificing a certain level of image detail, resulting in a softer appearance that may be noticeable and disliked by some. Due to the image processing used in this setting, your ability to shoot continuously in bursts will be greatly reduced.
- **Multi-Shot Noise Reduction**: Once this feature is enabled, the camera captures four consecutive shots in rapid succession. It aligns the images to account for any movement and merges them using the dark-frame subtraction technique to eliminate random pixels caused by noise, ensuring a professional result. The outcome is an image of superior quality compared to the High setting. For optimal results, it is recommended to use Multi Shot NR when the camera is securely mounted on a tripod and the subject remains still. This feature is not accessible in certain scenarios, such as when Image Quality is set to RAW or RAW+JPEG/HEIF or Dual Pixel RAW, when using flash, live view, shooting multiple or Bulb exposures, or performing auto exposure/white balance bracketing.

Frequently Asked Questions

1. What are the different shooting menu options?
2. How do you set the image quality?
3. How do you set the custom white balance?
4. How do you set the anti-flicker shooting?
5. How do you set the high-speed display?
6. How do you set the high ISO speed noise reduction function?

CHAPTER TWELVE
THE PLAYBACK AND WIRELESS MENUS

Overview

Here, you will learn the playback and wireless menus in the Canon EOS R6 Mark II and learn the various playback menu options

Playback Menu Options

The seven Playback menus are where you can choose options for the display, review, transfer, and printing of your photos. The majority of these entries consist of functions rather than settings. Consequently, only a handful of them possess specific default values. For instance, Image Jump with Main dial has a default value of 10 images, Magnification has a default value of 2X, and Control over HDMI is set to Disable by default.

Protect Images

- **Options:** Select Images, Select Range, All Images in Folder, Unprotect All Images in Folder, All Images on Card, Unprotect All Images on Card

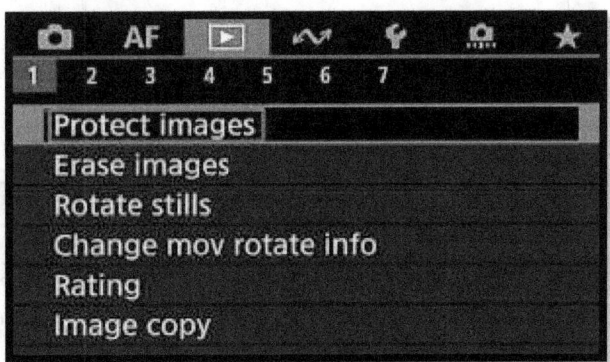

- **RECOMMENDATIONS:** Use your preferred settings.

Once an image is protected, it cannot be deleted using the camera's erase function. In order to delete a protected image, you need to first disable the protection. By removing all the images, only the protected ones will be left. This feature is incredibly useful for efficiently deleting multiple unnecessary images in one go. This entry is the first of six in the Playback 1 menu. To prevent accidental erasure of an image, you have the option to mark it for protection. This will ensure that the image remains safe and untouched, even if you press the Erase button or access the Erase Images entry in the Playback menu.

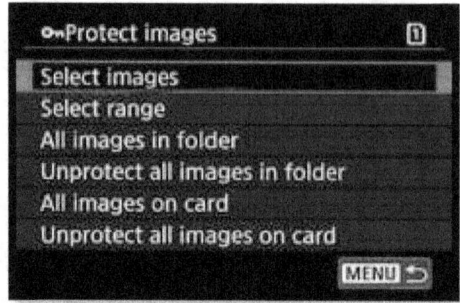

Use the Protect option found in the Playback version of the Quick Control menu (which will be explained shortly), or select this menu item. To ensure the safety of your images, simply press the **MENU button** while viewing an image and select the Protect option from the Playback 1 menu.

Erase Images

- **Options:** Select and Erase Images, Select Range, All Images in Folder, All Images on Card
- **RECOMMENDATIONS:** N/A

By selecting this menu entry, you will have access to four options: Select and Erase Images, Select Range, All Images in the Folder, and All Images on the Card. With the first three options, you can selectively remove images, while the fourth option allows you to delete all the pictures on a card. Images that are protected will not be deleted. However, using the Format command typically results in a quicker and more comprehensive outcome.

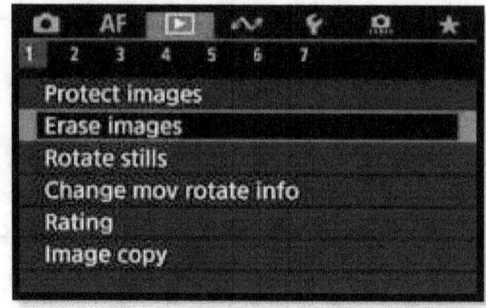

When no Image Search Conditions have been set, the default screen will appear, presenting you with the following options:

- **Choose and erase images**: Scroll through the images on your card using the left/right directional controls to view them. To mark an image for deletion or to remove a checkmark, simply press the **SET button**. Once you have made your selections, simply press the **Q button** and a confirmation prompt will appear. Select either Cancel or OK and press **SET** to complete the process.

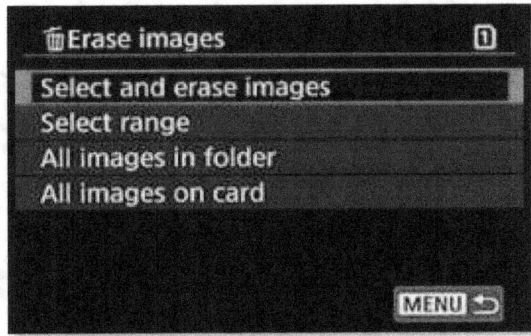

- **Select Range**: Functions like the previously mentioned range protect option. To mark the first image in a series, simply highlight it and press SET using the Select Range feature. Next, locate the final image that needs to be deleted and press the **SET button** once more. Press Q to confirm and delete the images.
- **All Images in Folder:** You will be presented with a list of the folders that are currently accessible on your memory card. Choose **SET**, and a prompt will pop up, asking for your confirmation and reminding you that protected images will not be deleted.

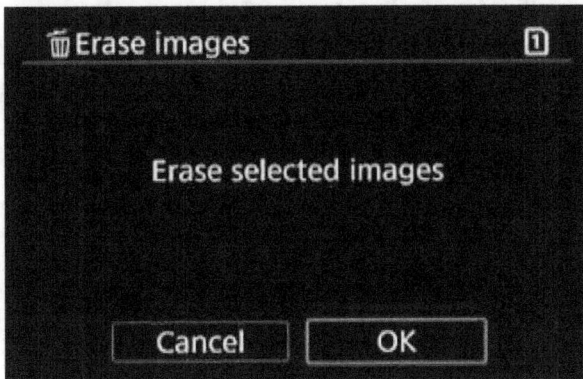

- **All Images on Card**: You will be prompted to confirm this step. All images on the card, except for the ones marked with the Protect command, will be removed when selecting the All Images on Card option. This step solely focuses on removing images and does not involve any reformatting of the memory card.

Rating

- **Options:** Select Images (Individual images, Range, All Images in Folder, All Images on Card); One to five stars, None
- **RECOMMENDATIONS:** N/A

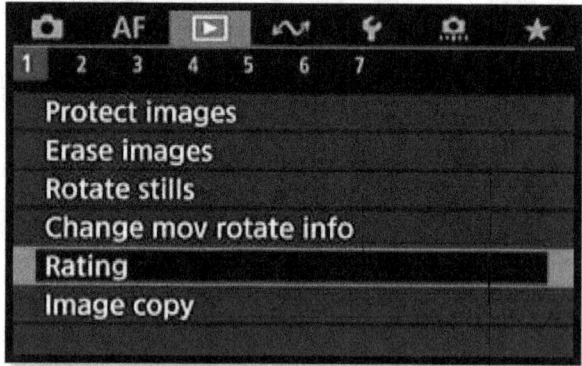

To apply a rating to your images or movies, simply press the **RATE button** multiple times during playback. This will allow you to assign a quality rating or represent other criteria. Alternatively, you can use this entry to assign ratings to images using a scale of one to five stars or disable the rating system altogether. The Image Jump function is capable of displaying images based on their rating. Imagine you were capturing the excitement of a track meet with various events.

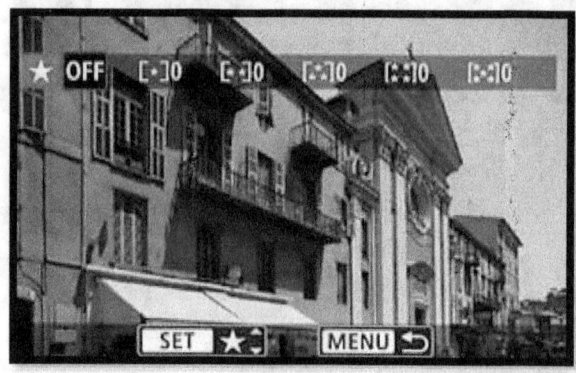

Assigning ratings to different track and field events can help provide a professional evaluation. For jumping events, a one-star rating can be applied, while relays deserve a two-star rating. Throwing events deserve three stars, hurdles warrant four stars, and dashes deserve the highest rating of five stars. Additionally, with the Image Jump feature, you can exclusively review images of a specific type.

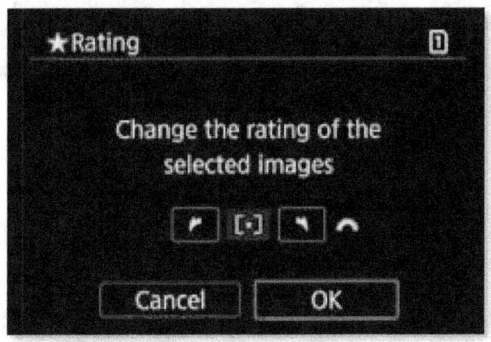

Change Movie Rotate Info

- **Options:** Change playback orientation
- **RECOMMENDATIONS:** N/A

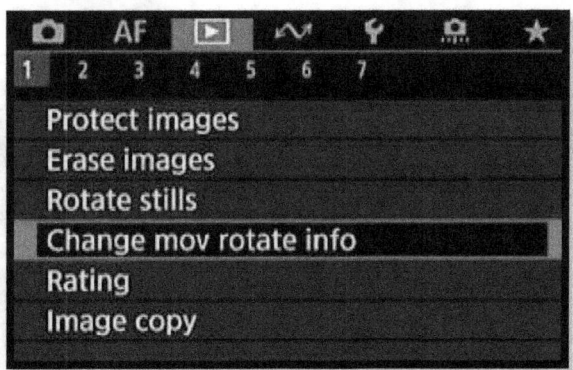

For those with experience in smartphone movie recording, it's common knowledge that the device's orientation can range from horizontal to vertical and even upside-down. With this feature, you can adjust the orientation of your camera's videos for optimal viewing on different devices. Your movies will be displayed horizontally on the camera's screen, while the option only affects how they appear on your smartphone and other devices. To activate the Add Movie Rotate Info option, navigate to the Set-up 1 menu.

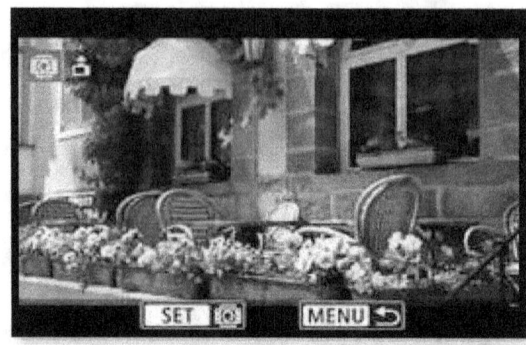

(Choosing a movie)

To select this entry from the Playback 1 menu, simply choose a movie by rotating the QCD-1. A symbol located in the upper-left corner of the screen displays an arrow that indicates the orientation of the movie frame when the video is played. With every press of the SET button, the orientation seamlessly transitions between the top (the default), right side, and left side.

RAW Processing (RAW/DPRAW)

- **Options:** Select Images, Select Range; Use Shot Settings; Set Up Processing: JPEG; Set Up Processing: HEIF
- **RECOMMENDATIONS:** Use your preferred settings.

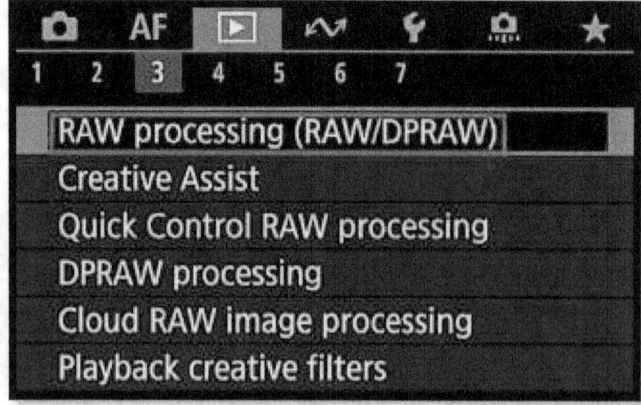

Note that this is the first entry on the Playback 3 menu page. This entry is capable of handling both Dual Pixel RAW files and standard RAW files with ease.

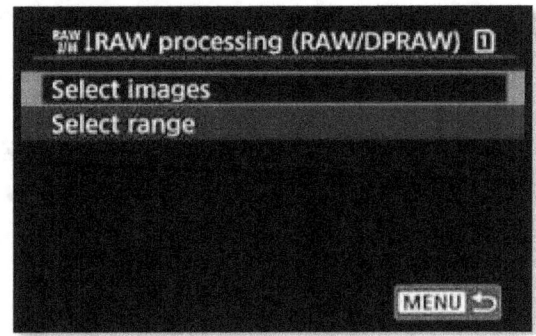

With this option, you can generate JPEG or HEIF versions of your full-size RAW images directly within the camera, excluding S RAW files. The original RAW shot remains unaltered. When you choose this menu option, you will only be shown RAW and DPRAW images that are compatible with your selection.

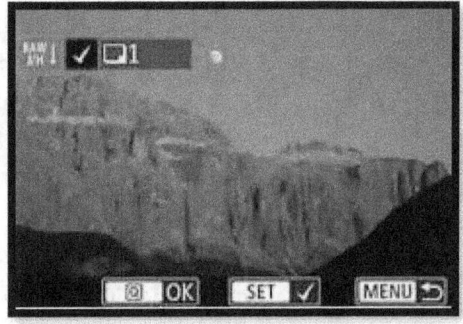

Photobook Set-up

- **Options:** Select Images, Multiple
- **RECOMMENDATIONS:** N/A

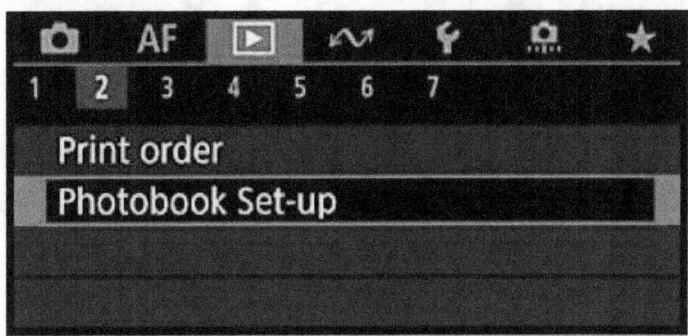

It is possible to choose a maximum of 998 images from your memory card and effortlessly transfer them to a designated folder on your computer using the EOS Utility. This method allows you to selectively transfer images to a designated folder, which is particularly beneficial when curating photos for a photobook. Unfortunately, RAW images and movies are not compatible with photobooks. **Here are the options available to you:**

- **Select images**: Select specific images from any folder on your memory card.
- **Multiple**: You have the option to select a range, choose all images in a folder, clear all in a folder, select all images on a card, or clear all on a card. be aware that the Multiple option does not include the collection of movies or RAW images.

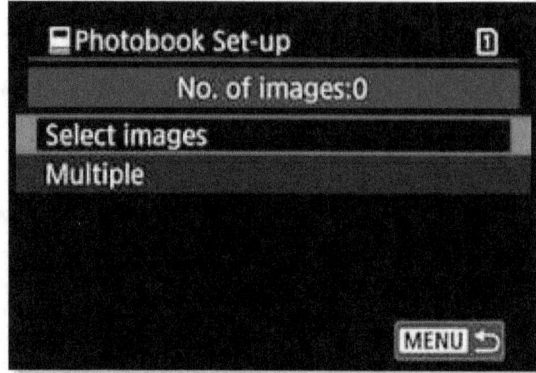

After selecting the desired images for transfer, use the EOS Utility to efficiently copy them to the designated folder.

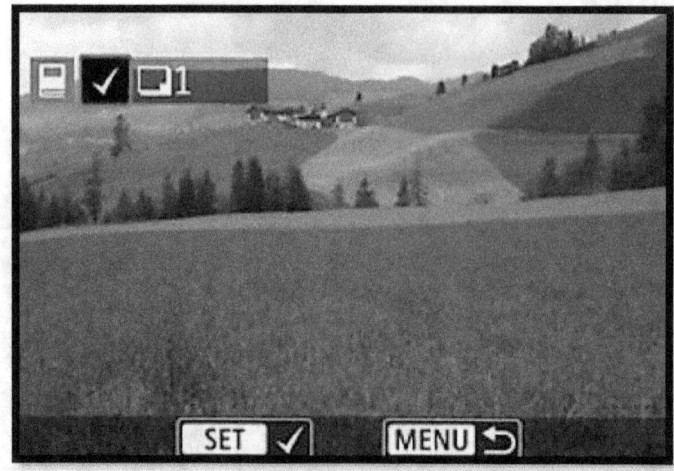

Quick Control RAW Processing

- **Options:** Creative Assist, RAW Processing
- **RECOMMENDATIONS**: N/A

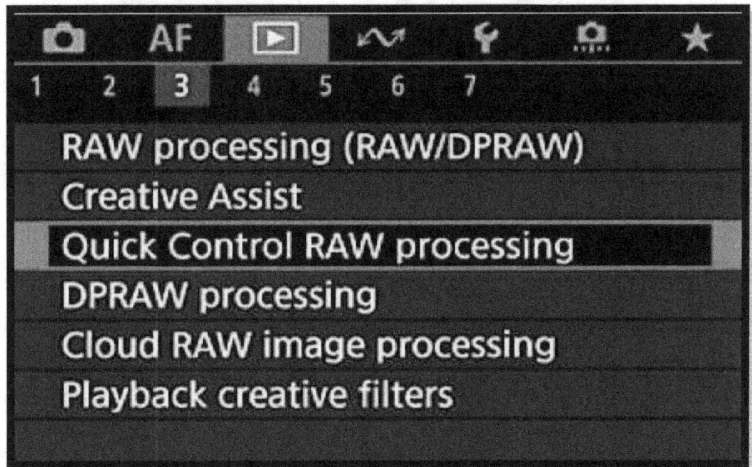

Access RAW Image Processing and Creative Assist directly from the Playback version of the Quick Controls screen. You can indicate which of the two is currently active with this entry.

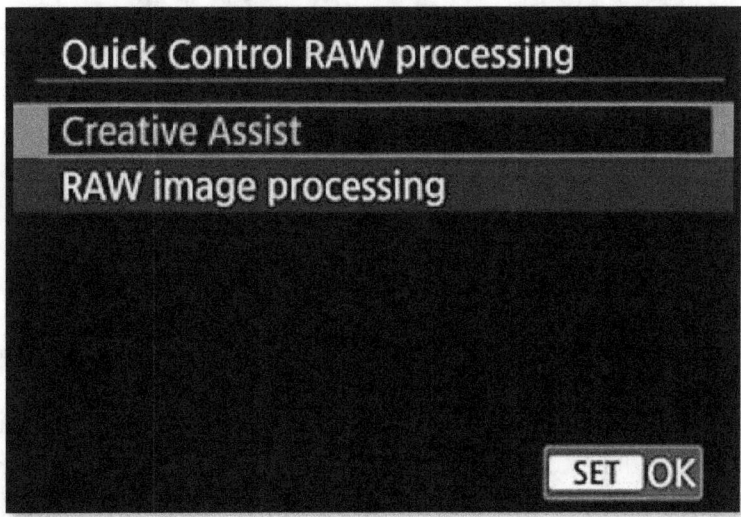

The Creative Assist icon is typically found in the Quick Controls screen, positioned as the second icon from the bottom in the right column.

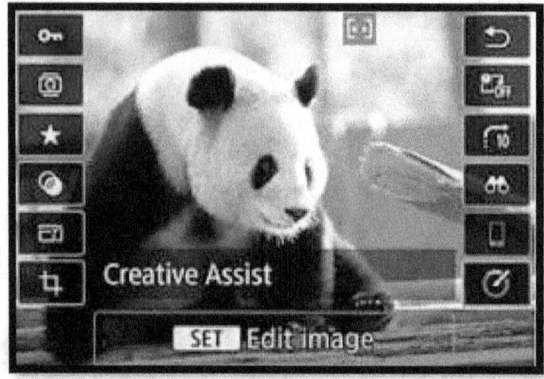

To call for the RAW processing instead, simply highlight it on the screen that appears when you access this menu, and press **SET** like a pro.

Cloud RAW Image Processing

- **Options:** Quantity Selected, Processing Capacity, Last Updated, Check Processing Capacity (Refresh), Add Images to Process, Check/Remote Selected Images, [Send]
- **RECOMMENDATIONS:** N/A

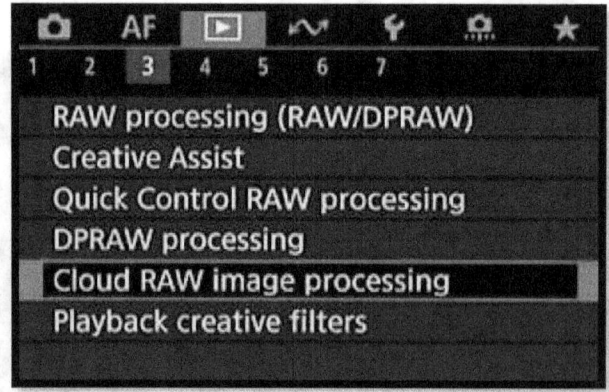

From a technical standpoint, it's worth noting that this particular menu entry is not considered an official R6 II feature. This feature serves as a gateway to Canon's subscription service, offering cloud-based RAW image processing that surpasses the camera's internal capabilities. This service uses advanced neural network processing to effectively reduce noise, false color, moiré, and jagged lines, and perform various other functions. According to Canon, the service is particularly useful for optimizing images like night scenes and astronomical shots captured at high ISO, images taken in low-light conditions with a moving subject, images featuring fine stripes, and images showcasing buildings with tile or brick patterns.

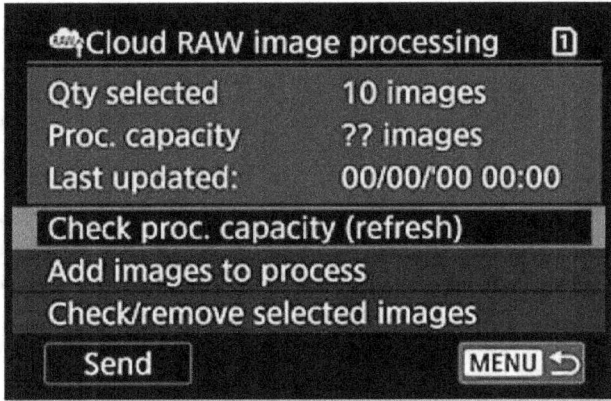

RAW images and processed images will be securely stored in Canon's cloud storage for 30 days, maintaining their original quality. You have the option to effortlessly transfer them to your computer or other services like Google Photos. An account on image.canon is free, but to access Cloud RAW Image Processing, a monthly subscription fee of $4.99 is required. This subscription allows you to process up to 80 images. If you exhaust your monthly allowance, you have the option to purchase additional processing in increments of 80 images for $4.99 each.

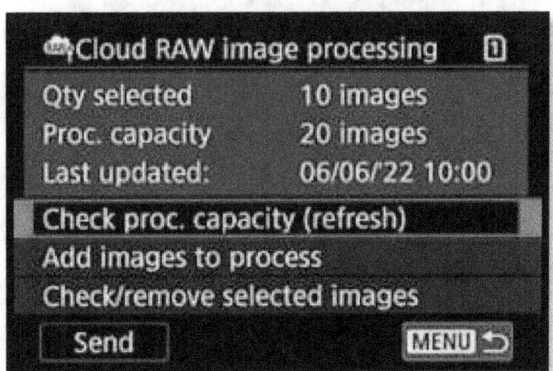

This menu option allows you to conveniently monitor your account status, choose images, and effortlessly transmit them to the Canon server when your R6 II is connected to the Internet. Once the processing is complete, Canon will promptly send you an email to inform you that your images are ready.

HEIF→JPEG Conversion

- **Options:** Convert to JPEG

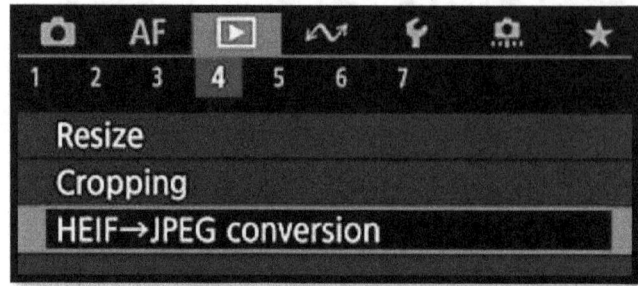

If you require a conventional image, it is possible to convert HEIF images taken with HDR Shooting and PQ (perceptual quantization) enabled to JPEG format. Choose this menu option to exclusively view HDR images that are compatible.

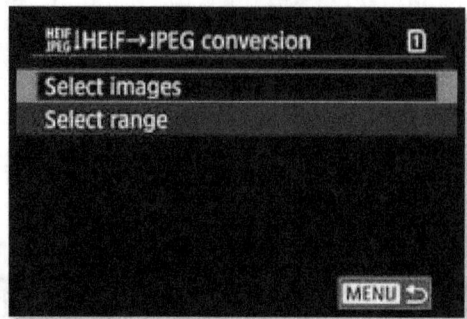

When you press **SET**, a message will pop up saying "**Converting to JPEG**." After that, you will see a prompt asking you to save the file as a new one. It's as simple as that. The original file remains unaltered.

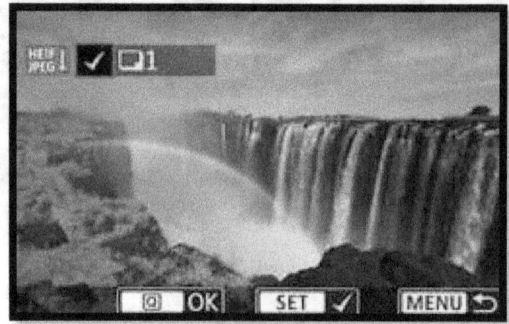

Magnification

- **Options:** 2X (default), 4X, 8X, 10X, Actual size, Same as last magnification
- **RECOMMENDATIONS:** Same as last magnification

You can set the initial magnification for the magnified view during playback and choose the starting position on the screen. Select your initial magnification level based on the frequency with which you typically examine your images up close during the review process. If you have a keen eye for detail, you may prefer a thorough 10X view whenever you zoom in on your image. **Here are the available options:**

Magnification. There are three options available to you:

- **2X, 4X, 8X, 10X, starting from the center of the frame**: Choose the initial magnified view to be either 2X, 4X, 8X, or 10X, centered around the middle of the frame.
- **Actual size (from a selected point)**: The magnified view begins at 100 percent and is centered on the auto-focus point that was used to achieve focus. If manual focus was used, the image would be centered in the middle of the frame.
- **Same as last magnification (from the center point):** The camera uses the magnification value that was previously selected, with the focus centered around the middle of the frame.

Magnified Position. This sets the starting point for applying magnification. You have the option to select either From the Centre or Focus Point.

Maintain position. One option is to keep your current position in the frame while browsing images. It can be quite handy when you need to compare the same area of an image, such as a subject's face, in a series of consecutive shots.

Switch Main Dial/Quick Control Dial 2

- **Options:** Disable: Main dial: Image Jump, Quick Control dial 2: Magnify/Index view (default); Enable: Main dial: Magnify/Index view, Quick Control dial 2: Image Jump
- **RECOMMENDATIONS:** Default

With this setting, you have the option to switch the functions of the Main dial and QCD-2, giving you more control over your device. By default, the Main dial smoothly transitions between images on playback, based on the Jump method you've chosen. The QCD-2 allows for precise image adjustments, seamlessly transitioning between zoomed-in views and full-frame or index views. Select the "**Enable**" option to switch each of these behaviors to the other dial.

Highlight Alert

- **Options:** Enable, Disable (default)
- **RECOMMENDATIONS:** Enable

Select the Enable option to have the LCD screen blink on overexposed highlight areas during picture review, commonly referred to as "**blinkies**". If you find this alert distracting, you can set it to disable. Experienced users often use the histogram displays while playing back footage for a more accurate assessment of overexposure and underexposure.

HDMI HDR Output

- **Options:** Off, On (default)
- **RECOMMENDATIONS:** N/A

With this feature, you can effortlessly enjoy the stunning quality of RAW or HEIF images on your HDR TV by simply connecting your camera with an HDMI cable. Television innovations come and go, but Canon is always staying ahead of the game, constantly keeping up with the latest trends. Unlike 3D TV, which faced challenges with content availability and consumer interest and eventually faded away by 2018, High Dynamic Range (HDR) TV has proven to be a lasting innovation. If your current television lacks HDR, your next one will probably come equipped with it, along with a 4K display. With this capability, you can effortlessly showcase your camera's RAW images on your impressive new display. They will appear impressive (according to others). For optimal viewing, it's important to ensure that your TV is HDR-compatible and that the input settings are properly configured to display HDR images. When viewing HDR output from your camera, certain features like RAW processing may not be accessible. When displaying multiple-exposure RAW images and photos shot with the L (ISO 50 equivalent) sensitivity setting, the camera will send JPEG images to your HDR TV.

AF Point Disp.

- **Options:** Enable, Disable (default)
- **RECOMMENDATIONS:** N/A

Choose **Enable**, and the precise AF point(s) used to establish focus will be visually emphasized in red. If you used automatic AF point selection, you might notice that multiple points are highlighted.

Frequently Asked Questions

1. What are the different playback menu options?
2. How do you set the option to protect images?
3. How do you set up photobook?
4. How do you erase images?
5. How do you change movie rotate info?
6. How do you set the cloud RAW image processing function?

CHAPTER THIRTEEN
SET-UP MENU

Overview

Learn everything there is to know about the setup menu in the Canon EOS R6 Mark II and know how you can implement them.

File Numbering

- **Options:** Numbering: Continuous (default), Automatic Reset; Manual Reset
- **RECOMMENDED:** Continuous

Each picture you capture will be assigned a unique file number, ensuring a seamless and organized system for all your photos. This numbering system remains consistent across various memory cards, restarting anew when a new card is inserted or when you manually reset the numbers. Numbers are assigned sequentially, ranging from 0001 to 9999. Once the count reaches 9999, the camera automatically generates a new folder on the card, starting with folder 100. This allows for a continuous numbering system, with folder 100 containing files numbered from 0001 to 9999, and the count restarting in folder 101.

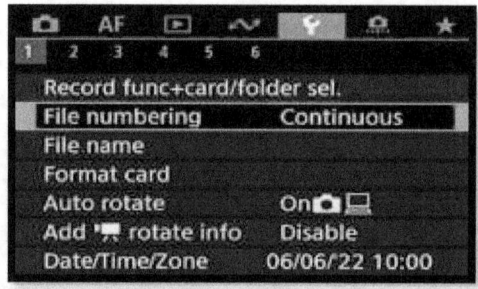

The camera efficiently maintains a record of the most recent number used in its internal memory. It's important to be aware of a few quirks that may arise.

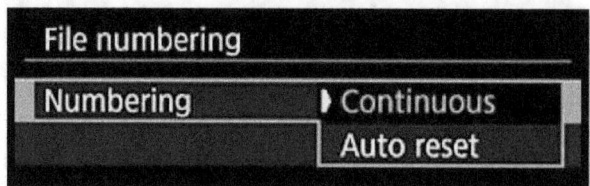

At first glance, the numbering system appears straightforward: Within the menu, you have the option to select Continuous, Automatic Reset, or Manual Reset. **Allow me to explain how each of them functions:**

- **Continuous**: When using a blank or reformatted memory card, the system will assign a number that is one higher than the number stored in the camera's internal memory. When the card is not blank and has images, the next number will be incremented by one compared to the highest number on the card or in internal memory. To ensure consistent continuous file numbering, it is essential to always use a blank or freshly formatted card.
- **Automatic Reset**: When using a blank or reformatted memory card, the subsequent photo captured will be assigned the number 0001. When using a non-blank card, the subsequent number will be incremented by one compared to the highest number recorded on the memory card. Whenever a memory card is inserted, the subsequent number will be either 0001 or one digit higher than the current highest number on the card. Keep in mind that if your Folder number reaches 999 (which could mean a significant number of folders on one card!) and that folder contains 9999 images, you won't be able to keep shooting until you swap out the card for a new one.
- **Manual Reset:** A new folder is created with a higher number than the previous one, and it resets the file numbers to 0001. The camera will use the numbering scheme that has been selected, whether it is Continuous or Automatic Reset, whenever a new memory card is inserted, regardless of whether it is blank or contains data. During a manual reset, you have the opportunity to customize the folder name instead of using the default CANON or any other five-character name you have previously set.

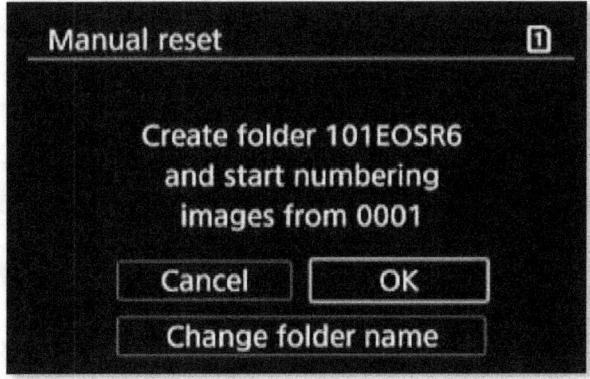

File Name

- **Options:** Change User Setting 1, Change User Setting 2
- **RECOMMENDATIONS:** Use your preferred settings.

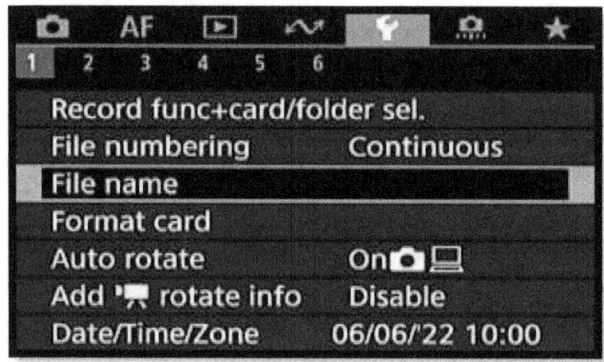

File names are composed of four alphanumeric characters, followed by a four-digit file number and file extension. You can change the initial four alphanumeric characters, which are originally assigned to each camera and established during the camera's shipment. The file name consists of a four-digit alphanumeric string, followed by the four-digit image number. Examples of these file names include BE3B0001.jpg, BE3B001.hif, or BE3B0001.cr3. The initial four characters are preconfigured during the manufacturing process and are exclusive to your camera. Additionally, you have the option to create two custom User Settings: Setting 1, which allows for four characters of your choosing, and Setting 2, which allows for three characters. With this menu option, you can modify the names assigned to your photos. However, it is important to keep in mind that there are specific limitations that must be adhered to. When it comes to making changes to file names, there are certain rules and industry conventions that professionals follow. In this case, you can modify four out of the eight characters in the file name, specifically the BE3B (or the equivalent on your camera), according to the guidelines set by the Design Rule for Camera File System (DCF) specification. The DCF standard restricts file names generated by compliant digital cameras. These names are limited to a maximum of eight characters, along with a three-character extension (e.g., .jpg, .hif, or cr3) that indicates the file format. Out of the eight available characters, four are used to indicate the type of camera employed in creating the image, more professionally. Canon will automatically use the initial four characters that were set at the factory. The remaining four digits are used for numbers ranging from 0000 to 9999. This explains why the numbering "rolls over" to aaaa0000 once the limit of 9999 numbers is reached. **When the camera is manufactured, it is set up to offer three different file-naming options:**

- **Factory Preset Code**: This feature is exclusive to your camera. Each camera is equipped with its unique preset code. When enabled, your images will be automatically assigned names such as aaaa0001.jpg when using the sRGB color space. When you switch to Adobe RGB, the industry convention is to replace the first character with an underline, resulting in file names like _EOS0001.jpg or _EOS001.cr3. This feature is quite impressive; allowing you to easily identify which of your multiple R6 II cameras (although unlikely) was used to capture a specific image.

- **User Settings 1**: This is one of two customizable naming schemes. By default, the camera is programmed to save images as IMG_0001.jpg/cr3/mov (for video) when using the sRGB color space. Alternatively, it will save them as _IMG0001.jpg, etc., when using Adobe RGB. On the other hand, if you want to achieve a more professional look, you have the option to customize all four initial characters for this setting. By doing so, you can have a file name like EOSR0001.jpg instead, especially when working with sRGB. When using Adobe RGB, the first characters in the file name are still replaced by the underscore. When selecting OHIO, you will find OHIO0001.jpg for sRGB and _HIO0001.jpg for Adobe RGB.

- **User Setting 2**: With this customizable setting, you have the option to indicate just the first three characters out of the initial four. IMG is the default for those characters. The camera uses the fourth position to indicate the code that represents the quality of the image recording. If your initial three letters are ABC, you could have file names such as _BCL0001.jpg or ABCL001.jpg.

Format Card

- **Options:** Format Card, Low-Level Format
- **RECOMMENDATIONS:** Use your preferred settings.

Use this item to wipe clean your memory card and establish a pristine file system, fully prepared for use. Upon selecting Format Card, a display will appear, giving you the option to choose between Card 1 or Card 2. Once you have selected your card, a screen will appear showing the card's capacity and the amount of space currently in use. At the bottom of the screen, you will find two options: Cancel or OK to proceed with the format. If you wish to perform a low-level format, simply press the Trash button. This is a simplified format that eliminates all sectors on the card and generates new ones. This can enhance the performance of a slow card by eliminating any "**bad**" sectors that may have been left behind from previous use. A progress bar will be displayed on the screen to indicate the formatting step.

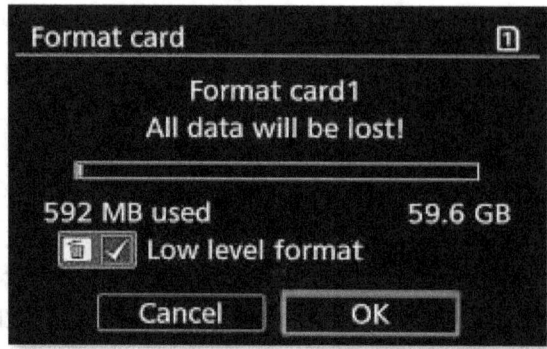

Add Movie Rotate Information

- **Options:** Enable, Disable (default)
- **RECOMMENDATIONS:** Disable if you don't transfer your video to smart devices often.

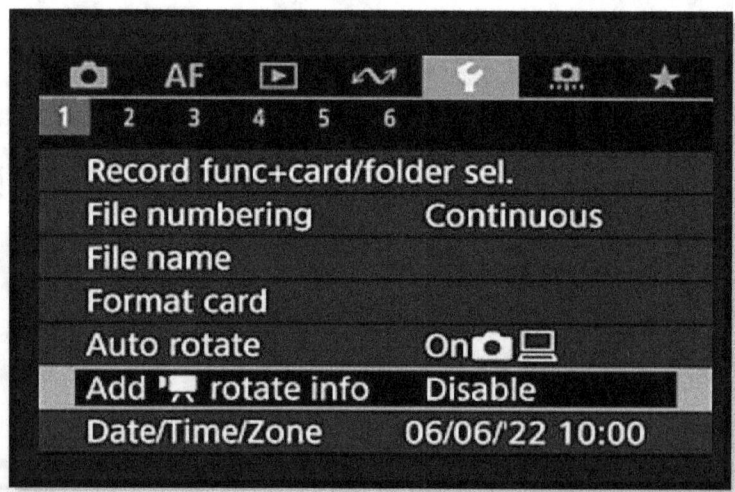

With this feature, you can effortlessly include orientation indicators in your video clips, ensuring seamless playback on any device. This setting does not affect video playback on the camera or when using an external monitor connected via an HDMI cable.

Date/Time/Zone

- **Options:** Date, Time, Zone, Daylight Savings
- **RECOMMENDATIONS:** Use your preferred settings

Use this feature to configure the date and time settings, which will be automatically included in the image file along with exposure details and additional data.

Here are the steps to set the date and time:

1. To access this menu entry, navigate to the Set-up 1 menu.
2. Adjust the QCD-1 to shift the highlighting to the Date/Time entry.
3. To access the Date/Time setting screen, simply press the **SET button** located in the center of the QCD-1.
4. Adjust the QCD-1 to choose the desired value for modification. To adjust the desired format, press the **SET button** when the gold box highlights the month, day, year, hour, minute, or second. A set of triangles appears above the value, one pointing up and the other pointing down.
5. Adjust the value up or down by rotating the QCD-1. Press the **SET button** to confirm the value you have entered.
6. Perform steps 4 and 5 for each of the remaining values you wish to modify. You have the option to change the date format to yy/mm/dd or dd/mm/yy instead of the default mm/dd/yy. Additionally, you can toggle Daylight Savings time and select the most suitable time zone.
7. After completing the task, you can rotate the QCD-1 to choose between the options of OK (if you are happy with your modifications) or Cancel (if you prefer to go back to the Set-up 2 menu without making any alterations). Press the **SET button to** confirm your selection.
8. After you have successfully set the date and time, you can either press the **MENU button** to exit or simply tap the shutter release.

Auto Rotate

- **Options:** On: Camera, Computer (default); On: Computer Only; Off
- **RECOMMENDATIONS:** Camera+Computer

You have the option to enable or disable this feature. When enabled, the display screen automatically rotates vertical pictures, allowing for comfortable viewing without having to physically adjust the camera. On the other hand, this orientation results in the image being displayed with its longest dimension using the shortest dimension of the display, resulting in a size reduction. There are three options available to you. The image can be automatically rotated when viewed in the camera or on your computer screen using your image-editing/viewing software.

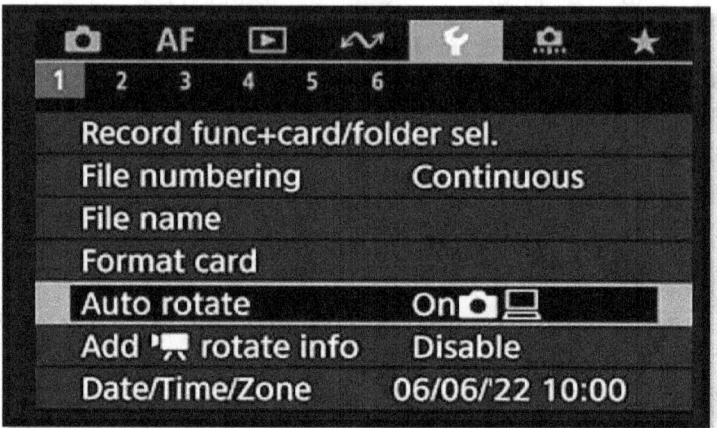

This option is indicated by a pair of camera and computer screen icons. You can enable auto rotation for your images by using your image editor or viewing software. Simply look for the computer screen icon to access this feature. This feature enables you to effortlessly rotate your computer screen while still being able to fully maximize the image on your camera display. Off is the third option available. The image will remain in its original orientation when viewed on the camera or computer. It is important to keep in mind that disabling the Auto Rotate feature will prevent any pictures taken during that time from automatically rotating when you re-enable Auto Rotate. The decision to apply autorotation is based on the information embedded in the image file at the time the photo is captured.

Language

- **Options:** 29 languages
- **RECOMMENDATIONS:** Use your preferred language.

This entry is the first one on the Set-up 2 page. Select from a wide range of 29 languages for menu display. Use the Quick Control Dial 1 or the multi-controller joystick to easily navigate and highlight your desired language. Activate by pressing the **SET button**.

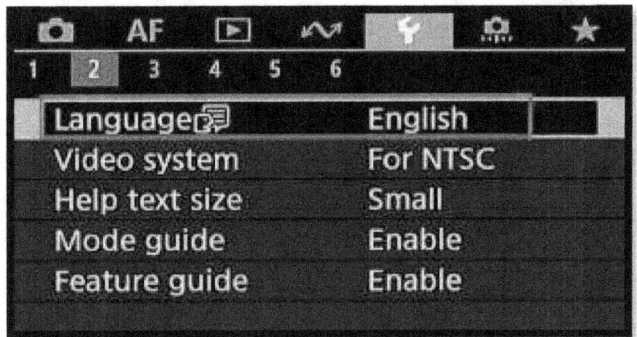

Video System

- **Options:** For NTSC, For PAL
- **RECOMMENDATIONS:** N/A

This setting allows you to control the output through the HDMI cable when you are displaying images on an external monitor. There are two options available for selection: NTSC, commonly used in the United States, Canada, Mexico, and many Central, South American, and Caribbean countries, as well as various Asian countries and other nations, or PAL, which is used in the UK, a significant portion of Europe, Africa, India, China, and certain parts of the Middle East.

Mode Guide

- **Options:** Enable (default), Disable
- **RECOMMENDATIONS:** Disable

When Mode Guide is activated, a professional-looking graphic screen will appear every time you rotate the Mode dial to a different setting. This screen will give you a concise description of the specific mode's functionality. Its usefulness diminishes after the initial weeks of camera ownership. Once you have familiarized yourself with the new mode, you can start working with it right away without any further reminders. To access the Quick Controls screen for Scene Intelligent Auto, SCN, or Creative Filter modes when the Mode Guide is disabled, simply press the **Q/SET button** after selecting the corresponding Mode dial position.

Feature Guide

- **Options:** Enable (default), Disable

- **RECOMMENDATIONS:** Disable

When activated, it provides a concise explanation of the features of the choices in the Quick Control screen. Once you become familiar with your R6 II, you'll find that the Mode Guide becomes unnecessary.

Beep

- **Options:** Enable (default), Disable
- **RECOMMENDATIONS:** Disable

This entry is the initial option in the Set-up 3 menu. A built-in beeper emits a useful chirp to indicate different functions, including the countdown of your camera's self-timer, when an image is in focus, and during touch operations. If you prefer, you have the option to completely turn it off to avoid the beep, which can be bothersome, rude, disruptive (such as at a concert or museum), or simply unwanted for any other reason. On the Beep screen, select the option to activate or disable the beeps according to your preference. Press the **SET button** to confirm your selection and exit.

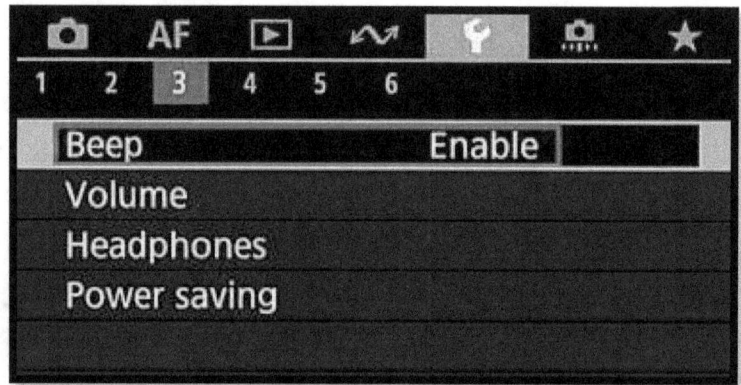

Choose the USB Connection App

- **Options:** Photo Import/Remote Control, Canon App(s) for iPhone
- **RECOMMENDATIONS:** N/A

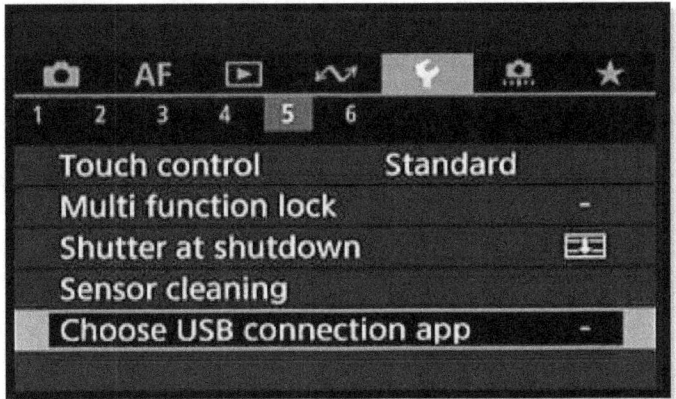

This entry will guide you on how to transfer images to an Android or iOS smartphone or computer using a compatible USB cable, just like a professional. Opt for Photo Import/Remote Control to use computer applications like EOS Utility, dedicated Android applications accessible from the Google Play Store, or the Apple iOS version of Photos.

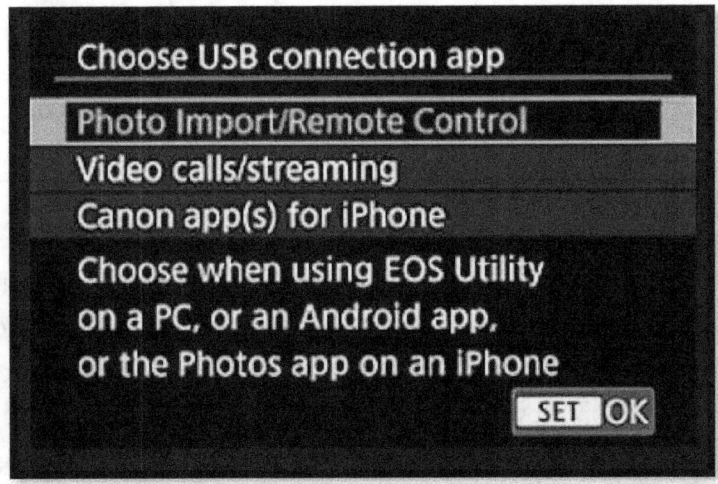

If you plan on connecting your camera to your iPhone using a USB cable, consider using the Canon App(s) for iPhone.

Custom Shooting Mode (C1–C3)

- **Options:** Register Settings; Clear Settings; Auto Update Settings: Enable, Disable
- **RECOMMENDATIONS:** Any settings work just fine.

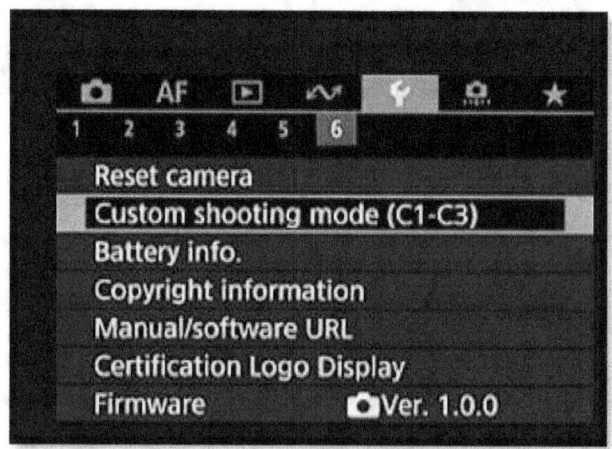

Reset Camera commands do not cancel Custom Shooting modes. With this feature, you can effortlessly save and retrieve your preferred camera shooting settings by assigning them to the C1, C2, or C3 positions. Simply press the MODE button to access them whenever you need. This action will overwrite any previously stored settings at that position. Additionally, you have the option to individually reset the settings for any of the three MODE positions, restoring them to their original factory default values. Save your preferred settings to easily access them in specific situations. If you switch to C1, C2, or C3 and happen to forget the settings you've made for that slot, simply press the INFO button to easily view the current settings. Note that My Menu settings are not stored individually. There is a single roster of My Menu entries that is accessible across all the positions on the Mode dial. There are three options available in this menu: Register Settings, Clear Settings, and Auto Update Settings. Register Settings allows you to store your current settings in either C1, C2, or C3. Clear Settings, on the other hand, erase the settings in C1, C2, or C3. Lastly, there is Auto Update Settings. Enabling this option allows you to save any modifications you make to your settings in C1, C2, or C3 modes. On the other hand, disabling it will keep your registered settings unchanged, disregarding any adjustments you made while using the Custom Shooting mode. It is important to use this menu entry to clear your settings.

To complete these tasks, simply follow these steps:

1. Configure your settings. Choose a different exposure mode on the camera, not Scene Intelligent Auto.
2. Access the user settings for the camera. Go to the Custom shooting mode option in the Set-up 6 menu and press **SET** with expertise.

3. Select a function. If you wish to save your camera's current settings in C1, C2, or C3, opt for Register Settings. On the other hand, if you want to remove the settings stored in either location, go for Clear Settings. To access the settings screen for your choice, press SET.

4. Manage your settings. The screens for storing and clearing are almost indistinguishable. Use the QCD-1 to effectively emphasize the Custom Shooting Modes: C1, C2, or C3. Simply press SET to conveniently store or clear the settings for that particular position. (You will have the option to proceed or cancel initially.)

5. Automatic updates. It is important to remember that if you make adjustments to a setting while using a custom shooting mode, your saved settings can be automatically updated to reflect the changes. Choose the **Auto Update Set** and select **Enable** to activate this option. If you prefer to keep your custom settings until you choose to update them manually, choose the **Disable option** instead.

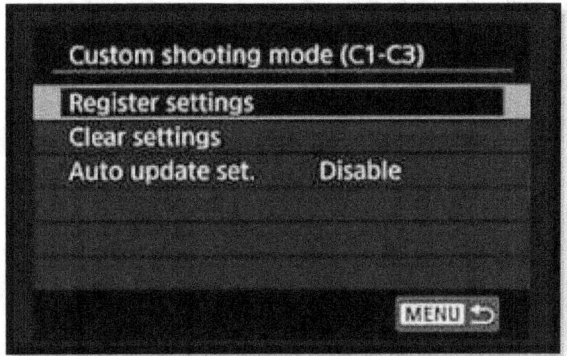

6. After confirming, you will be directed back to the Set-up 6 menu. To exit the menu system entirely, you can either press the **MENU button** or simply tap the shutter release button.

Frequently Asked Questions

1. What are the different set up menu functions?
2. How do you set the file name?
3. How do you set the file numbering?
4. How do you set the date and time zone?
5. How do you add movie rotate information?

CONCLUSION

In line with its competitors, the Canon EOS R6 II offers exceptional image quality. It also stands out among its peers with its precise autofocus and impressive video shooting capabilities. This combination is highly appealing; with superior autofocus compared to the Nikon Z6 II and a video quality that surpasses the Sony a7 IV. The sensor of the R6 MKII is highly competitive with other cameras available in the market, surpassing them in terms of High ISO performance and color fidelity. One standout feature of this camera is its impressive shooting speed of up to 40fps, along with the ability to pre-buffer bursts. This allows you to effortlessly capture those crucial moments with ease. The rolling shutter of this device may not be optimal for capturing extremely fast movement, but it is still quite useful in practical situations. The EOS R6 II is a pleasure to use, going beyond just its impressive specs and capabilities. The menus are extensive, yet the grip is ergonomically designed for comfort. The controls are thoughtfully positioned, and careful attention has been paid to the number of control points required. It exudes a sense of expertise as if it has been meticulously crafted by individuals with extensive experience in the field of photography.

INDEX

(

(QCD-1) Quick Control Dial 1, 44
(QCD-2) Quick Control Dial 2, 44

1

140 CRAW files, 4
1-Point AF, 45, 95
1-point autofocus, 37

2

2 shots, 70
24.2MP full-frame sensor, 1

4

40fps shooting, 2

5

580EX, 145, 149, 150, 151, 152, 153, 154

A

A Tiny Slice of Time, 106
ability to save settings individually, 7
about mastering the focus mode, 85
absolute darkness, 77
AC Adapter Kit AC-E6N, 31
Accentuates camera shakiness, 129
acceptable level of noise in the image, 61
access lamp, 21
Access lamp, 46
accessible surface, 32
accessing the onscreen quick menu, 8
Accessory positioning holes, 50
Accessory shoe, 50
accidental damage, 33
account on image.canon, 186

accurate color reproduction, 9
achieve a blur effect caused by subject motion, 63
achieve a professional-looking effect, 63
achieve flawless results, 74
achieve sharp focus, 36, 84, 88
achieving precise color accuracy in-camera, 69
achieving proper exposure, 57
action-packed moments, 1
activate automatic sensor, 28
activate automatic sensor cleaning, 28
activate back-button focus, 104
activated with ISO expansion, 67
active focus points, 36
Actual size, 188
adapted manual-focus lenses, 4
Adapting to flexible priority (Fv), 65
Add Movie Rotate Information, 195
Added controls, 41
adding an "**interesting**" texture, 67
addition of exposure compensation, 8
additional directional operations, 44
additional shutter release, 32
Add-on Speedlite, 30
adequate depth of field., 63
Adequate maximum aperture, 118
adjust exposure with ISO settings, 56, 84
adjust the AF/MF selector, 36
Adjust the camera's contrast setting, 79
Adjust the contrast of the scene, 79
adjust the exposure, 60, 64, 65, 68, 73, 80, 109, 141
adjust the orientation and tilt of the screen, 22
Adjust the screen to a different position., 22
Adjusting Diopter Correction with expertise, 33
adjusting exposure settings, 6, 122
Adjusting Exposure with ISO Settings, 66
adjusting the contrast of the scene, 79
adjusting the ISO, 58, 64, 66, 130
adjusting the shutter speed, 69
adjustment of ISO speeds for still images, 66
adjustments for camera shooting functions, 52
adjustments made, 52
adjustments to the exposure, 12, 57, 58
adoption of mirrorless technology, 85
advanced intelligent subject detection, 1

advanced subject recognition, 2
advanced subject recognition autofocus system, 2
ADVANCED TECHNIQUES, 105
advanced techniques including continuous
    shooting, 105
Advantage, 132, 133
**Advantage - Lighting preview—Continuous
    lighting**, 132
AE lock/FE lock, 32, 51, 93
AE/FE, 45
AF (autofocus) and the stabilizer switch, 33
AF area, 8, 37, 45, 88, 89, 95, 97, 99
AF Area, 10, 95
AF menu, 35, 44
AF Menu Defaults, 53
AF multi-controller joystick, 6
AF operation, 36, 96, 97
AF Operation, 36, 92
AF Pixel Layout, 88
AF Point Disp., 189
AF point movement, 45
AF point selection button, 37, 45, 49, 95, 96, 114
AF point selection controls, 32
AF tracking, 3, 11
AF/MF switch, 82, 98
AF-assist beam, 81, 100, 142
affordable model, 1
affordable RF lenses, 7
AF-ON, 32, 44, 92, 102, 103
AI Focus, 93, 94, 97
All Images in Folder, 176, 177, 178, 179
All Images on Card, 176, 177, 179
allowing users to control their cameras remotely
    over Wi-Fi, 5
analyze your image and select the optimal
    exposure, 35
Anatomy of the Menus, 155
Android and iOS devices, 5
animals, 3, 11, 37, 75, 95, 97
Animals, 97
Anti-Flicker Shooting, 163, 164, 165
Aperture priority, 62
Aperture-priority, 58, 59, 61, 62, 84, 139, 141, 143
Aperture-priority mode, 58, 139, 143
Aperture-Priority Mode, 62
apparent size of the light source, 57
applying noise reduction, 12
appropriate shutter speed, 59, 67
approximately 3 percent of the image area, 35
APS-C cameras, 31

articulated design, 9
assess exposure with precision, 9
astigmatism, 130
Attach the protective cover, 15
Auto Detecting, 164, 166, 167
auto exposure/flash exposure, 45
Auto Image Align is activated, 74
Auto Lighting Optimizer, 52, 75, 79, 81
Auto Lighting Optimizer Off, 52
Auto or Manual Focus?, 85
Auto Picture Style, 81
Auto range, 66
Auto Rotate, 196, 197
Autofocus, 42, 49, 54, 81, 87, 100, 101, 155
autofocus and impressive, 203
Autofocus area selection mode, 49
autofocus mode, 36, 81, 87, 92, 99, 105
autofocus points, 13
autofocus remains operational, 3
Autofocus/Manual, 42
Autofocus/Manual focus switch, 42
automatic and manual focus., 42
automatic exposure bracketing, 69, 72
automatic HDR modes, 76
Automatic ISO, 52
Automatic Reset, 191, 192
Automatic White Balance, 52
automation like Scene Intelligent Auto, 65
Av mode, 62, 63, 65, 67, 69, 140
available include PASM, 13
available ISO speeds, 66
available option, 8, 76
available settings, 34
avoid potential wide-angle problems, 131
avoid sync-speed problems, 146
avoid telephoto lens problems, 131
**Avoid using high shutter speeds in conjunction
    with electronic flash**, 107
Avoiding Potential Wide-Angle Problems, 128
Avoiding Sync-Speed Problems, 138

B

Back-Button Focus, 101, 102
background's vertical lines, 12
back-panel LCD monitor, 30
basic navigation, 34
Batteries gradually lose their charge over time, 15
battery charger, 16
battery compartment, 17, 41, 51

Battery compartment cover, 51
Battery compartment cover/lock/door/door
    release, 51
Battery Grip BG-R10, 32
battery is running out of power quickly, 16
Battery life lasts for approximately 450 shots, 13
Battery Pack LP-E6NH, 29
Battery Power, 6
Battery Removal Procedure, 18
battery's recharge performance, 16
beautiful bokeh effects, 120
becomes increasingly apparent in the level, 13
becoming increasingly popular among creative
    photographers, 85
Beep, 93, 199
Begin by opening the cover., 20
Black-and-white photos, 78
blue sticker on the battery, 15
body-only option, 2
bracketed shots, 70, 72
Bracketing Auto Cancel, 71, 73
bracketing for exposure, 52
Bracketing is a technique used by photographers to
    capture multiple exposures, 69
Bracketing Parameters, 69
Bracketing Sequence, 70
brand-new camera straight, 28
breathtaking 6K RAW video, 1
bright conditions, 9
Build and Handling, 6
building quality., 6
Bulb exposures, 109, 175

C

calculate exposure with precision, 59
Camera & Imaging Products Association, 31
camera and prompt, 39
camera and various devices, 5
camera bag, 33, 119
camera captures footage, 12
Camera cover RF-5, 29
camera determine the optimal aperture, 59
camera features a high-resolution, 1
camera offers a range of settings to work, 81
camera settings like Drive mode, 53
camera shake, 63, 74, 83, 84, 109, 119, 127, 129,
    130, 143
camera temperature, 21
camera's built-in diopter adjustment, 33

camera's buttons and dials, 47
camera's firmware, 5
camera's functionality, 8
camera's imaging resolution, 89
camera's in-body image stabilization, 4
camera's interior, 33
camera's processing capabilities, 74
camera's recommended exposure settings, 64
camera's sensitivity setting, 67
Canon autofocus lenses, 42
Canon BR-E1 wireless remote control, 31
Canon carefully considered the feedback from
    users of the EOS R6, 1
Canon DSLR gear, 28
Canon E-77 II and LP1319, 29
Canon E-77 II and LP1319 lens case, 29
Canon EF 11-24mm, 31
Canon EF and EF-S lenses, 30
Canon EF-mount 24-105mm lens, 28
Canon EOS 5D-series DSLRs, 6
Canon EOS R6 II digital camera, 28
Canon EOS R6 Mark II, 1, 2, 5, 6, 9, 10, 11, 13, 14,
    34, 39, 40, 52, 85, 132, 176, 191
Canon EOS R6 Mark II establishes a new standard,
    1
Canon RF, 6, 13, 116, 117, 118, 124, 131
Canon service support, 29
Canon Speedlite 270EX II, 139, 151
Canon Speedlite 320EX, 151
Canon Speedlite 430EX II, 151
Canon Speedlite 430EX III, 151
Canon Speedlite 470EX AI, 151
Canon Speedlite 580EX II, 151
Canon Speedlite 600EX II-RT, 30
Canon Speedlite EL-1 or the 600EX-RT/600EX
    II-RT, 151
Canon Speedlite EL-100, 30, 152
Canon Speedlite EL-5, 151
Canon Tilt/Shift TS-E 17mm f/4L lenses., 31
Canon's CRAW format, 4
Canon's estimates, 30
Canon's higher-end RF lenses feature, 6
Canon's RF lens range, 6
Canon's wireless flash system, 149, 150
capture motion, 1, 61
capture of 190 JPEG, 4
Capture revealing photos, 108
capture selfies, 9
capture stunning HDR images, 76
capture stunning shots in broad daylight,, 110

Capture your photo sequence., 72
capturing a great photo, 56
capturing a well-composed image, 57
capturing bursts, 12
capturing HDR images of moving subjects, 76
capturing still images, 8
capturing stunning 24.2MP full-frame stills, 1
capturing stunning footage, 4
capturing the moment, 93
Car Battery Cable CB-570, 32
Card 1, 19, 20, 194
Card 2, 19, 20, 194
Card slot cover, 45
careful attention, 203
causing excessive discharge, 16
Caution, 21
CBC-E6 Car Battery Cable, 32
CDAF, 87
center-weighted, 13
Center-weighted averaging, 36, 59, 60
central lock position, 7
Certain types of lighting, 74
change movie rotate info, 190
Change Movie Rotate Info, 180
change other important settings, 8
change the interface language, 39
Change the Interface Language, 27
Changing Default Settings, 52
Channels, 150
characteristics of Canon's signature reliability, 11
charge the battery, 15
Charge the battery., 14
Charging in low temperatures, 15
Charging the Battery, 14
charging time of the battery, 15
Choose and erase images, 178
Choose from high-speed continuous, 72
Choose **Language**., 27
Choose the **Back Button**, 103
Choose the **Date/Time/Zone option**., 24
choose the desired zone for focusing, 37
Choose the preferred language., 27
Choose the time zone., 25
Choose the USB Connection App, 199
Choosing a Focus Mode (AF Operation), 36
Choosing a Metering Mode, 35, 59
Choosing a Shooting Mode, 61
CHOOSING YOUR LENS ARSENAL, 116
chosen settings for image quality and ISO speed.,
    22

CIPA, 31
Circles of Confusion and Focus, 90
Clear All Custom Functions, 52
Clear All Speedlite C.Fn's, 146
Clear Flash Settings, 146
Clear Settings, 142, 146, 200, 201, 202
Close the cover., 17, 19
Close-up, 84
Cloud RAW Image Processing, 185, 186
CMOS sensors, 67, 89
Color fringes observed, 130
Color space, 81
combine images using HDR techniques, 70
Communication Settings, 52
company's Dual Pixel CMOS AF technology, 10
comparable amount, 56
Compatible with all image formats, 88
Compensation feature, 130
Complete the warranty and registration card,
    29
complete your photo-taking session, 38
composing and viewing your images, 9
compromising quality, 4
computers, 5
concert or museum, 199
concise overview of the factors, 57
concise overview of the various permutations,
    147
CONCLUSION, 203
Configure Menu Settings, 54
Configure your settings, 201
Confirm your selection, 72
connect a plug adapter, 16
Connectivity, 5
Connectors, 6
consider a Speedlite as an essential accessory., 30
consider adjusting the depth, 8
consider lens accessories, 29
Consider using a tripod if it is available, 74
consider using the Canon App(s) for iPhone, 200
considering a photo's tonality, 77
considering readings, 35
considering the **RF 70-200mm f/4L IS USM lens**,
    121
continue capturing stunning shots, 32
Continuous, 13, 82, 94, 99, 105, 106, 132, 133,
    142, 191, 192
continuous AF. Canon, 11
Continuous Flash Control, 142
continuous lighting, 132, 133

Continuous Lighting Basics, 133
continuous shooting, 12, 75, 81, 82, 83, 94, 111, 143, 160, 164, 173
Continuous shooting, 13, 105
Continuous Shooting, 105
continuous shooting performance, 12
continuous shots, 74, 106, 174
Contrast Detection, 87
contrast-detection autofocus, 87
control dials, 7
control flash units, 154
Control ring, 42
controller for various functions, 44
Controlling Flash Units, 148
convenience of in-camera charging, 6
convenient access to various settings, 7
convenient Bluetooth remote control, 5
convenient feature, 9
conveniently adjust pairs of settings simultaneously, 7
conveniently update the camera's firmware using your smartphone, 5
Converging lines, 128
Convert to JPEG, 187
Copyright Information, 52
corresponding mount, 50
Cost of lenses, 118
country or region, 16
create a bracketed set, 84
create a shallow depth of field, 62, 84
Create light trails, 110
Create streaks, 110
Creating a Bracketed Set, 71
creation of smaller raw files, 4
Creative Assist, 82, 184
crucial moments, 203
current DSLR users, 2
current exposure, 58
Current focal length, 114
Current focus point, 114
Current settings, 156
Curves in various image editors, 79
Custom Function 1 menu, 70, 71, 72, 73
Custom Functions (C.Fn),, 52
Custom Functions 3 menu, 52, 102
custom options, 10
Custom Shooting Mode (C1–C3), 200
Custom Shooting Modes, 52, 202
Custom White Balance, 167, 168
customizable My Menu feature, 9

Customize Dials settings., 52
Customized Controls, 52
Customized Quick Controls, 52
customizing the shooting menu and its options., 155
CUSTOMIZING WITH THE SHOOTING MENU, 155

D

darker environments, 76
darkest tones, 12
Date/Time/Zone, 24, 196
Daylight, 132, 133, 134, 135, 168, 196
days of film photography, 34
DC coupler cable access, 41
deactivate various controls on the camera, 7
dealing with submenus, 43
Dealing with Visual Noise, 67
decrease exposure, 10, 68
Decreased contrast due to flare, 131
Dedicated wireless infrared signals, 148
Dedicated wireless optical signals, 148
default settings, 52, 55, 163
Default, All Purpose, Sports, 55
delayed exposures, 105
Delayed Exposures, 110
depth-of-field preview, 10
desired equivalent exposure combination, 58
detail and color accuracy, 13
determine exposure, 142, 146
determine the optimal f/stop, 63
determining exposure, 137
Determining Exposure, 138
Dial-up functions, 49
different combination of f/stop and shutter speed, 64
different directions, 35
different file types, 6
different kit options, 28
different lighting conditions, 62
different manufacturers, 86
different pairs of functions, 7
different types of memory cards, 18
digital nature of your images, 78
digital sensors, 57
Dioptric adjustment control, 43
Direct connection, 148
Disable/OFF, 162, 163
Disadvantage, 132, 133
discontinued predecessor, 2

Discovering Basic Zone Modes, 80
discovering the anatomy of the menus, 155
discreet sound, 11
discuss the 24.2MP Dual Pixel CMOS AF II sensor, 2
display's bottom left corner, 45
Distance, 141, 146
distribution of dark and light tones, 77
document DC-002., 31
drawing inspiration from Canon's EOS DSLRs, 6
drive, 7, 12, 52, 72, 111, 173
Drive mode, 81, 82
Dual Pixel CMOS AF, 2, 10, 89, 90
Dual Pixel RAW, 90, 159, 175, 181
Dual Pixel RAW Focus Adjustments, 90
duplicates the setting adjustment function, 35
Dust Delete Data, 52, 169, 171
Dynamic Range Mode, 76

E

effectively double the exposure, 56
effortless operation, 5
effortless retrieval of shadow, 12
effortlessly capture a series of pictures, 105
EF-S 18-135mm, 31
either raw or JPEG files, 12
EL-1, 141, 145, 147, 149, 150, 151, 152, 153
electrical contacts, 17, 51, 124
Electronic contacts, 41, 51
ELECTRONIC FLASH BASICS, 137
electronic levels, 9
electronic shutter, 12, 13, 30, 75, 90, 106, 114, 173
electronic viewfinder, 13, 30, 43, 46, 47, 115, 171
Elements of Wireless Flash, 147
eliminating the need for extra software installation, 5
embarking on a photography session, 32
enabling Bluetooth, 11
Enabling flicker control, 105
enabling users, 7
Enhance your shooting capabilities, 32
enhanced Dial Function option, 7
enhanced precision, 69
enhancements, 1
Enjoy a 3-inch fully articulated **screen**, 13
ensure optimal protection, 33
ensure sharp and accurate images, 94
Ensure that the battery is completely inserted into the charger., 14
Ensure that the battery is securely inserted by locking it in place., 17
Ensure that the card's label side, 19
Ensure that you have ample lighting, 107
Ensure the battery is fully charged before use., 15
ensure the system functions correctly, 4
ensuring a professional look., 29
ensuring optimal performance, 4
ensuring precise adjustments, 69
enthusiast camera, 28
entire frame, 10, 96
EOS R3, 2, 3, 9, 11, 171
EOS R6 Mark II showcases exceptional speed, 11
EOS R6 Mark II,, 11
Erase button, 46, 177
erase images, 190
Erase Images, 177
Erasing custom white balances and Dust Delete Data., 52
ergonomically designed for comfort, 203
ES icon, 114
E-TTL II Metering, 142
EV correction features, 66
EV increments, 13
Evaluative, 52, 59, 60, 81, 93, 142
Evaluative and Center-weighted averaging modes, 59
excellent choice, 28, 118, 122
excellent condition, 2
Excellent for shooting above crowds, 47
excels in single-shot AF, 11
exchange exposure, 50
Exciting new video features, 4
Exercise caution when handling cards., 21
exhilarating ways, 1
Expand Area AF, 45
Expand the AF, 37
expected level of protection, 6
expert shooters, 47
explore Canon's new mirrorless system, 28
Exposing to the Right, 80
exposure calculations, 61
exposure compensation, 9, 42, 44, 52, 65, 68, 120, 172
Exposure compensation, 13, 65
exposure lock indicator, 45
exposure mode dial, 6
exposure modes, 7, 36, 50, 59, 66, 139, 140, 141
Exposure modes, 13
exposure modes for video recording, 7

Exposure plays a crucial role, 56
exposure scale, 65, 66, 68, 73
Exposure settings, 58
exposure triangle, 56, 61, 65
Extend the charger prongs and securely insert, 14
extensive control, 5
extensive experience, 203
extensive zoom range, 118
External Auto/External Manual, 144
external design, 6
External microphones, 13
external monitor, 5, 172, 195, 198
external recorder, 4
external Speedlite, 30, 50, 83, 137
External Speedlite, 137, 140, 142
extra features, 32
extra lens control functions, 48
extreme lighting differences, 10
extremely low light conditions, 3
Eye detection, 98

F

---

face obstacles or limitations., 127

'

'face only AF', 4

F

Factory Preset Code, 194
fantastic accessories, 29
fast movement, 203
Fast/close focusing, 118
faster options feature, 12
faster speed and minimal impact, 38
feature for low-light shooting, 4
Feature Guide, 198
feature provides convenient access, 7
field preview button, 8, 41
File Name, 193
File Numbering, 191
finely adjust the settings, 76
fine-tune your autofocus, 104
fine-tuning the tonal range, 77
firm's EL-5 flash, 4
First and foremost, turn off the camera., 38

First of all, turn off the camera., 39
First things first, 28
fix exposures with histograms, 84
Fixed ISO, 65
Fixing Exposures with Histograms, 77
Flash C.Fn Settings, 145
Flash Combinations, 147
flash exposure compensation, 7, 52, 144
Flash Exposure Compensation and FE Lock, 141
Flash Firing, 142
Flash Function Settings, 144
Flash mode, 144
Flash Range, 141
Flat faces in portraits, 130
flexibility to customize exposure settings, 7
Flexible View, 46
Flexible Zone AF 1, 37, 96
Flexible Zone AF 2, 37
Flexible Zone AF 3, 37
Flexible-Priority (Fv),, 61
flickering outline, 12
fluorescent and LED illumination,, 74
Fluorescent Light/LEDs, 136
Focal length, 13, 141
focal plane mark, 50
Focus aids, 86
Focus Guide, 100
focus modes, 3, 7, 92
focus on a darker area, 11
Focus on any specific point, 88
focus on prioritizing the vehicles, 98
Focus Peaking, 99
Focus ring, 42
focus zone, 10
focusing on static subjects, 11
Food, 84
Format Card, 194
Formatting the Card, 20
forward-facing direction, 9
four-wheeled vehicles, 98
frequent ghost images, 76
front of the camera, 8, 10, 40, 41, 82, 111
Front View, 40
front windscreen of a vehicle, 11
full-resolution raw, 3
full-time depth of field preview, 10
fully charged Battery Pack LP-E6NH, 16
function that prevents the camera from attempting
    to refocus, 4

functionality of any of the previous four methods, 61

Fv mode, 58, 65

G

Gain a wider perspective, 126
gaining extra controls, 32
gaze from the viewfinder, 9
gently remove the rear lens cap, 33
Get objects closer, 126
Get your camera closer, 126
Getting a Handle on Exposure, 56
Getting closer, 91, 129
Getting Started with Electronic Flash, 139
Ghost Images, 137
glass fiber-reinforced polycarbonate shell, 6
Go to the initial screen, 114
Going Topside, 48
Google Photos, 186
gradual release of power current, 16
grayscale image, 77
greyscale tonal range, 78
Group photo, 83
Groups, 150
Guide Numbers, 139

H

halfway pushing, 44
Hand grip, 41
Handheld Night Scene, 84
handling of the R6 was exceptional, 6
hard-to-reach spot, 32
HDMI HDR Output, 189
HDR backlight control, 84
HDR photography, 73, 163
HDR Shooting [HDR PQ], 160
HEIF→JPEG Conversion, 187
High ISO Speed Noise Reduction, 174
high level of professionalism,, 11
high readout speed, 11
high refresh rate of 120fps, 9
high-dynamic range photography., 76
high-end EOS R3,, 2, 171
higher level of versatility and customization, 76
highest level of image sharpness, 63
Highlight Alert, 189
Highlight Tone Priority, 79, 161, 162, 163

highly appealing, 203
highly practical feature, 6
highly recommended, 30, 33, 60, 109, 124
high-quality images, 13, 149
high-resolution counterpart, 1
High-Speed Display, 173
Histogram Basics, 79
Hit the AF point selection button, 37
hood alignment mark, 42
hood bayonet, 42
Horizontal, 37, 99, 114
horses, 3
How do you add movie rotate information?, 202
How do you set the date and time zone?, 39, 202
How do you set the file name?, 202
How do you set the file numbering?, 202
How does focus mode work?, 104
How Electronic Flash Works, 137
How Focus Works, 86
how to select the autofocus areas on your camera, 37

I

IBIS, 1, 125
Icons representing loaded cards, 20
illumination present, 56
image data, 67
Image quality, 81, 82, 118
Image Quality, 90, 157, 158, 159, 175
Image quality and size, 81
Image Search Conditions, 178
image sensor, 35, 122
image stabilization, 42, 106, 114, 116, 119, 120, 121, 122, 125, 128, 129, 130, 140
Image Stabilization and You, 125
Image stabilizer switch, 42
impact exposure, 57
important buttons and components, 43
important moment of action, 4
impressive 30 frames per second, 3
impressive 33MP, 2
impressive 40 fps, 3
impressive 40fps, 1, 13
impressive dynamic range, 12
impressive EOS R6, 5
impressive eye control focus, 11
impressive feature set, 1
Impressive Performance, 11
improved accessibility, 7

Incandescent/Tungsten/Halogen Light, 136
include "**expanded**" settings like Low, 66
include accurate shooting information., 23
include aircraft, 3
include evaluative, 13
include Spot AF, 45
include the addition of an In-Body Image Stabilizer, 1
included in the package., 6
included power adapter, 32
including Canon's old FD-mount optics, 4
including the C positions, 7
including zebras, 3
inclusion of the customary front, 6
incorporate blur, 63
incorporate color temperature to EOS R6 Mark II, 136
incorporate focus breathing compensation, 4
increase or decrease sensitivity, 64
increasing exposure, 79
incredibly advanced system, 11
Increment between Exposures, 71
individual lens control dials, 7
individuals with less-than-optimal eyesight, 33
indoor photography, 66, 110
influence of noise, 13
INFO button, 35, 37, 46, 66, 77, 81, 95, 98, 109, 164, 201
Initial priority, 98
Initial Setup, 31
innovative technology, 10
Inserting and removing batteries, 16
Inserting and Removing Cards, 18
Inserting Cards, 18
Inserting the battery, 17
instant start-up., 11
Instructional guides, 29
intelligent capabilities, 35
interface adjustments, 2
interval shooting., 112
INTRODUCTION, 1
investing in a new battery., 16
ISO 50 equivalent, 64, 66, 189
ISO adjustments, 6
ISO adjustments in Auto ISO mode, 6
ISO and noise, 13
ISO performance, 203
ISO performance and color fidelity, 203
ISO range of 100-102,400, 1
ISO range of 100-102,400 (standard), 1

ISO sensitivity setting, 64, 66, 141
ISO sensitivity settings, 76
ISO setting, 56, 58, 62, 63, 64, 65, 66, 107, 139, 141
ISO settings can vary, 74
ISO speed, 22, 64, 66, 81, 161, 175
ISO Speed Settings, 66, 161
Issue, 128, 130, 131

J

joystick, 7, 45, 95, 134, 152, 153, 155, 156, 197
JPEG Fine Large, 52
JPEG Fine Large image quality, 52
JPEG/HEIF compression, 158
JPEG/HEIF, RAW, or both options, 158
Jump between tabs, 155
Just as accurate, 88

K

keep the battery stored with the protective cover, 16
keep your camera running, 32
Key features, 5
Key Wireless Concepts, 150
Kids, 83

L

lack of sensor stacking, 12
Landscape, 63, 83
landscape formats, 9
Landscape photography, 63
Landscape photography hand-held, 63
Language, 27, 197
Larger f/stops result in less depth-of-field, 56
latest version of the LP-E6NH, 30
LCD screen, 9, 13, 28, 30, 36, 43, 105, 132, 153, 172, 189
LC-E6, 14, 32
LC-E6E, 15, 32
LC-E6NH batteries, 32
least-reflective area, 78
Leaving the battery in the camera, 16
lengthening the shutter speed, 56
lengthy and cumbersome, 4
Lens, 13, 28, 33, 41, 42, 101, 128, 129, 130
lens control ring, 7

Lens mount, 13, 41
Lenses, 6, 116, 118, 121, 123, 126, 127, 129
Less confusion, 85
level of durability, 6
level of flexibility, 12
Light at its source, 57
Light is captured by the sensor, 58
Light passed by the lens, 58
Light passing through the shutter, 58
light performance, 2, 67
Light reflected, 57
Light reflected, transmitted, or emitted, 57
Light that's Available, 132
Light's duration, 57
lighting conditions, 62, 75, 77, 107
Lighting preview, 132
likelihood of motion blur, 56
Limit AF methods, 101
Limitations, 75
linear resolution, 13
lines that appear to be bowing outward, 128
Lines that exhibit a concave curvature, 130
lithium-ion power packs, 32
Living with Color Temperature, 134
lock button, 44, 45, 64, 141
lock in the current base exposure, 64
lofty sensitivity ratings, 67
long exposure, 105, 109
Long Exposure, 55
Long Exposures, 108, 109
longer for safety reasons, 15
Look sharp, 126
looking to capture the excitement of the action in
    real-time., 98
low light conditions, 10, 107
lower ISO settings, 56
lower-priced alternatives, 2
low-light performance comparable, 2
low-speed continuous, 72, 82
LP-E6N/LP-E6, 16
LP-E6NH lithium-ion battery, 31
LP-E6NH lithium-ion battery pack, 31
LP-E6NH/LP-E6, 30

M

macro work, 122
magnesium alloy chassis, 6
magnification, 1, 9, 13, 45, 99, 119, 122, 126, 188
Magnification, 45, 176, 188

Magnified Position, 188
Magnified View, 99
Magnify/Reduce button, 45, 99
Main Dial, 34, 188
mains charger, 6
Maintain position, 188
maintain the loyalty, 2
major components, 40, 41
majority of practical scenarios, 12
Make adjustments to the contrast in your image
    editor, 79
make EV changes, 84
making adjustments, 52, 54, 56, 94, 134
making decisions about your image, 57
Making EV Changes, 68
Manual (M),, 59
Manual exposure mode, 65
Manual Exposure Mode, 65
manual focus, 7, 36, 42, 82, 85, 86, 87, 90, 92, 98,
    100, 104, 120, 123, 170, 188
Manual focus, 82
Manual Focus, 85, 98
manual focus ring, 7
Manual mode, 65
Manual Reset, 191, 192
master available lights, 136
Mastering Autofocus, 10
Mastering Basic Navigation, 34
Mastering exposure, 56
MASTERING LIGHT, 132
Mastering the art of achieving the ideal exposure,
    57
Mastering the art of cycling, 10
MASTERING THE MYSTERIES OF FOCUS, 85
Mastering the Touch Screen, 46
mechanical shutter, 3, 12, 13, 84
mechanical/electronic shutter, 9
mechanical/electronic shutter selection, 9
MEET YOUR CANON EOS R6 II, 14
Memory card, 29
MENU button, 43, 49, 54, 68, 72, 155, 157, 168,
    177, 196, 202
menu settings is a feature available in Basic
    Settings, 52
Menu tabs, 156
menus are extensive, 203
merging process, 74
Metering and AF Start functions, 103
metering mode, 35
Metering mode, 35, 36, 81

Metering mode icon, 36
Metering Mode icon,, 60
metering modes, 59
Metering options, 13
meticulously unpacking the camera, 28
MF indicator, 36
M-Fn button, 32, 37, 45, 48
mid-tone areas, 60
million pixels, 43
minimize blurring caused by camera movement while in motion, 63
minimize blurring caused by the movement of the subject, 63
minimizing dust accumulation, 33
minimizing the impact of camera, 56
minimum size of 32GB, 29
mirrorless camera, 86, 121
mirrorless cameras, 87, 88, 125, 171
mirrorless cameras and dSLRs, 87
Misalignment, 74
mobile device, 5
Mode dial, 50, 61, 81, 83, 113, 114, 154, 166, 198, 201
Mode Guide, 83, 198, 199
moderately high settings, 13
modest improvement, 13
modify settings like shutter speed., 34
modify the ISO sensitivity setting to adjust exposures, 66
More depth-of-field, 127
More Exposure Options, 106
More foreground, 127
More lenses, 86
more precise control, 66
More speed, 126
Motion warning, 114
Motorsports, 62
Mount Adapter EF-EOS R, 124, 125
Mount Adapters, 30, 124
Mount lenses to use, 131
Move from page to page, 155
Movie shooting button, 49
Moving objects can create ghosts, 74
Moving subject, 75
Moving Subjects Mode, 76
MULTI, 144
multi-controller, 6, 45, 50, 66, 89, 95, 96, 100, 134, 155, 156, 197
Multi-controller, 35, 45
multi-function locking feature, 23

multi-function shoe, 4, 6, 13
Multi-function shoe, 6
Multiple, 182, 183
multi-purpose accessory shoe, 50
My Menu, 9, 47, 52, 54, 155, 156, 201
My Menu tab, 47

N

N1 rear lens cap., 29
NAILING THE RIGHT EXPOSURE, 56
Nana USM autofocus mechanism, 120
navigate to the AF operation icon, 36
navigate to the Metering mode entry, 35
necessary image edits, 38
Neck Strap, 29
new menu setting, 10
Nikon Z6 II, 203
noise reduction function, 175
northern hemisphere, 112
Not compulsory, 28
notable improvements, 5
noteworthy design, 2
noticeable artifacts, 12
noticeable change, 7
noticeably choppy view, 10
number of control points, 203
Number of Exposures, 70
numerous zones, 35

O

OM System's Pro Capture mode., 12
On subject, 98
On-camera flash used alone, 148
On-camera flash used as a trigger only for off-camera flash, 148
On-camera flash used simultaneously with off-camera flash, 148
One-Shot, 36, 40, 52, 81, 92, 93, 94, 95, 96, 97, 100, 101, 102, 104, 106, 172
One-shot AF/single autofocus, 93
Open the cover by sliding it., 18
optical distortions, 130
optical stabilization,, 4
optimal f/stop or shutter speed, 58
optimal performance, 20, 31, 33, 97, 117
optimal values for shadows, 79

optimal values for shadows and highlights from multiple images., 79
opting for a 64GB or larger card, 29
option in the Basic Settings menu, 52
optional Type-C-to-USB-A adapter., 39
orange boxes, 36
original EOS R6, 4, 7
original LP-E6 batteries, 30
Other menu options, 156
Output size, 13
overall appearance and atmosphere of an image, 56
Overexposure, 64
overlay grid lines, 9
overly contrasty image, 79
overshadowing the physical controls, 8
Overview, 14, 40, 52, 56, 85, 105, 116, 132, 137, 147, 155, 176, 191
OVF Sim View Assist, 171

P

packed group of ten controls, 8
Panasonic Lumix S5 II, 2
Panning, 84
Panoramic Shot, 83
Partial, 35, 60
PDAF, 87, 88, 89
People, 97
perceptual quantization, 187
perfect balance of tones and colors, 56
Periscope view, 47
personalized shooting experience, 8
Perspective distortion, 127
Phase Detection, 88
phase detection autofocus, 10
phase-detection autofocus, 87, 89
Photobook Set-up, 182
photographer and copyright information., 47
Photoshop Elements, 79, 134
pick photography parameters, 44
picture style, 8
Picture Style, 81
Placing AF sensors, 89
planning to track a pair of relay runners, 63
Playback button, 46
Playback mode, 45, 46
point using the face detection and tracking mode, 36
portable voltage, 16
portable voltage transformers, 16

Portrait, 81, 83, 84
Position it in your direction., 23
potential damage, 21, 33
potential risk, 11
Power Options, 31
power outlet., 14, 15
power outlets in foreign countries, 16
power switch, 7, 20, 21, 23, 28
Power switch, 49
Powered by an LP-E6N Li-ion battery., 13
practical benefits, 4
practical option, 1
practical option for most photographers, 1
practical situations, 203
practical updates, 9
precious moments, 3
precise autofocus and impressive video shooting, 203
precise autofocus and impressive video shooting capabilities, 203
precise focus calculation, 36
precise preview, 9
predecessor, 1, 6, 13
predecessor's strengths, 1
predictive AF technology, 94
presence of in-body stabilization in the R6 II., 120
press the AF Area button, 10
press the **MENU button**, 54
press the **SET button**, 54
pressing the M-Fn button, 7, 37
pressing the SET button, 11, 83, 197
pressing the shutter button, 3, 12, 105
preventing dust from entering your camera, 29
Preview AF, 93, 100, 104
Preview of lighting, 132
previous model, 2, 30
Price, 1, 13
primary controls, 44
prior knowledge, 10
prioritizes safeguarding your equipment, 33
priority (Tv) modes, 58
priority (Tv) operates differently, 62
Priority Mode, 62, 65
Proceed to insert the battery., 17
Proceed to insert the card., 18
process of inputting the lens's focal length, 4
produce a slight sound, 28
Produce extraordinary images, 108
produces high-quality images at low ISOs, 13
professional experience, 9

professional look, 29, 79, 194
professional nature, 11
professional photographers, 11, 28, 109, 123
professional-quality photos, 83
Program AE Mode, 63
Programme (P),, 61
ProRes raw, 4
pros and cons, 56, 98
Protect Images, 157, 176
protective barrier, 33
protective cover in the opposite direction, 15
Push the card in gently and it will be ejected., 21
PZ-E1 Power Zoom Adapter, 31

Q

Q button, 8, 35, 60, 68, 82, 83, 93, 163, 164, 178
Quick Control dial 1, 34, 35, 43, 68
Quick Control dial 2, 35, 65, 188
Quick Control Dial 2, 44, 188
Quick Control dial,, 32
Quick Control menu,, 37, 164
Quick Control screen, 20, 34, 35, 36, 68, 82, 199
quick overview, 1

R

R system, 2
range of animals, 11
RATE button, 43, 100, 179
Rating, 179
raw burst mode, 3, 9, 12
raw burst mode option, 3
RAW file converter, 79
RAW Processing, 181, 184
RAW Processing (RAW/DPRAW), 181
rear control dials, 6
reasonable increase, 2
recalculate exposure, 45
Rechargeable batteries, 32
recharging process, 15
Recommendation, 28
RECOMMENDED, 29, 30, 52, 191
Recommended Default Changes, 54
recommended lens-mounting procedure, 33
recommended setting, 64
Record videos in stunning 4K resolution, 1
recording status, 10
rectify any alteration, 4

Reduced foreground/increased compression, 129
reducing the weight you need to carry, 30
reduction of actual frames per second, 105
Regarding autofocus, 3
Registering your camera by mail is optional, 29
Release shutter without card, 22
reliable and efficient data storage, 6
remarkable headline, 2
remarkable headline specifications, 2
remarkable speed and reliability, 11
Remember to remove the battery, 16
Remote controls, 31
Remote Recommendations, 31
Remove the card., 21
Remove the protective, 14
Remove the protective cover that comes with the battery., 14
removing cards, 21
removing the body cap, 33
Render people invisible, 110
replace your primary charger., 32
repurpose the video record button, 8
Reset Camera commands, 201
reset the Customize Buttons, 52
Resetting to Factory Defaults, 52
Resolution, 157, 158
Restoring the factory defaults, 52
Restoring the factory defaults for various settings, 52
RF 100-400mm f/5.6-8, 121
RF 100-500mm f/4.5-7.1L IS lens, 121
RF 14-35mm f/4 L IS USM, 119
RF 15-30mm f/4.5-6.3 IS STM lens, 119
RF 16mm f/2.8 STM, 122
RF 24-105mm f/4-7.1 IS, 116, 117, 120
RF 24-105mm STM lens, 1
RF 24-240mm f/4-6.3 IS USM lens, 120
RF 24mm f/1.8 Macro IS STM lens, 122
RF 28-70mm f/2L USM, 120
RF 35mm f/1.8 Macro IS STM, 122
RF 5.2mm f/2.8 L Dual Fisheye 3D VR lens, 122
RF 70-200mm f/2.8L IS USM, 120
RF lens mount index, 41
RGB live histogram, 9
Right-Side Controls, 44
rolling shutter, 11, 12, 203
Root Certificate, 52
Rotate the screen., 22
rotating the QCD-1, 49, 68, 181, 196

S

same 3.69m-dot EVF and 3in, 9
Scene Intelligent, 35, 36, 59, 61, 65, 66, 80, 81, 82, 94, 139, 141, 161, 198, 201
Scene Intelligent Auto mode, 36, 81, 82, 94
Scene Intelligent Auto Mode, 80
Screen protection, 47
Scroll among page entries, 156
seamless wireless connection, 5
seamlessly integrating the in-lens and in-body systems, 4
second QCD dial leaps, 44
secondhand market, 2
securely closed by applying pressure, 17
securely mount your camera on a tripod, 112
seemingly minor feature, 4
Select images, 183
Select Range, 176, 177, 178, 181
select the Metering mode, 35
select the number of bracketed shots, 70
Selected menu item, 156
selecting a shooting mode, 14
Selecting AF Area, 36
selecting aperture, 58
selecting certain options, 35
Selective focus, 129
Selfie mode, 46
Self-Timer, 111
Self-timer light with AF-assist beam, 40
semi-automatic with TV, 65
sense of expertise, 203
Sensitivity range, 13
Sensor, 13, 28, 50
sensor cleaning, 28
sensor cleaning settings., 28
sensor pixel, 10, 90
sensor-cleaning mechanism, 33
sensor's focus plane., 50
separate lock button, 7
Servo AF, 36, 38, 40, 81, 83, 92, 94, 96, 97, 99, 100, 102, 105, 106
Set daylight saving time., 26
set the anti-flicker shooting, 175
set the cloud RAW image processing function, 190
set the high-speed display, 175
set the image quality, 175
set the option to protect images, 190
Set the time zone with precision., 24
set up a receiver flash, 154

set up a sender/controller flash, 154
set up photobook, 190
Setting the Date, 23
Setting the Date, Time, and Time Zone, 23
Setting up a Receiver Flash, 153
Setting up a Sender/Controller Flash, 152
Settings option, 52
SET-UP MENU, 191
Set-up Menu Defaults, 54
shadow details, 9
shake correction, 4
Share the fun, 46
shielding the camera's USB terminal,, 39
Shoot at an impressive 40 frames per second., 1
shoot multiple exposures, 90
shoot panoramas, 115
Shooting 2, 44, 66, 68, 71, 72, 75, 140, 142
Shooting 2 menu, 66, 68, 71, 72, 75, 140, 142
Shooting 3 menu., 35, 155, 164
Shooting 4 menu of your camera, 79
shooting a soccer game outdoors, 62
shooting and playback., 45
shooting at 7fps, 12
shooting breathtaking 6K RAW video at 60p., 1
shooting experience, 9
shooting in raw format, 12
Shooting Information Display, 52
Shooting Menu Options, 157
Shooting menus, 44
shooting mode, 45, 46, 49, 54, 56, 61, 65, 72, 77, 84, 111, 166, 201, 202
Shooting mode, 45, 201
shooting modes like P, Tv, Av, and Manual, 65
shooting panorama, 105
Shooting Panoramas, 113
shooting screen, 20
shooting settings, 105, 201
shooting speed, 143, 164, 203
Shooting/Movie mode switch, 61
Shutter, 13, 40, 41, 47, 48, 58, 59, 61, 62, 63, 74, 81, 103, 112, 141, 143, 145, 161
shutter button, 7, 36, 40, 45, 51, 93, 99, 102, 170
shutter button or snap the image, 45
shutter release button, 33, 34, 40, 44, 48, 72, 81, 94, 103, 109, 111, 202
Shutter release button, 40, 48
shutter speed of approximately, 62
Shutter speeds, 13, 74, 143
Shutter-priority mode, 59, 62
Sigma Octantis, 112

signaling under or overexposure, 64

significant impact on the depth-of-field of your photos, 56

significant improvements, 6

significant level of compensation., 74

significant optical issue, 130

Silent shutter, 84

simultaneously record, 18

single AF point, 37

single battery, 30, 32

single burst, 4

Size, 81, 82, 118

skilled photographer, 65

slide an electronic flash, 50

slight optical adjustment, 33

Slow Synchro, 140, 143

smaller AF point., 37

smallest f/stop available, 62

smartphones, 5

Smooth and steady cam, 127

soft rubber eyecup/frame, 43

solid grasp of contrast, 89

some expert tips for using the R6 II's impressive built-in feature, 74

some important concepts, 147

Sony a7 IV, 203

Sony Alpha A7 IV, 2

Special Scene Mode, 83

specific area of the image, 10

specific shooting session, 66

specific type of noise, 67

Specify the minimum and maximum ISO sensitivity options, 66

specs and capabilities, 203

Speedlite 320EX, 154

Speedlite 430EX II, 154

Speedlite 430EX III/430EX III-RT, 154

Speedlite 600EX-RT/600EX II-RT, 154

Speedlite control section, 137

Speedlite EL-100, 152, 154

spherical aberration, 130

Sports, 55, 83

Spot, 35, 37, 45, 60, 95, 98, 99

Spot AF enables the manual selection of a single, 37

spot recognition setting available, 11

sRGB color mode,, 52

stacked architecture, 2

stacked sensor, 11

Stage Performances, 55

Stage Performances, Long Exposure, HDR, Portrait, 55

standalone body, 28

standard, 1, 2, 6, 11, 13, 35, 42, 69, 70, 72, 101, 106, 118, 120, 144, 163, 181, 193

Standard Picture Style, 52

standout feature, 203

Star Trails, 112

Star trails are a fantastic use for both long exposures, 112

stationary subjects, 76, 97, 110

ST-E2 and ST-E3-RT transmitter, 30

Stepping back, 127

Stereo microphones, 41

still experiencing issues, 11

Still Photo Shooting Menu Defaults, 53

stills/video mode selector, 7

Storage, 6

straightforward approach, 36

Strap mount, 50

struggled to adequately compensate for movement, 76

stunning shots, 110, 112, 122

subject detection AF system, 3

subject detection modes, 8

subject movement, 56, 87, 143

Subject Tracking, 96

substantial tonal adjustments post-shooting, 12

superior autofocus, 203

Super-sized subjects, 127

supplementary thumb dial, 6

swiftly focusing on a suitable subject, 85

Switch between different modes, 37

Switch subject, 98

Switching between automatic and manual focus, 36

T

tablets, 5

take continuous shooting, 115

teleconverters, 121

temporary ISO adjustments, 6

Terminal covers, 42

Text entry, 47

the "**selfie**" position, 46

the AF point or Zone AF frame, 47

The Auto Lighting Optimizer and Highlight Tone Priority features, 79

The battery charger, 16

the Battery Pack LP-E6NH, 29

The buffer has an impressive depth, 4
The Business End, 42
The camera features a 3-inch, 1.62m-dot vari-angle screen., 1
The camera has dimensions of 138.4 × 98.4 × 88.4 mm., 13
The camera itself, 28
The camera organizes, 54
The Camera Remote app, 5
The camera supports 2x UHS-II SD memory cards., 13
The camera's top surface, 48
the Canon EOS R6 II, 51, 105, 203
the Canon EOS R6 II offers exceptional image quality, 203
The Canon EOS R6 II,, 66
The Canon EOS R6 Mark II establishes a new standard for the performance of hybrid cameras., 1
The card in the back card slot is [1],, 19
the Custom Functions 5 menu, 52
the EOS R3, 11
The EOS R6 II, 90, 203
The EOS R6 II is a pleasure to use, 203
the EOS R6 Mark II, 1, 2, 3, 4, 5, 9, 11
The EOS R6 Mark II boasts a 24MP sensor, 13
The EOS R6 Mark II showcases exceptional speed and responsiveness, 11
The EOS R6 Mark III, 6
The E-TTL II mode, 144
The exposure zones, 60
the field of photography., 221
The indicated angles are only approximate., 22
The Mark II is compatible with the same BG-R10 battery grip, 6
The Moving Subject mode, 76
THE PLAYBACK AND WIRELESS MENUS, 176
The presence of light and dark areas is observed when using a polarizing filter, 128
The price for the body only is $3,561 / £2,779., 1
The program mode (P), 63
The Q (Quick Control) button, 46
The R6 could detect and track humans, 11
the R6 II provides various alternative methods for selecting the AF method, 37
the R6 II's anti-shake capabilities, 74
The R6 II's rear panel is jam-packed, 42
The range for stills, 66
The **RF 15-35mm f/2.8L IS USM lens**, 119
The **RF 24-70mm f/2.8L IS USM**, 119

The sensor of the R6 MKII, 203
The sequence consists of decreased exposure, 70
the Set-up 6 menu., 54, 202
the Speedlite 600EX II-RT, 137
the top-of-the-line EL-1, 30
the USB cable to a USB Type-C port, 39
three custom positions, 6
Time exposures, 109
Time Lapse and Interval Photography, 111
Timed exposures, 108
toggle toggles image stabilization on and off, 42
Tonal Range, 77
top plate, 6, 7
top priority, 3
top-notch full-frame sensors, 12
top-tier cameras, 9
Touch Operation, 47
Touch the shutter/focus point, 47
touchscreen, 7, 8, 9, 50
tough competition, 2
track-and-field events, 62
Tracking acceleration, 101
Tracking acceleration and deceleration, 101
Tracking sensitivity, 100
tracking system, 98
traditional **"exposure triangle."**, 56
traditional DSLR, 10
traditional SLR cameras, 10
trains, 3, 11
transfer images, 38, 39, 183, 200
transfer photos, 5, 39
transfer your images, 38
Transferring Photos to Your Computer, 38
translucent objects, 57
Tripod socket, 50
Turning on the Power, 23
TV mode, 65, 69, 140

U

ultimately reducing the battery's lifespan, 16
Underexposure, 64
Underneath Your Camera, 50
Understanding exposing, 80
Understanding exposure is essential for capturing great photos, 56
Understanding histograms, 77
Understanding Histograms, 79
Understanding histograms is crucial for fine-tuning the tonal range of an image, 77

Understanding the external flash's illumination, 141

Understanding the naming convention for color temperatures, 135

unexpected knocks, 33

unused AF methods, 101

Unwanted cropping, 74

unwanted light, 33, 42

USB Power Adapter PD-E1, 30

USB-C port provides a reliable connection., 5

use a speedlite as an optical sender, 154

use external speedlite control, 146

use telephoto and tele-zoom lenses, 131

Use the Display, 68

use the LC-E6 or LC-E6N batteries, 32

Use the Multi-Function Lock, 50

User Setting 2, 193, 194

User Settings 1, 194

using a Canon digital camera, 52

using a card reader, 38

using a semi-automatic shooting mode, 36

using a shutter speed of 1/8000th second, 64

using a sliding scale, 66

Using a Speedlite as an Optical Sender, 152

Using a wired or wireless remote control, 31

using an external flash, 45

using Av mode,, 62, 69

using Dual Pixel RAW, 105

using flash settings, 137

Using HDR Mode, 74

Using Interval Photography, 111

using Scene Intelligent Auto, 59, 66, 81, 94, 139

Using shutter-priority mode, 63

Using Telephoto, 129

using the aperture and shutter speed, 58

using the electronic shutter, 3, 11, 84

using the EVF, 47

using the face detection, 36

using the H setting, 67

using the LCD or viewfinder, 31

using the LCD or viewfinder to compose your shots., 31

using the QCD 1, 54

using the QCD-1,, 66

using the right thumb, 8

Using the Screen, 22

Using the Speedlite 430EX III-RT as Radio Sender, 153

using your camera extensively, 30

using your camera without a lens, 33

utilizing the front and rear dials, 7

V

valuable tools for adjusting contrast, 79

valuable update available for video mode., 10

variety of feature updates, 2

various distances, 4

Various factors can influence high-speed shooting, 105

various options available, 106, 147

vehicle battery option, 32

Vehicles, 97, 98

vehicle's lighter or accessory socket, 32

Vertical, 6, 37, 99

Vertical grip, 6

vertical shooting, 32, 51

video capabilities, 4

Video capabilities, 13

video quality, 203

Video System, 198

video-optimized interface, 7

Viewfinder and Screen, 9

viewfinder boasts impressive features, 9

viewfinder eyepiece, 43

Viewfinder eyepiece/eyecup, 43

viewfinder or LCD monitor, 85

Viewfinder sensor, 43

viewing experience reminiscent, 9

Visual image noise, 67

visualize the outcome of your images, 9

vloggers appreciate, 122

vlogging purposes, 9

W

Waist-level view, 47

WB bracketing, 69, 134

Weird colors, 74

well-organized, 8

What are the different playback menu options?, 190

What are the different recommended settings in your camera?, 55

What are the different set up menu functions?, 202

What are the different shooting menu options?, 175

What are the front controls and their functions?, 51

What are the three ways to take long exposures?, 115

What are the top controls and their functions?, 51
What can lenses do for you?, 131
What you see is what you get, 85
When the focus is difficult, 101
Which flashes can be operated wirelessly?, 154
Which Flashes Can Be Operated Wirelessly?, 150
While using the EVF, move the focus point, 47
white balance, 7, 9, 11, 12, 35, 50, 52, 81, 134, 168, 169, 175
White balance, 81, 167
White Balance Bracketing, 134
Whole Area AF, 37, 45, 96
whole-stop increments, 69
Why Use Wireless Flash?, 149
wide range of menu settings, 53
Wider field of view, 127
wider horizontal zone, 37
wider range of image formats., 87
Wireless Evolution, 147
work with different lighting in EOS R6 Mark II, 136
work with HDR, 79, 84
work with long exposures, 115
work with short exposures, 115
work with the AF system, 104
Working with HDR, 73

working with P, Tv, Av, or M exposure modes, 59
Working with Short Exposures, 107
Working with the AF System, 92
WORKING WITH WIRELESS FLASH, 147
WYSIWYG, 85
WYSIWYW, 85

Y

YOUR VISUAL ROADMAP, 40

Z

Zone AF 1, 45
Zone AF 2, 45
Zone AF 3, 45
Zoom in or out by turning this ring., 42
Zoom lenses, 119, 121
Zoom lock, 48
Zoom range, 118
Zoom ring, 42
Zoom scale, 48

www.ingramcontent.com/pod-product-compliance
Lightning Source LLC
Chambersburg PA
CBHW080945290526
45795CB00009B/2917